THE ENCYCLOPEDIA OF
DIY

SKILLS AND TECHNIQUES FOR SUCCESSFUL RESULTS

THE ENCYCLOPEDIA OF
DIY

SKILLS AND TECHNIQUES FOR SUCCESSFUL RESULTS

BLITZ EDITION

© Orbis Publishing 1998

Published by Blitz Editions
An imprint of Bookmart Ltd.
Desford Rd.
Enderby
Leicester LE9 5AD

This material has previously appeared in the parkwork *Jobmate*.

Printed in the Czech Republic
60184/2

ISBN 1 85627 374 1

CONTENTS

PLUMBING

WASTE WATER SYSTEMS

Each day every one of us uses an average of 160 litres (35 gallons) of water from the mains supply. When it's used it has to be got rid of – something we tend to take for granted. Here's how it's done.

The supply of hot and cold water to the taps in your house is really only half the domestic plumbing story. You also need a waste system to remove what you've used or don't want. And besides coping with the dirty water from the bath, basin and sink and the waste from the WC, the system also has to deal with the rainwater which falls on the roof.

The drainage system therefore has to be efficient and durable, and for obvious reasons of hygiene, self-cleansing. Waste matter mustn't be allowed to remain in the pipes and if blockages occur it should be possible to remove them easily.

How the drainage system works

There are several domestic drainage systems but each of them can be broken down into five separate sections. When waste water leaves an appliance of any sort, it will go immediately through a 'waste trap' – a 180° bend containing a water seal which fills the trap whenever the waste pipe empties. This keeps drain smells out of the room and prevents insects and the like from entering the home. With WCs it also makes self-cleansing easier. WC traps are cast as an integral part of the WC pan, but on other appliances they are separate, and are attached to the outlet pipe by a large retaining nut.

From the trap, waste water enters a branch pipe which leads to the main vertical drainage 'stack'. This takes it below ground level to the first underground section of the drainage system where it flows through at least one inspection chamber (covered with a manhole cover) and into the public sewer, which is usually situated underneath the road. The sewer is provided by the public health authority and it is their responsibility to remove all waste running into it.

Often rainwater from the roof is fed into the drainage system to flow into the public sewer. But some authorities provide a separate street drain for it or insist on the provision of soak-aways (pits filled with rubble and gravel which allow the water to soak into the surrounding earth) near the house. Tanks and cisterns rarely overflow, but when they do they discharge clean water, so it's not necessary for the overflow pipes to be located over a drain.

The water can fall directly onto the ground.

The cost of laying public sewers in rural areas means that the waste from many houses in these parts flows into a cess pool or septic tank. These are specially constructed pits for storing effluent (and in the case of a septic tank, for breaking it down into harmless matter). Both of these require periodic pumping out, cess pools much more often as they store all the waste. If you're buying a house with one of these systems, check how often this has to be done, who does it and how much you may have to pay.

How it all began

Proper plumbing systems have only been around for about 100 years. The large urban expansion which took place during the Industrial Revolution lead to squalid housing conditions, and disease was rife. Eventually, enclosed sewers were introduced along with piped water supplies and pottery WC pans. By the 1870s many homes were equipped with a basin, a WC and a sink; but an acute shortage of qualified plumbers lead to ridiculous installations which often produced as great a health threat as before. The London County Council took the lead in sorting things out by laying out a set of rules in 1900, establishing the 'two-pipe' system – one stack for waste water from basins and sinks, another for 'soil water' from WCs.

The amount of pipework needed with the two-pipe system, and the increased siphonage problems on tall buildings, led to the introduction of the 'one-pipe' system. This system was the forerunner of the modern 'single stack' system and abandoned the distinction between the soil and the waste pipe stacks. It was only used extensively on multi-storey buildings.

On the one-pipe system all discharges flowed into a single stack which had an open-ended outlet at roof level. All traps had deep seals and each branch pipe was also connected to a vent pipe which rose to eaves level.

The single stack system was developed in the UK in the late 1940s to overcome the drawbacks and complications of the two-pipe systems, and to simplify the installation – everyone must be familiar with the untidy cluster of pipes on the outside walls of houses with these systems.

The advent of light plastic piping helped in this development, as it made the production of accurate mouldings easier, and cut down the installation time because plastic was quicker to join than the old metal piping.

The single stack system

This consists of a single waste stack into which all the branch pipes discharge. However, ground floor waste doesn't have to go

TWO-PIPE WASTE SYSTEM

The traditional two pipe system takes all soil to the underground drain by one pipe, and all the waste from baths, basins etc down another. It is found in most pre-war houses, and is still used, particularly in bungalows where the installation is spread out.

Roof drainage may flow into the same underground drainage system; it may go into a separate storm drain (out in the street) in areas of high rainfall; or it may drain into a soakaway in the garden.

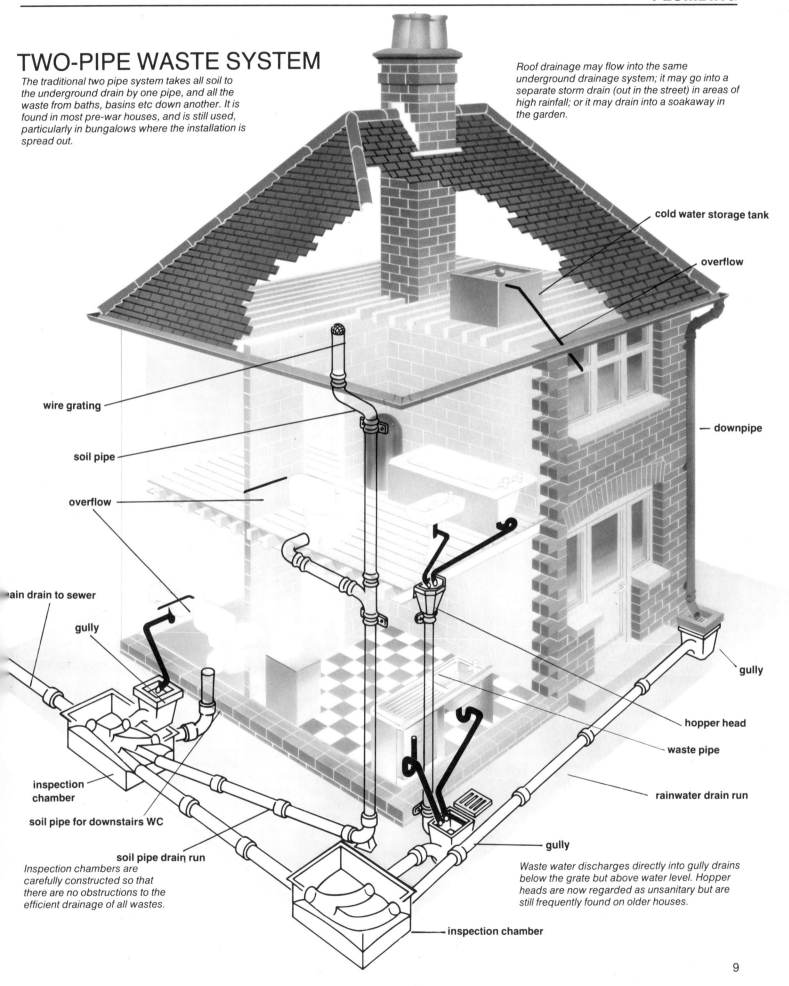

cold water storage tank

overflow

downpipe

wire grating

soil pipe

overflow

gully

hopper head

waste pipe

rainwater drain run

gully

ain drain to sewer

gully

inspection chamber

soil pipe for downstairs WC

soil pipe drain run

Inspection chambers are carefully constructed so that there are no obstructions to the efficient drainage of all wastes.

inspection chamber

Waste water discharges directly into gully drains below the grate but above water level. Hopper heads are now regarded as unsanitary but are still frequently found on older houses.

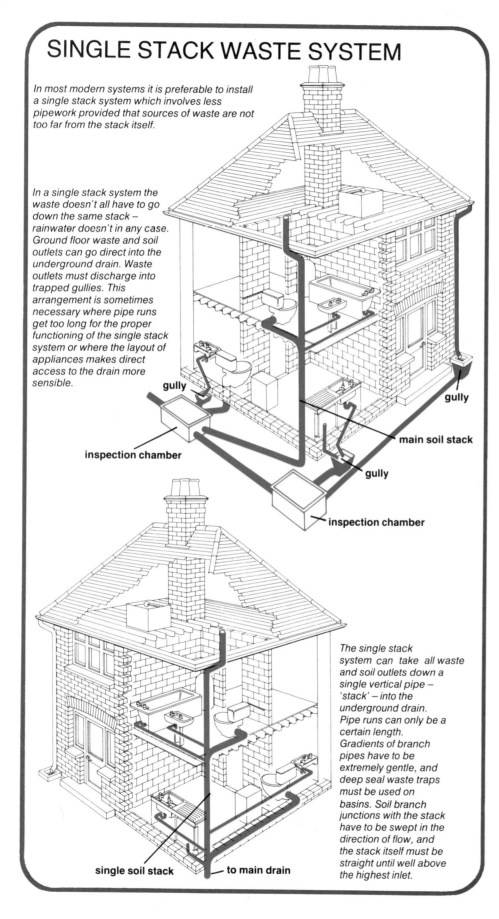

SINGLE STACK WASTE SYSTEM

In most modern systems it is preferable to install a single stack system which involves less pipework provided that sources of waste are not too far from the stack itself.

In a single stack system the waste doesn't all have to go down the same stack – rainwater doesn't in any case. Ground floor waste and soil outlets can go direct into the underground drain. Waste outlets must discharge into trapped gullies. This arrangement is sometimes necessary where pipe runs get too long for the proper functioning of the single stack system or where the layout of appliances makes direct access to the drain more sensible.

gully

inspection chamber

gully

main soil stack

gully

inspection chamber

The single stack system can take all waste and soil outlets down a single vertical pipe – 'stack' – into the underground drain. Pipe runs can only be a certain length. Gradients of branch pipes have to be extremely gentle, and deep seal waste traps must be used on basins. Soil branch junctions with the stack have to be swept in the direction of flow, and the stack itself must be straight until well above the highest inlet.

single soil stack

to main drain

into the stack. Sink waste water may flow into a trapped gully and ground-floor WCs may be connected directly into the underground drain. This avoids any risk that a blockage at the base of the stack (where it bends to join the underground drain) could lead to waste water being forced back along the waste pipes to ground-floor appliances.

In appearance the single-stack system is the simplest waste system of all and the most economical to install. As a result it is incorporated in the majority of new houses. But because the branches have to be comparatively short, the system is less useful in bungalows where appliances are likely to be spread out. Usually all the pipework is sited indoors, which means a neater appearance for the house exterior; it also reduces the possibility of frost damage. All you'll see of the system is a tell-tale vent pipe poking up through the roof.

In order to make the system work properly a number of technical regulations have to be taken into account when it's being installed. These relate to the length, diameter, bend radii and angles of bend of the branch pipes, the use of P-traps and S-traps on waste pipes other than WCs (see *Traps for each appliance*), the positioning of the stack connectors, and the dimensions of the stack itself. While the system may look simple, considerable research has been done to ensure that problems of siphonage aren't likely to occur.

The two-pipe system

The principles of the two-pipe system were based on a belief that all kinds of disease were caused by the 'bad air' in drains, and the system aimed to keep this out of homes. The basic principle was that the 'soil' discharge from WCs went directly down one stack into the underground drain. All other discharges, termed 'waste', went down another stack which led into a trapped gully (a cast drain incorporating a water trap) at ground level and from there joined the soil discharge under-ground. Sometimes waste had to fall into a channel at ground level before running into the drain.

All waste and soil pipework had to be fixed to the outside of the building. The soil pipe was continued upwards to eaves level where it terminated open-ended in a wire cover to keep nesting birds from causing a blockage. This allowed free passage of air from the underground drain.

When the two-pipe system came into existence, most homes only had an outside WC (quite often shared) and a kitchen sink, so discharge was entirely at ground level, but when upstairs bathrooms became popular waste was directed into hoppers attached to stand-pipes, which caused new problems. Hoppers were not self-cleansing and soapy water drying on the inside could start to smell; draughts could also blow up the pipe to the hopper, bringing smells from the drain at the bottom. This led to some authorities banning hoppers and insisting on discharge direct into another stack which meant installing an eaves-level vent as with the soil stack.

On buildings over two storeys high this created another problem known as 'induced siphonage'. When water flowing down the waste stack from one outlet passed another outlet where it joined the stack, it could cause a partial vacuum in the second pipe which could suck out the contents of the water trap. To cure this problem the upper part of each trap had to be connected to a branch vent pipe which either connected to a separate vertical stack to eaves level, or joined the vented waste stack at least 900mm (3ft) above the level of the highest waste connection. If you live in a tall house you may have this system, and any repairs to vent pipes should follow the existing system. The alternative is to take out the entire system and replace it with a single stack arrangement.

Traps for each appliance
The traditional trap was a simple U-shaped bend attached to a horizontal branch outlet – today called a 'P' trap. If the branch outlet is vertical this trap bends round again into a double 'U' or 'S' outlet. In systems with lead pipes, the traps were often formed from lengths of pipe, while with modern plastic waste systems the traps are separate and easily detachable. The plastic bottle trap, which performs the same function, is also now widely used, and this is more compact and neater in appearance.

The depth of the water-filled part of the trap is known as the 'depth of seal'. Shallow traps have a seal depth of around 50mm (2in), 38mm (1½in) or 19mm (¾in), while 'deep-seal' traps have a 75mm (3in) seal.

Lead traps usually allow access for clearing blockages, and this is obtained by unscrewing an access cap or 'eye'. Modern plastic traps are connected by screwed collars at both ends and can be completely removed for cleaning if blocked. The lower part of bottle traps likewise completely unscrews. Adjustable plastic traps are available for fixing to existing pipework where access is difficult and special adaptors are used to link to copper and iron pipes.

Traps must remain filled with water and it is against the bye-laws if they don't. This is the most important and lasting principle handed down from the waste disposal thinking of the last century.

The water seal can be lost from traps for lots of reasons. Siphonage is the worst problem and where it occurs it's usually due

to a badly designed system. Simply, if the air pressure beyond the trap is slightly less than the normal atmospheric pressure acting on the surface of the water in the trap, the water will drain away. This is more likely with 'S' traps than 'P' traps, and with shallow rather than deep traps. The problem of siphonage led to the introduction of venting systems and dictated the dimensions in the single stack system (and also excluded the use of 'S' traps).

Overflow pipes
There are two sorts of overflow pipes – those which are connected to storage cisterns and WC cisterns, and those which are attached to or form a part of appliances such as basins and baths. They are known in the trade as warning pipes. Both sorts should be fitted to avoid the risk of overflows damaging your home. This may be caused when you forget to turn off the bath, or by mechanical failure when the ball-valve on the water storage tank jams open.

In sinks, basins and baths the overflow must discharge into the branch waste pipe between the trap and the appliance, or into the trap above the water level of the seal, and must be able to cope with the flow of water from one tap turned full on.

Sink and basin overflows are usually built into the design of the appliance, while those for baths are supplied as part of the plumbing and connect to a slot in the waste outlet casting.

Overflows from tanks and cisterns consist of a length of pipe of a minimum 22mm (⅞in) internal diameter, capable of discharging water as quickly as any incoming flow. They usually emerge through the outside wall and stick out far enough to avoid any water flow sluicing down the wall surface, which could be a potential source of damp.

Pipe and trap materials
All waste and soil pipes are today mainly manufactured in plastic. Branch pipes were made of lead or copper, stack pipes of cast iron, traps of lead or brass and underground pipes of vitrified clay. Only the latter still predominantly utilize the traditional material.

Your legal position
Drainage regulations fall under the Public Health Acts as well as the Building Regulations, so it's important to know where you stand. The householder is responsible for the entire drainage system until it enters the public sewer – even though this is usually beyond the boundary of the property. While blockages beyond the lowest inspection chamber are rare, any clearance work can be very expensive – particularly if you use a '24-hour' plumbing service. The public

SINGLE STACK SYSTEMS

Single stack waste systems must be built and modified correctly in order to be acceptable to the authorities and to work properly. Here are some rules to remember:

● 'P' traps must be used on all appliances – 'S' (integral) traps are only allowed on WCs – and the depth of seal should always be 75mm (3in)

● wash basins and bidets need a 32mm (1¼in) diameter trap and branch pipe, if the branch is up to 1.7m (5ft 7in) long. If more – up to a maximum of 2.3m (7ft 6in) – use a 38mm trap and pipe

● baths, sinks and showers use a 38mm (1½in) diameter trap and branch pipe

● washing machines use a vertical stand pipe (usually about 600mm/24in high) with a 32mm (1¼in) diameter trap at the bottom ('P' or running 'P'). There must be an air gap where the hose enters the standpipe

● WC branch pipes are usually 100mm (4in) in diameter to correspond with the outlet; branch lengths can be up to 6m (20ft) long

● branch pipe gradients should be at a minimal angle – preferably 1-2½° (18-45mm fall per metre or ¾-1¾in per 39in)

● ground floor WCs can connect directly into the underground drain as long as the top of the trap is less than 1.5m (5ft) from the point of entry into the main drain

● there should be no connection nearer than 200mm (8in) below the WC branch connection from the opposite side of the stack

● the lowest connection to the stack must be at least 450mm (18in) above the bottom of the bend at the base of the stack

● the bend at the base of the stack (below ground) must have a radius of at least 200mm (8in)

● stack pipes must be at least the same diameter as the WC outlet

● the top of the stack pipe, capped with a grille, must be above the eaves and at least 0.9m (35in) above any window which is within 3m (10ft) of the pipe.

sewer is provided by the public health authority and is their responsibility.

If your house was built as one of a group of houses, then it's quite possible that you'll have shared drainage facilities. This means there is one drainage pipe collecting the waste of several homes before it discharges into the public sewer. The system was adopted because it saved installation costs. If your house was built before 1937, it's still the responsibility of the local authorities to cleanse the shared drainage runs, although you're responsible for clearing blockages and for maintenance. But if you live in a post-1937 house then the responsibility for the shared drains rests collectively on all the owners concerned and if a blockage is caused by someone else you will have to pay a proportion of the bill. It is therefore important when moving house to check out the exact position. If this is difficult to ascertain, try the Environmental Health Officer for advice; he should also be consulted if you want to change the system.

PLASTIC WASTE TRAPS

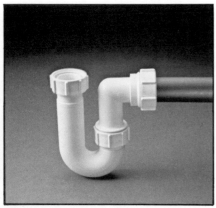

The modern U-bend *is made from one of several plastic materials.*

A U-bend with telescopic extension *can be adjusted to existing appliances.*

An S-bend *is designed for use where the outlet is vertical.*

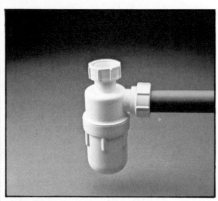

A bottle trap *gives a neater appearance, but is less efficient.*

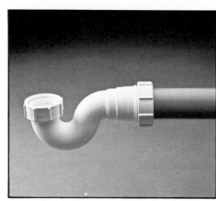

A shallow trap *is used beneath a bath or shower where space is crucial.*

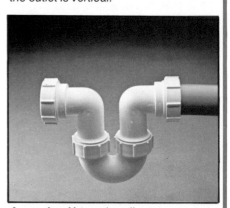

A running U-trap *handles two or more untrapped appliances piped together.*

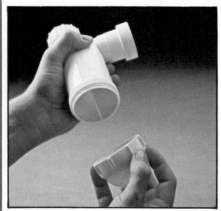

A dip partition bottle trap *has a base which unscrews.*

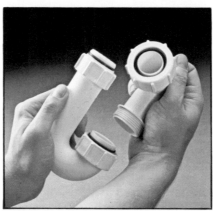

All modern traps come apart for easy cleaning and installation.

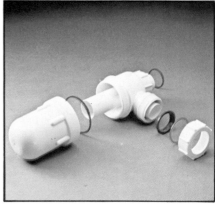

A dip tube trap taken apart to show the O rings and washers.

UNDERSTANDING WATER SUPPLY

Each one of us uses about 160 litres (35 gallons) of water a day, and takes it for granted. Only in a long spell of dry weather comes an awareness that we should use it carefully. Our use is controlled by the supply system – this is how it works.

In the last 50 years the consumption of water has almost doubled. Rising standards of living have given rise to increased consumption, and a greater awareness of the need for hygiene has also played a large role in increasing the demand. Faced with this high demand, supply sources have been hard pressed to keep up.

Where it comes from

Water is supplied by the local water authority (or the 'Undertaking' as it is known in the plumbing trade). After falling as rain it is collected in reservoirs which are fed by streams and rivers, or is pumped from underground wells. Water varies a lot in its chemical makeup since it picks up minerals and gases as it flows. If it picks up calcium, magnesium and sodium salts it will be 'hard' – the menace of pipe systems. Before being distributed it is usually filtered through sand and pebble beds to remove solids and organisms, and may have chlorine added to it to ensure that it is 'potable' – drinkable. Fluoride is also sometimes added for the protection of teeth.

Distribution is carried out by a network of pipes starting with 'trunk mains' which may be as much as 610mm (24in) in diameter. These split into mains and sub-mains which run underneath streets and side streets. It is these sub-mains which are tapped by individual houses for their supply.

The house system may be 'direct' in which all cold water supplies are piped direct from the rising main, with the cistern only being used to supply the hot water tank. Or it may be an 'indirect' system in which all cold-water supplies are taken from the cistern, with the exception of a direct supply to the kitchen sink for drinking purposes.

For water to flow through the trunk mains – and eventually into your house – it must be under a certain amount of pressure. This pressure is assisted by pumps but it is vital that somewhere in the mains system the water should reach a height in a reservoir or water tower, higher than any domestic system it has to supply. The vertical distance through which the water 'falls' is known as the 'pressure head' and without it our

cisterns would never fill up without a lot of expensive additional pumping. The storage cistern also provides a pressure head inside the house, which is why it's preferable to have it in the roof space.

The house system

The sub-main underneath the road is tapped by the 'communication pipe' which ends at the authority's stop-valve. This is usually situated under the pavement about 300mm (1ft) outside the boundary of your property. The stop-valve is located at the bottom of a vertical 'guard' pipe – about 1 metre (39in) deep – which is covered at the surface by a hinged metal cover. It should only be operated by the water authority and requires a special key to turn it. But in a real emergency you may be able to turn it yourself. In old houses it may be the only way of turning off the water supply. After this stop-valve the water enters the service pipe and from then on all pipes become your responsibility.

The service pipe continues under the wall of the property at a depth of at least 750mm (2ft 6in) to protect it from frost – though some water authorities insist that it should be 900mm (3ft) deep. As it travels under the house wall or foundation it usually goes through an earthenware pipe to protect it

INDIRECT COLD SUPPLY

The most common system of water supply in the UK is called 'indirect' because most taps take water from the storage cistern in the roof and not direct from the mains. The cistern is fed by the rising main which in turn is fed by the distribution pipe from the mains.

Water input to the cistern is controlled by a high pressure ball-valve. If this valve jams open the water level rises to flow out of the overflow or 'warning' pipe which should stick well out from the wall.

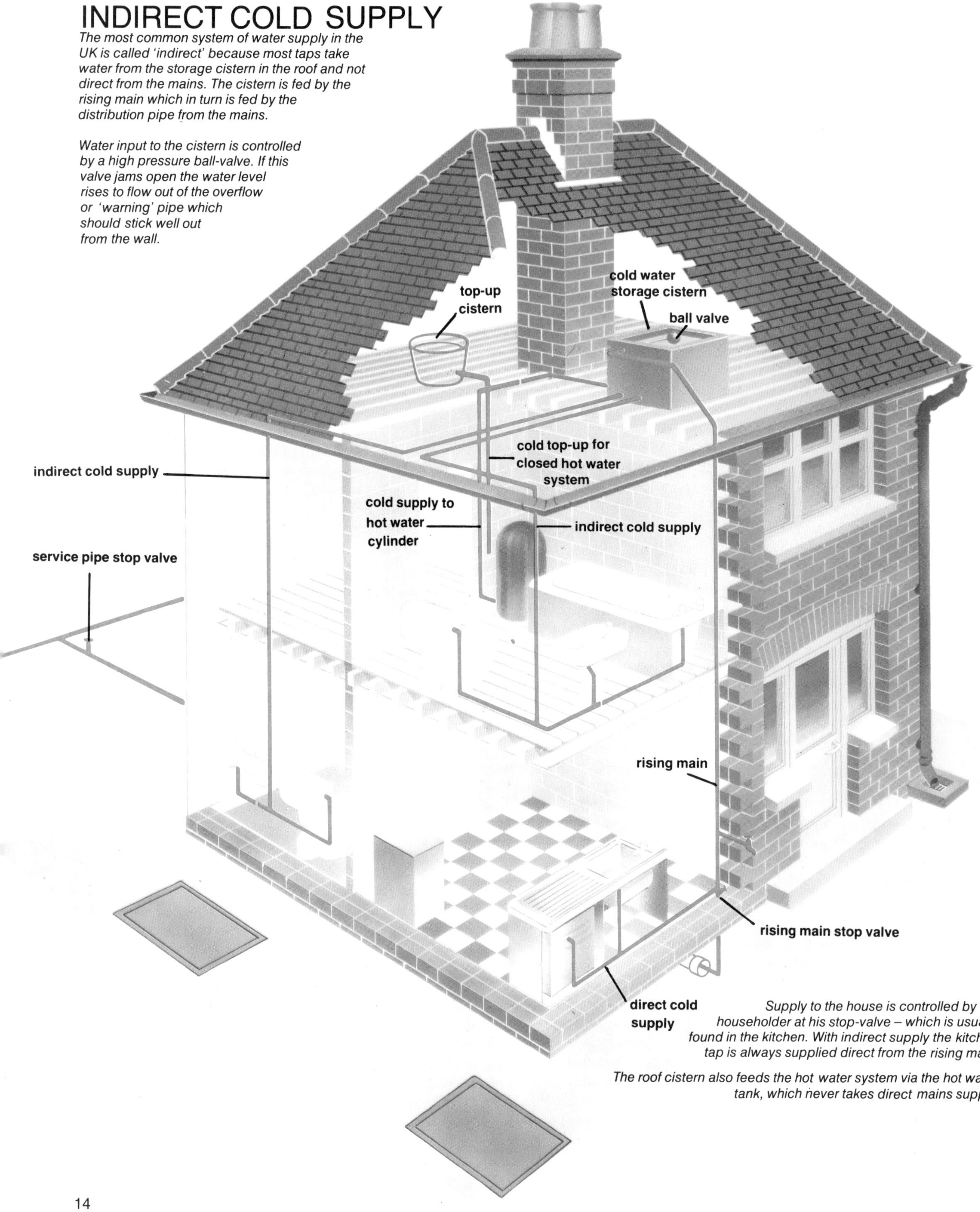

David Pope

top-up cistern

cold water storage cistern

ball valve

cold top-up for closed hot water system

indirect cold supply

cold supply to hot water cylinder

indirect cold supply

service pipe stop valve

rising main

rising main stop valve

direct cold supply

Supply to the house is controlled by the householder at his stop-valve – which is usually found in the kitchen. With indirect supply the kitchen tap is always supplied direct from the rising main.

The roof cistern also feeds the hot water system via the hot water tank, which never takes direct mains supply.

from possible settlement which might cause it to fracture. To prevent any risk of freezing in cold weather the service pipe should not emerge above ground level until it is at least 600mm (2ft) inside the inside wall surface.

Up to about 40 years ago, service pipes were usually made of lead (in fact the word plumbing originally stemmed from the Latin word for lead – *plumbum*). Today copper and polythene are used instead. The latter is particularly good as it is a poor conductor of heat and is less prone to freezing and fracture.

The service pipe

The service pipe continues under the wall near the kitchen sink, which means that it is often attached to the inner face of the outside wall. This is contrary to the recommendation that it should be attached to an inside wall, and so such a pipe should be lagged with insulation material. The pipe should also be insulated if it comes through any sub-ground floor cavity where it would be subjected to the icy blasts of winter from under-floor ventilation. Again these precautions are both intended to minimise the risk of frost damage.

When the service pipe rises above the ground floor it is called the 'rising main' and it eventually terminates in the supply cistern, which is usually in the roof cavity. The householder's main stop-valve is usually found on the rising main a little way above floor level. This is the most important 'tap' in the house. In any plumbing emergency – when bursts or leaks occur, for example, your first action should be to turn this tap off, thus isolating the house system from the mains water supply. The stop-valve should always be turned off when you go away if the house is going to be empty. In old houses the location of the stop-valve may vary considerably, it may be in the cellar, under the stairs, or even under a cover beneath the front path – or it may not exist at all, in which case the authority's stop-valve is the only control.

Branch supply pipes

At least one 'branch' supply pipe leaves the rising main close above the stop-valve and drain tap – this is to the tap over the kitchen sink. This tap must be supplied direct from the main supply as it is supposed to provide all drinking and cooking water. Water which has been in a storage cistern is no longer considered drinkable, sometimes termed 'potable', as it may be slightly contaminated by debris in the storage cistern.

Other branches may be taken at this point to an outside tap, or to a washing machine or dishwasher.

The rising main continues upwards and while its ultimate destination is the cold water storage cistern the pipework in between will vary from house to house, depending on

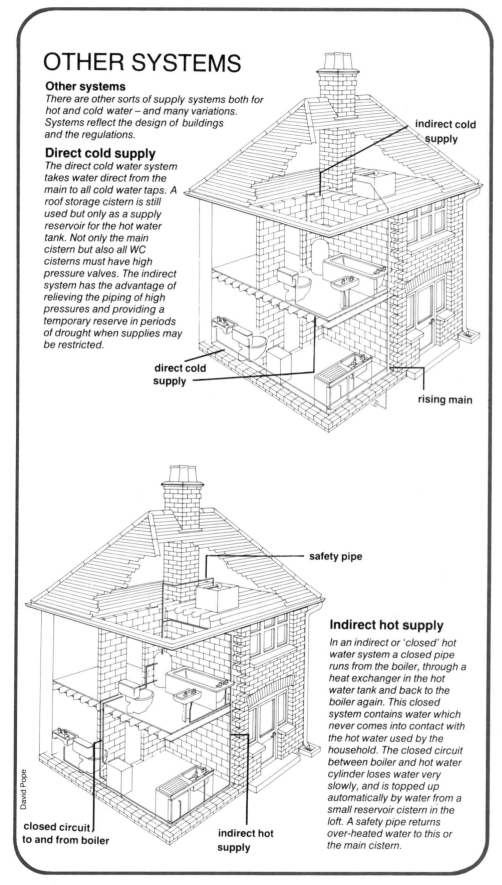

OTHER SYSTEMS

Other systems
There are other sorts of supply systems both for hot and cold water – and many variations. Systems reflect the design of buildings and the regulations.

Direct cold supply
The direct cold water system takes water direct from the main to all cold water taps. A roof storage cistern is still used but only as a supply reservoir for the hot water tank. Not only the main cistern but also all WC cisterns must have high pressure valves. The indirect system has the advantage of relieving the piping of high pressures and providing a temporary reserve in periods of drought when supplies may be restricted.

indirect cold supply

direct cold supply

rising main

safety pipe

Indirect hot supply

In an indirect or 'closed' hot water system a closed pipe runs from the boiler, through a heat exchanger in the hot water tank and back to the boiler again. This closed system contains water which never comes into contact with the hot water used by the household. The closed circuit between boiler and hot water cylinder loses water very slowly, and is topped up automatically by water from a small reservoir cistern in the loft. A safety pipe returns over-heated water to this or the main cistern.

closed circuit to and from boiler

indirect hot supply

David Pope

DIRECT HOT WATER SUPPLY

The direct or 'open' system of hot water supply is based on the water being supplied to the hot water tank from the cold water cistern, passed to the boiler for heating, returned to the tank for storage and then piped to the supply taps.

The cold water cistern is always used to supply water to the hot water cistern. Direct feed from the mains supply should never be used as the pressure would be too great.

David Pope

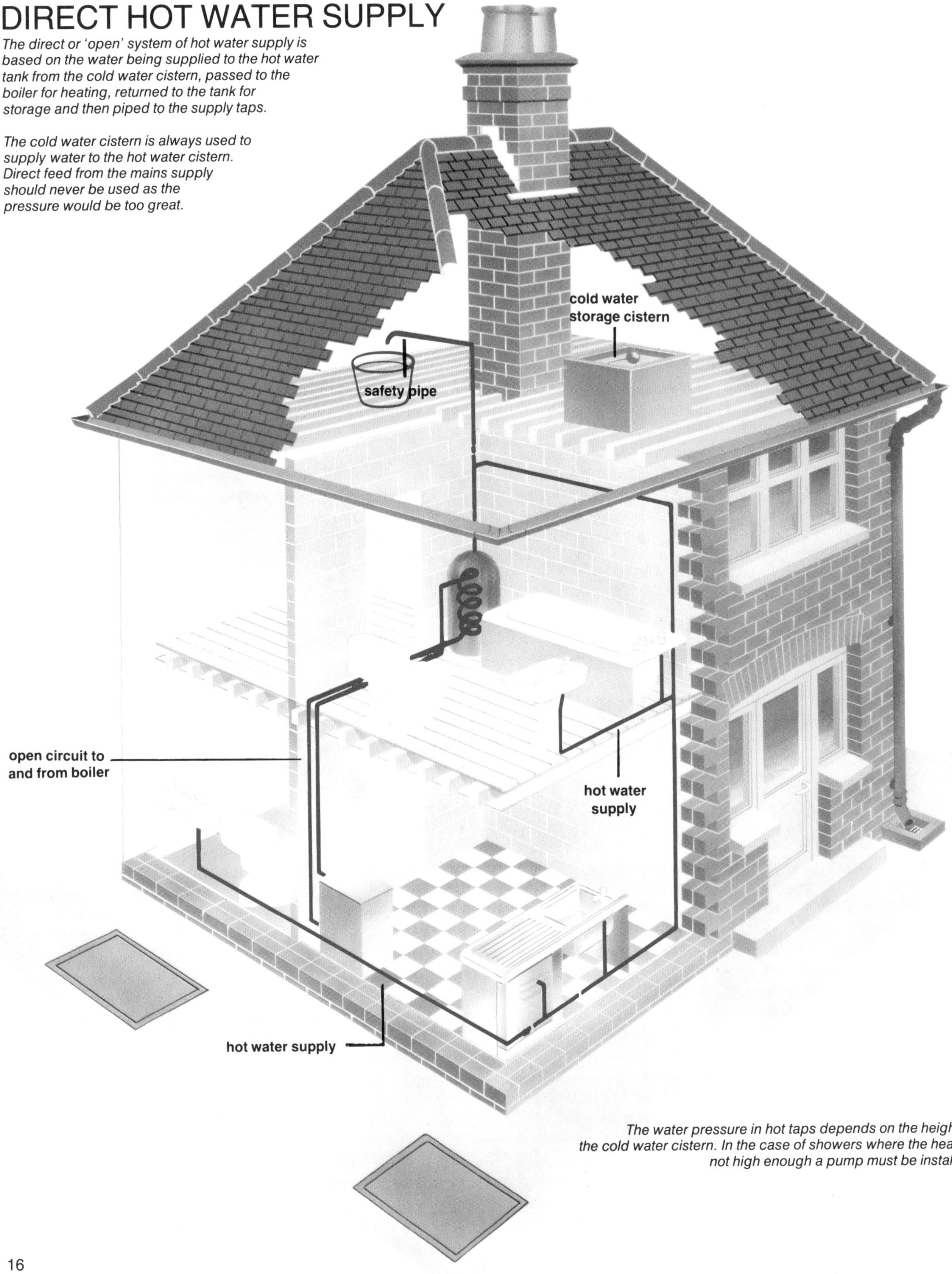

cold water
storage cistern

safety pipe

open circuit to
and from boiler

hot water
supply

hot water supply

The water pressure in hot taps depends on the height of the cold water cistern. In the case of showers where the head is not high enough a pump must be installed.

16

whether a 'direct' or 'indirect' system has been installed.

In many areas indirect systems must be installed in new buildings, yet in Western Europe direct systems are the rule. Indirect systems have been encouraged because of the difficulty in maintaining constant mains pressure particularly at times of peak demand. Routing of most supplies through the storage cistern evens out fluctuations, and it also rules out the risk of 'back siphonage' whereby dirty water could be sucked back into the mains supply – though this rarely occurs. The 1976 drought in the UK provided good reason for indirect systems, since each house had an emergency supply in the storage cistern if the mains water had to be shut off.

Cisterns

The 'tank' in your loft or attic is in fact a 'cistern'. Cisterns are not sealed – though they should be covered – and so are subject to atmospheric pressure. Tanks are completely sealed – as with a hot water storage tank – and are not subject to atmospheric pressure.

Cold water cisterns ‚have traditionally been made of galvanised mild steel and it is quite likely that you will find one like this in your loft. They are still available, but are not usually installed in new houses. Other materials used have been asbestos, cement, copper and glass fibre, but today the most common material is plastic, of which glass fibre reinforced polyester (GRP), polythene and polypropylene are the most common varieties.

The advantages plastics have over all other cistern materials are their lightness in weight, resistance to corrosion and flexibility. Galvanised steel is heavy and liable to corrode, while asbestos and cement are not only heavy but can become porous and are prone to accidental damage. Don't forget the capacity of a typical cistern is 227 litres (50 gallons), and this water alone weighs nearly 0.25 tonne (¼ ton), so all cisterns must be fully supported on the joists. With rigid materials such as steel the cistern can rest across the joists, but with plastic and glass fibre a platform should be installed to support the whole area of the bottom, otherwise the material may develop local weaknesses.

Cisterns should be covered to prevent any contamination of the water. Where the underside of the roof is exposed dust and dirt are liable to fall in. The top and sides should also be insulated to minimise the risk of freezing. The bottom is left uncovered to allow rising warm air from rooms below to keep the water above freezing point, and so you shouldn't insulate the roof space under the cistern.

Cisterns were often installed before the roof was put on and if you want to replace yours, perhaps because it's made of steel and is

corroding, you may not be able to get it through the trap door. While it is sometimes suggested that a cistern should be cut up to get it out this is in fact a very heavy and arduous job in such a confined space and it would be better to manoeuvre it to one side and leave it in the loft, installing a new cistern alongside. Modern plastic cisterns can literally be folded up so they can be passed through small loft hatches.

Pipes and taps

Water leaves the storage cistern in distribution pipes which are usually 22mm (¾in) or 15mm (½in) in diameter. In a direct system, supply from the cistern will usually be to the hot water tank, and in an indirect system this link must also be direct – but other distribution pipes are used with branches to supply the other appliances – basins, baths and WC cisterns. Distribution pipes usually end in taps but in the case of a WC a low pressure ball-valve controls the flow.

The WC in an indirect system has a low pressure ball-valve because when the water leaves the storage cistern it is no longer at mains pressure but at normal atmospheric pressure which is pressing down on the surface of the stored water. This means that the higher up the house a tap or other outlet is situated the lower will be the water pressure. In practice this means that you can't have a tap in an indirect system which is above the level of its distribution outlet from the cistern. Showers are particularly affected by this difference of pressure, and if there is not sufficient 'head' to 'drive' the shower a special pump may have to be installed.

Cold water supplied to the hot water tank is heated in two different ways again called indirect and direct systems – or, respectively, closed and open. In the latter the cold water is circulated through the boiler, where it is heated, and returned to the tank from where it flows to tapped outlets. In the indirect system the cold water supplied never actually goes to the boiler, instead it is heated in the tank by a coiled pipe or jacket containing hot water which is continuously circulating through the boiler. In either case a pump often helps the water flow through the boiler, and supplementary or alternative heat may come from an immersion heater. If there is no boiler but only an immersion heater in the tank the system is essentially direct with the heating of the water taking place in the tank rather than in the boiler.

Draining the system

Just above the rising main stop-valve should be a drain cock. With the stop-valve turned off the drain cock can be used to drain part of the cold water system when repairs are necessary – the hot water system has its own drain cock.

Ready Reference

PIPE SIZES AND THEIR USES

Distribution pipes
● 22mm (¾in) pipe – water supply to bath and hot water cylinder
● 15m (½in) pipe – WC, basin, bidet and shower supplies
● 28mm (1in) pipe – for use with multiple appliances, but usually unnecessary.

Warning pipes (Overflows)
● these must have a diameter greater than that of the inlet pipe to prevent cold water cisterns and WC cisterns from overflowing.

CONNECTIONS AT COLD WATER CISTERN

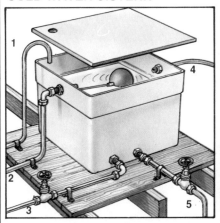

1 safety pipe   3 cold supply to taps
2 rising main   4 overflow
    5 cold supply to hot water tank

DRAINING THE SYSTEM

To drain the system from the mains stop-valve to cistern, turn off the stop-valve and attach one end of the hose to the drain cock, which should be just above the stop-valve, and run the other end to a drain. Then open the drain cock.
Drain remainder of system by turning off

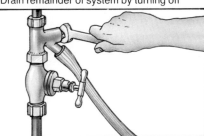

mains supply and opening cold water taps. The hot water system has its own drain cock, usually found close to the boiler.

JOINTS FOR COPPER PIPE

Joining copper pipe is one of the basic plumbing skills. Compression and capillary joints are easy to make and once you've mastered the techniques, you'll be prepared for a whole range of plumbing projects.

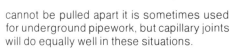

Connecting pipes effectively is the basis of all good plumbing as most leaks result from poorly constructed joints. For virtually all domestic plumbing purposes you will only have to use compression or capillary joints. Compression joints are easy to use but expensive, while capillary joints are cheap but need some care in fitting.

If you are making a join into an existing pipe system remember to make sure the water supply has been turned off at the relevant stoptap or gatevalve (see pages 139–141 and 142–143 for more details), and the pipe itself completely drained of water.

Preparing the pipes
Before joining the pipes together, check that the ends are circular and have not been distorted. If they have been dented, cut back to an undamaged section using a hacksaw with a sharp blade or a wheel tube cutter (see pages 149–151).

The ends should also be square and a simple way of checking this is shown overleaf (see *Ready Reference*). Use a file to make any correction and remove ragged burrs of metal. If you're using a capillary joint clean up the sides of the pipe with abrasive paper or steel wool.

Compression joints (friction joints)
A compression joint, as its name implies, is made by compressing two brass or copper rings (known as olives or thimbles) round the ends of the pipes to be joined, so forming a watertight seal. There are two main types of compression joint – the non-manipulative fitting and the manipulative fitting.

Although not the cheapest means of joining a pipe, a non-manipulative joint is the easiest to use and requires only the minimum of tools. It comprises a central body made of brass or gunmetal with a cap-nut at each end which, when rotated, squeezes the olive tightly between the pipe end and the casing. This is the most commonly used type of compression joint suitable for most internal domestic plumbing purposes.

A manipulative joint is now rarely used in indoor domestic water systems. Because it

cannot be pulled apart it is sometimes used for underground pipework, but capillary joints will do equally well in these situations.

The joint usually comprises a male and a female union nut. These are slipped over the pipe ends which are then flared ('manipulated') using a special steel tool called a *drift*. Jointing compound is smeared on the inside of the flares and a copper cone is inserted between them. The nuts are then screwed together to complete the seal.

How a compression joint works
The olive (thimble) is the key part of a non-manipulative compression joint. When the cap-nut is rotated clockwise the olive is forced between the casing and the pipe and is considerably deformed in the process.

A watertight seal is dependent upon the pipe ends having been well prepared so they butt up exactly to the pipe stop in the casing. This forms a primary seal and ensures that the pipe is parallel to the movement of the rotating cap-nut. An even pressure is then

applied to the olive so that it does not buckle under the strain of tightening.

What size of pipework and fittings?
Pipework is now sold in metric dimensions, but plumbing in your home may be in imperial sizes. The metric sizes are not exactly the same as their imperial equivalents – check the table *(Ready Reference, right)* which shows the different ways pipe can be bought.

These differences can cause problems. With capillary joints you have to use adaptors when converting pipe from one system to another. Adaptors are also needed for some compression joints although the 12mm, 15mm, 28mm and 54mm sizes are compatible with their imperial equivalents. This means if you already have imperial compression joints you can connect in new metric pipework, without replacing the joints.

Adaptors are made with different combinations of metric and imperial outlets to fit most requirements. A supplier will advise on what replacements to use.

HOW OLIVES MAKE A WATERTIGHT SEAL

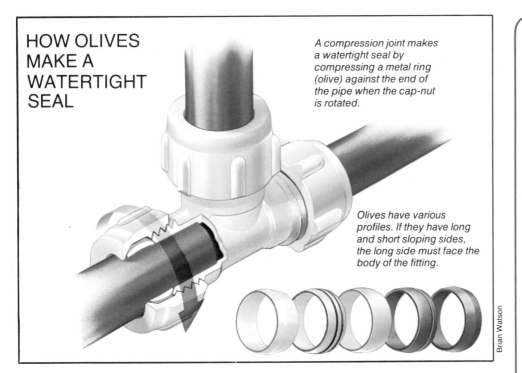

A compression joint makes a watertight seal by compressing a metal ring (olive) against the end of the pipe when the cap-nut is rotated.

Olives have various profiles. If they have long and short sloping sides, the long side must face the body of the fitting.

Brian Watson

Capillary joints

A capillary joint is simply a copper sleeve with socket outlets into which the pipe ends are soldered. It is neater and smaller than a compression joint and forms a robust connection that will not readily pull apart.

Because it is considerably cheaper than a compression joint it is frequently used when a number of joints have to be made and is particularly useful in awkward positions where it is impossible to use wrenches.

Some people are put off using capillary fittings because of the need to use a blow-torch. But modern gas-canister torches have put paid to the fears associated with

paraffin lamps and are not dangerous.

How a capillary joint works

If two pipes to be joined together were just soldered end to end the join would be very weak because the contact area between solder and copper would be small. A capillary fitting makes a secure join because the sleeve increases this contact area and also acts as a brace to strengthen the connection.

Molten solder is sucked into the space between the pipe and fitting by capillary action, and combines with a thin layer of copper at the contact surface thus bonding the pipe to the fitting. To help the solder to

What happens when solder melts

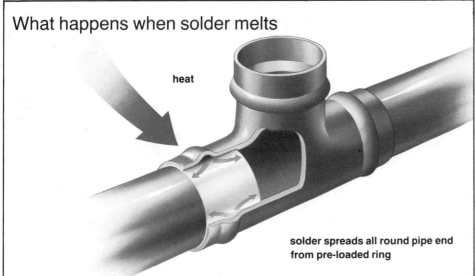

heat

solder spreads all round pipe end from pre-loaded ring

Brian Watson

MAKING A COMPRESSION JOINT

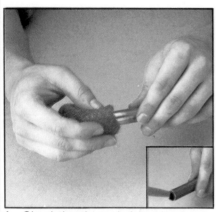

1 Check that the end of the pipe is square using a file to make any correction and to remove burr. Clean pipe end and olive with steel wool.

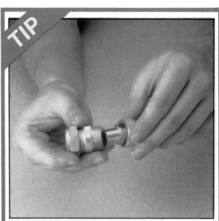

2 The olive goes on after the cap-nut. If it has both long and short sloping sides, make sure the long side faces the main body of the compression fitting.

3 Push pipe end firmly into body of fitting so that it rests squarely against pipe stop. Screw up cap-nut tightly with your fingers.

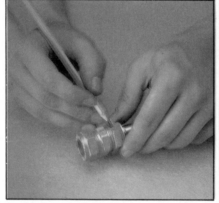

4 Make pencil mark on cap-nut and another aligning on body of fitting to act as guide when tightening cap-nut with wrench.

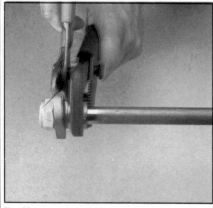

5 Use one wrench to secure body of fitting and the other to rotate the cap-nut clockwise. About 1½ turns is sufficient to give a watertight seal.

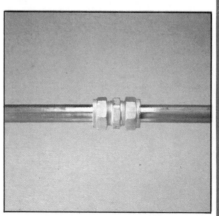

6 Repeat operation to join other pipe to fitting. If water seeps through when supply is turned on, tighten cap-nut further by half a turn.

'take' the copper needs to be clean and shining. Therefore flux is applied to prevent oxides forming which would impair the solder-copper bond.

Types of capillary joint

The most common type of capillary joint has a ring of solder pre-loaded into the sleeve. It is known as an integral ring or 'Yorkshire' fitting – the name of a leading brand.

The 'end feed' type of capillary joint is virtually the same as an integral ring fitting, but you have to add the solder in a separate operation. The sleeve is slightly larger than the pipe and liquid solder is drawn into the space between by capillary action.

Flux and solder

Essential in the soldering operation, flux is a chemical paste or liquid which cleans the metal surfaces and then protects them from the oxides produced when the blow-torch heats the copper so a good metal-solder bond is formed. Mild non-corrosive flux is easy to use as it can be smeared onto the pipe and fitting with a clean brush or even a finger. Although it is best to remove any residue this will not corrode the metal. There is an acid-corrosive flux which dissolves oxides quickly, but this is mostly used with stainless steel. The corrosive residue must be scrubbed off with soapy water.

Solder is an alloy of tin and lead or silver and is bought as a reel of wire. Its advantage in making capillary joints is that it melts at relatively low temperatures and quickly hardens as it cools. Lead-free solder must now be used on pipes carrying drinking water.

Blow-torches

A blow-torch is an essential piece of equipment when making capillary joints. It is easy, clean and safe to use providing you handle it with care. Most modern torches operate off a gas canister which can be unscrewed and inexpensively replaced (larger cans are relatively cheaper than small). Sometimes a range of nozzles can be fitted to give different types of flames, but the standard nozzle is perfectly acceptable for capillary joint work.

Using a blow-torch

When using a blow-torch it's most convenient to work at a bench, but you'll find most jointing work has to be carried out where the pipes are to run. Pipework is usually concealed so this may mean working in an awkward place, such as a roof space, or stretching under floorboards. However, always make sure you are in a comfortable position and there's no danger of you dropping a lighted blow-torch.

MAKING A CAPILLARY FITTING

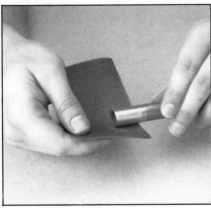

1 Make sure the pipe end is square, then clean it and the inner rim of the fitting with steel wool or abrasive paper until shining.

2 Flux can be in liquid or paste form. Use a brush, rather than your finger, to smear it over the end of the pipe and the inner rim of the fitting.

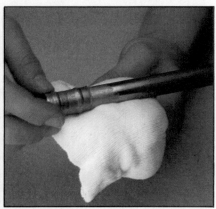

3 Push pipe into fitting so that it rests against pipe stop, twisting a little to help spread the flux. Remove excess flux with a cloth.

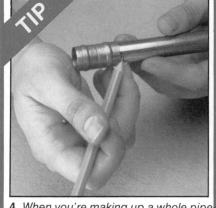

TIP

4 When you're making up a whole pipe-run, it helps to make corresponding pencil marks on pipe ends and fittings as a guide for correct lining up.

5 Make other side of joint in same way, then apply blow-torch. Seal is complete when bright ring of solder is visible at ends of fitting.

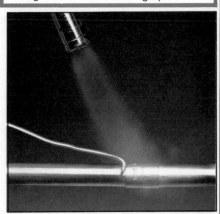

6 For an end feed fitting, heat the pipe, then hold the solder to mouth of joint. A bright ring all the way round signifies a seal.

Jem Grischotti

Ready Reference

WHICH TOOLS?

For cutting pipe:
● hire a **wheel tube cutter** (which ensures perfectly square pipe ends)

or use a **hack saw**
● use a **metal file** for removing ragged burrs of metal and for squaring ends of pipe that have been cut with a hacksaw. A half-round 'second-cut' type is ideal.

For compression joints:
● use two adjustable **spanners** or **pipe wrenches** (one to hold the fitting, the other to tighten the cap-nut)

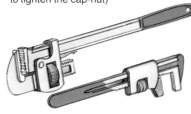

● **steel wool** to clean the surface of pipes before assembling a joint.

For capillary joints:
● a **blow-torch** to melt the solder
● **steel-wool** for cleaning pipe surfaces
● **flux** to ensure a good bond between the solder and copper
● **solder** because even if you're using integral ring fittings (which already have solder in them) you may need a bit extra
● **glass fibre** or **asbestos mat** (or a ceramic tile) to deflect the torch flame from nearby surfaces.

TIP: CUTTING PIPE SQUARELY

For a perfect fit, pipe ends must be cut square. If you're using a hacksaw, hold a strip of paper round the pipe so its edges align and saw parallel to the paper edge. Use the same trick if you have to file an inaccurately-cut end.

TIP: PROTECT NEARBY JOINTS

With capillary fittings, the heat you apply could melt the solder in nearby fittings. To help prevent this, wrap them in wet cloths.

When working near to joists and floor-boards, glass, paintwork and other pipework with capillary joints it is important to shield these areas with glass fibre matting or a piece of asbestos.

Applying the heat

When making a capillary joint gradually build up the temperature of the copper by playing the flame up and down and round the pipe and then to the fitting. When the metal is hot enough the solder will melt and you can then take away the flame. The joint is complete when a bright ring of solder appears all round the mouth of the fitting. Stand the torch on a firm level surface and turn it off as soon as you have finished. Where two or more capillary joints are to be made with one fitting, for example the three ends of a tee, they should all be made at the same time. If this is not possible wrap a damp rag round any joints already made.

Repairing a compression joint

If a compression joint is leaking and tightening of the cap-nut doesn't produce a watertight seal you'll have to disconnect the fitting and look inside – after turning off the water supply. If a cap-nut is impossible to move, run a few drops of penetrating oil onto the thread. If that doesn't do the trick, you'll have to cut it out and replace the fitting and some piping.

Once you have unscrewed one of the cap-nuts there will be enough flexibility in the pipe run to pull the pipe from the casing. Usually the olive will be compressed against the pipe. First check that it is the right way round (see page 152) and if it isn't replace it with a new one making sure that it is correctly set.

Sometimes the olive is impossible to remove and needs to be cut off with a hacksaw – make the cut diagonally. Reassemble the joint following the procedure on

page 154 and repeat the operation for the other end of the pipe. Turn on the water supply to check that the repair is watertight.

Repairing a capillary joint

Poor initial soldering is usually the reason why a capillary fitting leaks. You can try and rectify this by 'sweating' in some more solder but if this doesn't work you'll have to remake the joint.

Play the flame of the blow-torch over the fitting and pipe until the solder begins to run from the joint. At this stage you can pull the pipe ends out of the sockets with gloved hands. You can now reuse the fitting as an end feed joint or replace it with a new integral ring capillary connection.

If you reuse the fitting clean the interior surface and the pipe ends with abrasive paper or steel wool and smear them with flux. Then follow the procedure for making an end feed capillary joint.

REPAIRING A COMPRESSION JOINT

1 *Unscrew cap-nut using wrenches. There's enough flexibility in pipe run to pull pipe from casing. Check that olive fits, and isn't damaged.*

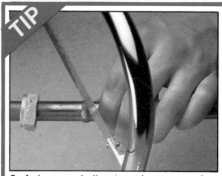

2 *A damaged olive must be removed. Use a hacksaw and to make it easier make the cut on the diagonal – but take care not to cut into the pipe itself.*

3 *Prepare end of pipe with steel wool or abrasive paper. Slip on new olive and finger tighten cap-nut. Rotate cap-nut 1½ turns using wrenches.*

REPAIRING A CAPILLARY JOINT

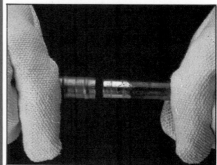

1 *Drain pipe and wrap a damp cloth round nearby joints. Play flame on fitting and pull pipe from rim using gloved hands.*

2 *If you remake both sides of joint use a new fitting. A spent integral ring fitting, thoroughly cleaned, can be used as an end feed joint.*

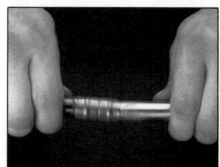

3 *Use steel wool to clean end of pipe and inside of fitting. Brush with flux and push pipe into socket. Apply blow-torch to melt solder.*

CUTTING & BENDING COPPER PIPE

One of the advantages of domestic copper pipe is that it's easy to cut and bend. Few tools are required and even if you've only a few bends to make in a pipe run, it makes sense to know how it's done. Making accurate bends may need some practice, but it's cheaper than buying specially-shaped fittings.

In all plumbing water has to be carried from a source to a fixture and often then to some type of exit where it can disperse as waste. Basic to all of this is that water must run smoothly with nothing causing resistance to the flow — an important factor when the pressure is low.

Generally the best plumbing practice is to make pipe runs as straight and direct as possible. But sometimes bends are unavoidable (like, for example, when pipe has to go around a room or to turn down into an area below) and if available fittings are neither right for the angle nor attractive to look at, then you'll have to bend the pipe to suit.

Copper piping, because it is both light and resistant to corrosion, is a popular choice for home plumbing work. It can be joined with either capillary or compression fittings (see pages 154–156 for more details) and when bends are needed you can create the angles in several ways.

The first essential is to accurately work out the pipe lengths you require. Once you've made the measurement double check it — it's quite easy to forget to allow for the pipe that will fit into the socket ends of the joints. You can make the actual marks on the pipe with pencil as this is clearly visible on copper and is a good guide when you come to cutting.

Cutting pipe accurately

For smaller pipe sizes, a sharp-bladed hacksaw is the best tool to use to make the cut. You'll need to hold the pipe firmly, but if you use a vice be careful not to over-tighten the jaws and crush the bore of the pipe (see *Ready Reference*).

It's important to cut the pipe square so that it butts up exactly to the pipe stop in the joint. This will ensure the pipe is seated squarely in the fitting which is essential for making a watertight seal. It will also help to make that seal. It's surprising how near to square you can get the end just cutting by eye. But the best way to make a really accurate cut is to use a saw guide. This can be made very easily by placing a small rectangle of paper round the pipe with one long edge against the cut mark. By bringing the two short edges of the paper together and aligning them you effectively make a template that's square to the pipe. All you then have to do is hold the paper in place and keep the saw blade against it as you cut. Any burr that's left on the cut edges can be removed with a file.

If you intend to carry out a lot of plumbing, or are working mainly in the larger pipe sizes, it may be worthwhile buying (or hiring) a wheel tube cutter. Of course using one of these is never absolutely essential, but it does save time if you've more than, say, half a dozen cuts to make. And once you have one you'll use it for even the smallest jobs. It's quick to use and will ensure a square cut without trouble every time. You simply place the pipe in the cutter and tighten the control knob to hold it in place. The cutter is then rotated round the pipe and as it revolves it cuts cleanly into the copper. This circular action automatically removes burr from the outside of the pipe, but burr on the inside can be taken away with the reamer (a scraping edge) which is usually incorporated in the tool.

Bending copper pipe

If a lot of changes of direction are necessary in a pipe run it's cheaper and quicker to bend the pipe rather than use fittings. This also makes the neatest finish particularly if the pipework is going to be exposed. Under a pedestal wash-basin, for example, the hot and cold supply pipes rise parallel to each other in the pedestal before bending outwards and upwards to connect to the two tap tails.

GETTING BENDS RIGHT

The trickiest part of bending copper pipe is getting the bends in the right place.
To avoid mistakes
● don't try to make too many bends in one pipe length
● mark the position for one bend at a time.

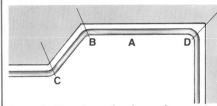

Example: To make up the pipe run in our sketch, plan to divide up the run at A; here two pipe lengths will be joined by a straight coupling after the bends have been formed.
● form bend B at approximately the right distance from point A
● offer up bend B to the wall, mark the start of bend C where the pipe touches the corner point
● form bend C and check for fit.
To get bend D in the right place on the second length of pipe
● measure the distance from A into the corner of the wall
● form bend D at this distance from the pipe end
● lay the two lengths in place, cut off any overlap and connect them with a straight coupling.

23

Using fittings in this situation would be costly while the cheaper alternative, making bends, means the pipework is less conspicuous. The pipe can also be bent to the exact angle required so this method of changing direction is not limited by the angles of the fittings. And with fewer fittings in a pipe system there are fewer places where leaks can occur.

The smaller sizes of copper pipe, those most commonly used in domestic plumbing, can be bent quite easily by hand. The technique of annealing — heating the pipe to red heat in the vicinity of the bend to reduce its temper (strength) and so make bending easier — is unnecessary when working in these pipe sizes. But the pipe will need support, either internally or externally, as the bend is made otherwise the profile will be flattened and this would cause a reduction in the flow of water at the outlet point.

For small jobs a bending spring is the ideal tool, supporting the pipe internally. It is a long hardened steel coil which you push into the pipe to the point where the bend will be made. It's best used for bends near the end of the pipe, since the spring can be easily pulled out after the bend is made. However, it can be used further down the pipe if it is attached to a length of stout wire (which helps to push it into place, and is vital for retrieving it afterwards).

Bending techniques
You actually bend the pipe over your knee, overbending slightly and bringing back to the required angle. The spring will now be fixed tightly in the pipe and you won't be able simply to pull it out. However, its removal is quite easy. All you have to do is insert a bar – a screwdriver will do – through the ring at the end of the spring and twist it. This reduces the spring's diameter and will enable you to withdraw it. It's a good idea to grease the spring before you insert it as this will make pulling it out that much easier (also see *Ready Reference*).

Slight wrinkles may be found on the inside of the bend, but these can be tapped out by gentle hammering. It's wise not to attempt this before taking out the spring. If you do you'll never be able to remove it.

Bending springs are suitable for 15mm and 22mm diameter pipe. But although it is possible to bend 28mm pipe as well, it's advisable to use a bending machine instead. This is also preferable if you have a lot of bends to make. And if you don't want to go to the expense of buying one, you can probably hire a machine from a tool hire shop quite easily.

A bending machine consists of a semi-circular former that supports the pipe externally during the bending operation and a roller that forces the pipe round the curve when the levers of the machine are brought together. The degree of bend depends on how far you move the handles.

Flexible pipe
Although not yet available in Australia, this is a kind of corrugated copper pipe which can be bent easily by hand without any tools. It has either two plain ends for connection to compression joints, or has one end plain and one with a swivel tap connector for connection to a tap or ball-valve.

As it's the most expensive way of making a bend, it's not cost effective to use it when you have to make a number of changes of direction in a pipe run. It's not particularly attractive to look at so it is best used in places where it won't be seen — like, for example, when connecting the water supply pipes to bath taps in the very confined space at the head of the bath. This kind of pipe can make the job of fitting kitchen sink taps easier, particularly when the base unit has a back which restricts access to the supply pipes.

CUTTING COPPER PIPE

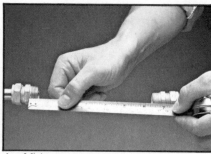

1 Make an accurate measurement of the proposed pipe run. It is important to allow for the pipe that will fit into the joints.

2 Use a simple paper template to help you cut pipe squarely. Wrap the paper round the pipe and align the edges.

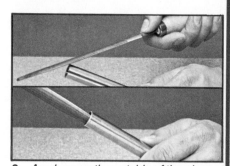

3 Any burr on the outside of the pipe can be removed with the flat side of a file. The curved side can be used to clean the inside of the pipe.

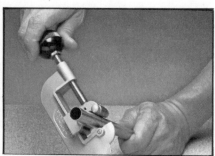

4 When using a wheel tube cutter, the cutting mark on the pipe is put against the edge of the cutting wheel and the control knob is tightened.

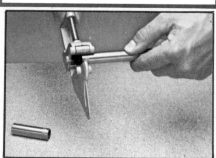

5 Once the pipe is clamped in place, the cutter rotates to make an even cut. The rollers on the tool will keep the blade square to the pipe.

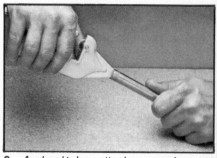

6 A wheel tube cutter leaves a clean cut on the outside of the pipe, but any burr on the inside can be removed with the reamer (an attachment to the tool).

Ian Grischotti

BENDING COPPER PIPE

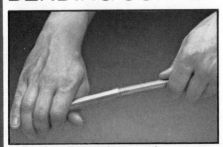

1 *The bending spring must be compatible in size with the pipe. Smear it with petroleum jelly.*

2 *Overbend the pipe slightly, and then bend it back to the required angle.*

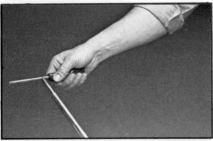

3 *Put a screwdriver through the ring at the end of the spring. Twist it, then pull the spring out.*

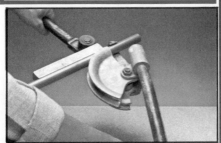

4 *To use a bending machine, open the levers, place the pipe with the straight former on top.*

5 *Raise the levers so the wheel runs along the straight edge and the pipe is forced round the circular former.*

6 *Bend the pipe to the required angle, then remove by opening the levers, taking out the straight former.*

FLEXIBLE COPPER PIPE

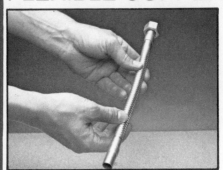

1 *Flexible pipe is frequently used in Europe for making awkward bends in the pipe run when connecting to taps.*

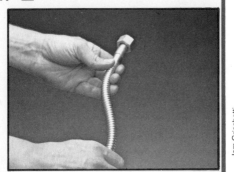

2 *It's easy to hand bend the pipe to the required shape, but don't continually flex it or the thin wall will split.*

Jem Grischotti

Ready Reference

PIPE LENGTHS

Measure the length of the run then work out:

● how many 2 metre lengths you'll need
● where to join them in on the straight (not at a bend)
● how many fittings you'll need to connect the pipes to each other.

TIP: CUTTING PIPE

Copper pipe can be crushed in the jaws of a vice so use a bench hook when cutting with a hacksaw. Pin a scrap of wood beside it to hold the pipe snugly.

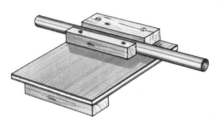

BENDING AIDS

For small diameter pipe use a *bending spring* to match the pipe size. It's a flexible coil of hardened steel about 600mm (2ft) long.

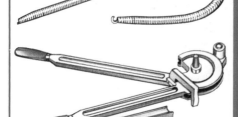

For pipe over 25mm diameter hire a *pipe bending machine* which supports the outside of the pipe wall as it bends.

TIP: REMOVING BENDING SPRINGS

For bends over 600mm (2ft) from the pipe end use a wire coathanger with a hooked end to turn and withdraw the spring.

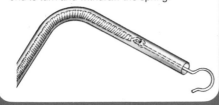

JOINING PLASTIC PIPING

Most waste pipes installed today are made of plastic, which is cheap, lightweight and easy to work with. A little practice and careful measuring will enable you to replace all parts of your system. Here's how to join them together.

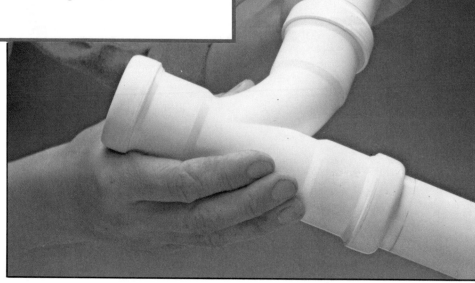

Waste systems draining baths, basins and sinks used to be made of lead, heavy galvanised steel with screwed joints, or copper. Soil pipes from WCs were traditionally cast iron, as was all the outside pipework for both waste and soil disposal. Nowadays waste and soil pipes are made of one or other of a variety of plastic materials, which may be used for repairs, extension work or complete replacement of an existing system.

These plastic pipes are lightweight and easily cut, handled and joined. They are made of materials usually known by the initials of their chemical names – UPVC (unplasticised polyvinyl chloride), MPVC (modified polyvinyl chloride), ABS (acrylonitrile butadiene styrene) and PP (polypropylene). CPVC (chlorinated polyvinyl chloride) is usually used for hot and cold water supply pipes. Pipes and fittings are available in white, grey or a copper colour, depending on type and manufacture.

All these materials are satisfactory for domestic waste systems and – with one exception – can all be joined in the same way: either by push-fit (ring-seal) jointing or by solvent welding.

The exception is PP pipe. This was first developed because of its good resistance to very hot water and chemical wastes, and was therefore extensively used in industry. Nowadays, however, it is frequently used in the home for waste or rainwater drainage. The big difference between PP and other plastic pipes used in waste drainage is that it cannot be solvent-welded. All joints must be push-fit. In most situations this is no great disadvantage but it does make it important to be able to distinguish PP from other plastics. It has a slightly greasy feel and, when cut with a fine toothed saw, leaves fine strands of fibrous material round the cut edges.

Sizes

When buying plastic pipe and components it is wise to stick to one brand only. Pipes and fittings from different makers, though of the same size, are not necessarily interchangeable. Most suppliers stock the systems of only one manufacturer, although the same

PREPARING THE PIPE ENDS

1 To make sure that you cut the pipe squarely, hold a sheet of paper around it so that the edges meet and overlap each other. This is your cutting line.

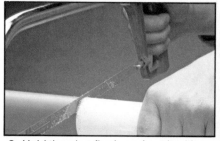

2 Hold the pipe firmly and cut it with a hacksaw, using gentle strokes. You may find it easier to use a junior hacksaw, which gives a finer cut.

3 When you've cut the pipe, use a piece of fine glass paper to clean off the burr left by sawing.

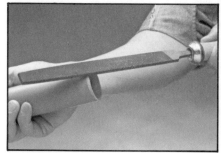

4 Now take a file and chamfer the end of the pipe all round the edge to a 45° angle. Try to keep the chamfer even.

SOLVENT-WELD JOINTING

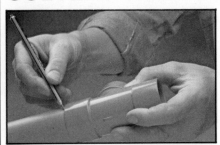

1 *Push the end of the pipe into the socket of the fitting as far as it will go. Mark the pipe at this point with a pencil as a guide to the length within the joint.*

2 *Take the pipe out of the fitting and, with a file, roughen the whole of the end surface that will be inside the fitting up to the pencil mark.*

3 *Take the fitting itself and roughen the inside of the socket with fine glass paper. This will provide a key for the solvent cement.*

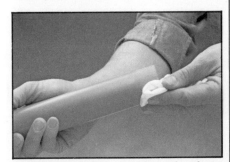

4 *Now clean off the roughened surface of the pipe and socket with spirit as recommended by the manufacturer to remove all dust and debris.*

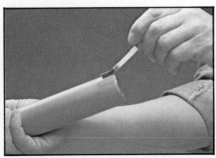

5 *Apply the solvent cement to the roughened end of the pipe, making sure that the whole roughened area is covered. Try and keep it off your fingers.*

6 *Also apply solvent cement to the socket of the fitting. Try to use brush strokes along the line of the pipe.*

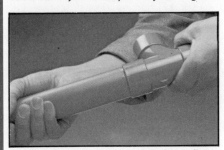

7 *Gently push the pipe fully home into the socket. Some manufacturers suggest a slight twisting action in doing this but check their instructions first.*

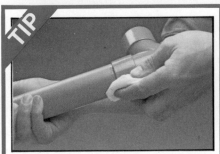

TIP

8 *Remove any excess solvent at the edge of the socket with a clean cloth, hold the joint in position for 15 seconds.*

Ready Reference

THE TOOLS YOU'LL NEED
● hacksaw – a junior or larger – for cutting the lengths of pipe as you need them
● piece of paper – to help cut the pipe truly square
● tape measure
● file – for chamfering the pipe ends
● fine glasspaper – to abrade pipes and sockets for solvent-welding, and for cleaning up the ends of pipes where you have cut them
● pencil – for marking the cutting points and socket depths to find the working area of the pipe.

VITAL ACCESSORIES
● solvent cement – for solvent-welding
● cleaning fluid – for cleaning the pipe ends and socket fittings when making solvent-weld joints
● petroleum jelly – for lubrication when inserting the pipe into the socket in push-fit joint assemblies
● tissues or rag for cleaning off excess solvent or petroleum jelly.

TYPES OF PIPE
Unplasticised PVC (UPVC) is used for all waste pipe applications.
Modified PVC (MPVC) has rubber or some other plasticiser added to make it more resistant to shock.
Chlorinated PVC (CPVC or MUPVC) is used where very hot water discharge occurs, such as washing machine out-flows.
Polypropylene (PP) is an alternative to PVC and can withstand hot water – but it expands a lot and is only suitable on short runs.
Acrylonitrile butadiene styrene (ABS) is stronger than UPVC and is used for waste connection mouldings.

SAFETY TIPS
● don't smoke when you are solvent-weld jointing – solvent cement and solvent cement cleaner become poisonous when combined with cigarette smoke
● don't inhale the fumes of solvent-weld cement or cleaning fluid – so avoid working in confined spaces
● don't get solvent-weld cement on any part of the pipe you're not joining as this can later lead to cracking and weaknesses, especially inside sockets where the solvent cement can easily trickle down
● hold all solvent-weld joints for 15 seconds after joining and then leave them undisturbed for at least 5 minutes – if hot water is going to flow through the pipe don't use it for 24 hours.

PUSH-FIT JOINTING

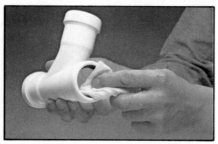

1 *Cut the pipe squarely as in solvent-weld jointing and remove the burr, then take the fitting and clean the socket out with the recommended cleaner.*

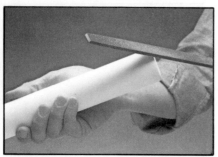

3 *Now chamfer the end of the pipe to an angle of 45°, and smooth off the chamfer carefully with fine glass paper so that no rough edges remain.*

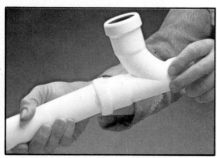

5 *Push the pipe into the socket gently but firmly. Then push it fully home and check that all is square, otherwise you may damage the sealing ring.*

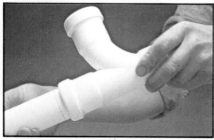

7 *Gently pull the pipe out from the fitting so that your pencil mark is about 10mm (³/₈in) away from the fitting to allow for expansion when hot water is flowing.*

2 *Check that the rubber seal is properly seated in the socket. You may find seals are supplied separately and you will have to insert them.*

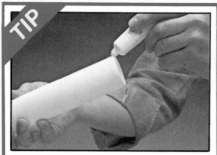

4 *Lubricate the end of the pipe with petroleum jelly over a length of about 5mm (3/16in).*

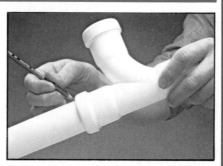

6 *Now make a pencil mark on the pipe at the edge of the socket – you can easily rub it off later if you want to – to act as a guide in setting the expansion gap.*

8 *The joint is now complete. Wipe off any excess petroleum jelly. Don't lose the expansion allowance when joining the other side of the fitting.*

manufacturer may make both PP and either PVC or ABS systems.

It is worth asking the supplier if there is an instruction leaflet supplied by the maker. There are slight variations in the methods of using each particular make of pipe and fitting. The manufacturer's instructions, if available, should be followed to the letter.

Buying new pipe

Existing waste pipe is likely to be imperial in size – 1½in internal diameter for a sink or bath and 1¼in internal diameter for a wash basin.

Metric sized plastic pipes are normally described – like thin-walled copper tubes – by their external diameter, though at least one well-known manufacturer adds to the confusion by using the internal diameter. Both internal and external diameters may vary slightly – usually by less than one millimetre between makes. This is yet another reason for sticking to one make of pipe for any single project.

The outside diameter of a plastic tube that is the equivalent of a 1¼in imperial sized metal tube is likely to be 36mm and the inside diameter 32mm. The outside diameter of the equivalent of a 1½in pipe is likely to be 43mm and the inside diameter 39mm. If in doubt, it is usually sufficient to ask the supplier for waste pipe fittings for a basin waste or – as the case may be – a bath or sink waste. Plain-ended plastic pipe is usually supplied in 3m (10ft) lengths, though a supplier will probably cut you off a shorter piece.

Joining solvent-weld types

Solvent-weld fittings are neater and less obtrusive than push-fit ones and they offer the facility of pre-fabrication before installation. However, making them does demand a little more skill and care and – unlike push-fit joints – they cannot accommodate the expansion (thermal movement) that takes place as hot wastes run through the pipe. A 4m length of PVC pipe will expand by about 13mm (just over ½in) when its temperature is raised above 20°C (70°F). For this reason, where a straight length of waste pipe exceeds 1.8m (6ft) in length, expansion couplings must be introduced at 1.8m intervals if other joints are to be solvent-welded. This rarely occurs in domestic design, however, and use of push-fit or solvent-weld is a matter of personal preference.

Although the instructions given by the different manufacturers vary slightly, the steps to making solvent-weld joints follow very similar lines. Of course, the first rule is to measure up all your pipe lengths carefully. Remember to allow for the end of the pipe overlapping the joint. When you've worked out pipe lengths cutting can start.

JOINING SOIL PIPES

These pipes are joined in the same way as plastic waste pipes but are much bigger – about 100mm (4in) in diameter – so they take longer to fit. They also have some different fittings, such as a soil branch for use where the outlet pipe joins the stack, and access fittings with bolted removable plates for inspection. There are also special connectors to link to the WC pan, via a special gasket, and to link to the underground drainage system which is traditionally made of vitrified clay.

The accurate moulding of the fittings and the ease of assembly means that you can confidently tackle complete replacement of a soil system.

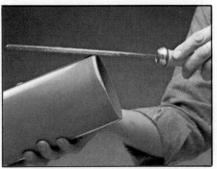

1 Soil pipes are joined in the same way as their narrower waste counterparts, but as they're bigger take special care with cutting and chamfering.

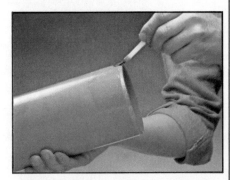

2 You have got a lot more area to cover with the solvent cement so you must work speedily – but don't neglect accurate application.

3 The soil branch pipe has a swept entry into the main stack fitting. This is one of the most important joints in the system, so make sure you get it right.

4 When you finally push the pipe into the fitting socket make quite sure that it goes right home against the pipe stop inside the fitting.

Cut the pipe clean and square with a hacksaw or other fine-toothed saw. A useful tip to ensure a square cut is to fold a piece of newspaper over the pipe and join the edges beneath it. The paper will then act as a template.

Remove all internal and external 'burr' or roughness at the end of the pipe, then use a file to chamfer the outside of the pipe end to about 45°. Not all manufacturers recommend this, but it does provide an extra key for the solvent.

Insert the pipe end into the fitting and mark the depth of insertion with a pencil. Using medium grade abrasive paper, or a light file, lightly roughen the end of the pipe, as far as the pencil mark, and also roughen the interior of the socket. Thoroughly clean the roughened surfaces of the socket and the pipe end using a clean rag moistened with a spirit cleaner recommended by the manufacturer of the fittings.

Select the correct solvent cement (PVC pipes need a different solvent cement from ABS ones; once again, buy all the materials needed at the same time from the same supplier). Read the label on the tin and stir only if instructed.

Using a clean paintbrush apply the solvent cement to the pipe end and to the

Ready Reference

TYPES OF FITTINGS
A number of fittings are available in both solvent-weld and push-fit systems – here are just a few of them. Check the complete range before you plan a new system – special bends and branches may exist that will make the job much easier.

Solvent-weld 92¹/₂° bend

Push-fit 157¹/₂° bend

Expansion coupling solvent-weld/push-fit

Push-fit double socket

Solvent-weld adaptor

inside of the fittings, brushing in the direction of the pipe. It is usually necessary to apply two coats to ABS pipes and fittings. The second coat should be brushed on quickly before the first has dried.

Push the pipe fully home into the fitting (some, but not all, manufacturers suggest that this should be done with a slight twisting action). Remove excess solvent cement and hold the assembled joint securely in position for about 30 seconds. If hot water will be flowing through the pipe, don't use it for 24 hours to give time for the joint to set completely.

Joining ring-seal types
Preparation for ring-seal or push-fit jointing is similar to that for solvent welding. The pipe end must be cut absolutely squarely and all the burr removed. You should draw a line round the cut end of the pipe 10mm from its end and chamfer back to this line with a rasp or shaping tool, then clean the recess within the push-fit connector's socket and check that the sealing ring is evenly seated. One manufacturer supplies sealing rings separately, and they should be inserted at this point. The pipe end should now be lubricated with a small amount of petroleum jelly and pushed firmly into the socket past the joint ring. Push it fully home and mark the insertion depth on the pipe with a pencil. Then withdraw it by 10mm (which is the allowance made for expansion). The expansion joint that is inserted into long straight lengths of solvent-welded waste pipe consists of a coupling with a solvent-weld joint at one end and a push-fit joint at the other.

As with solvent-weld jointing, individual manufacturers may give varying instructions. Some, for instance, advise the use of their own silicone lubricating jelly. Where the manufacturer supplies instructions it is best to follow these exactly.

Fittings
PVC pipe can be bent by the application of gentle heat from a blow-torch, but this technique needs practice and it is best to rely on purpose-made fittings. Sockets are used for joining straight lengths of pipe, tees for right-angled branches, and both 90° and 45° elbows are usually available. If you need to reduce the diameters from one pipe to another you can use reducing sockets. These are really sockets within sockets which can be welded together, one taking the smaller diameter pipe and the other the larger. Soil outlet pipes from WCs are joined in the same way; they are merely bigger – usually 100mm (4in) – in diameter. Sockets work in the same way, but the branch-junction with the main soil stack must be of a specially 'swept' design.

HOW PLASTIC FITTINGS WORK
Solvent-weld joints
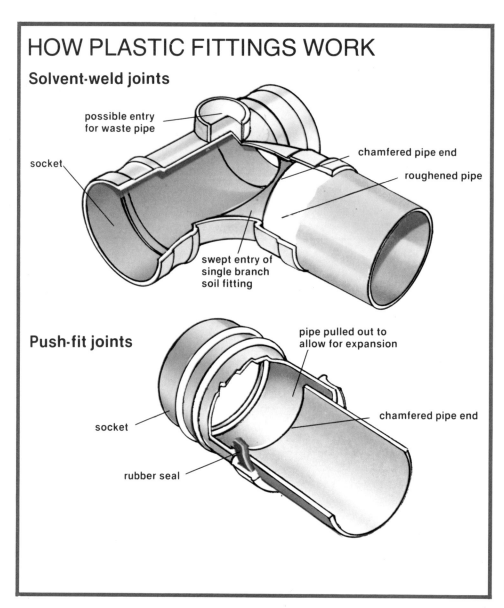

Push-fit joints

SPECIAL FITTINGS
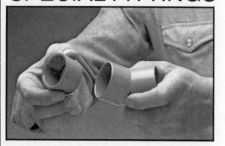

Special fittings are available when pipe fitting is not straightforward. This is a reducing adaptor for push-fit fittings where you need to join a

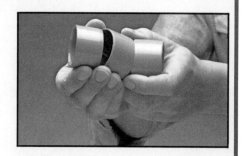

32mm pipe to a 40mm pipe. You join the relevant pipe to the mating part of the adaptor and then join the two adaptor parts together.

DRAINING PLUMBING SYSTEMS

When you are carrying out repairs or alterations to your plumbing or wet central heating system, you will usually have to drain water from the parts you are working on. Here's what you'll have to do.

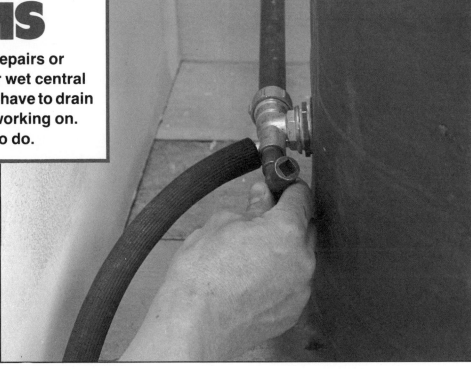

Virtually all major and many minor plumbing operations demand the partial or total drainage of either the domestic hot or cold water supply. If you have a 'wet' central heating system you'll also have to drain that before carrying out repairs or alterations. Before attempting this – long before the need for drainage arises, in fact – you should make yourself thoroughly familiar with the design and layout of these systems in your home. Here are some questions to which you should know the answers:

● Are all cold water draw-off points supplied direct from the rising main, or are the bathroom cold taps and the WC cistern supplied with water from a main cold water storage cistern (probably situated in the roof space)?

● Is the hot water system 'direct' or 'indirect'?

● If the system is direct, is the domestic hot water heated solely by means of an electric immersion heater, solely by means of a domestic boiler (gas, oil or solid fuel), or are both means of heating available?

● If hot water is provided solely by means of an immersion heater, is there a drain-valve at the base of the cold supply pipe from the storage cistern to the hot water cylinder?

● If hot water is provided by means of a boiler, is there a drain-valve on the pipework beside the boiler, or possibly incorporated into the boiler itself?

● If the system is indirect, is it a conventional indirect system (indicated by the presence of a small feed-and-expansion tank in the roof space, feeding the primary circuit) or is it a self-priming indirect system such as the Primatic?

● Is there a 'wet' central heating system provided in conjunction with hot water supply?

● Where is the main stop-valve, and are there any other stop-valves or gate-valves fitted into distribution or circulating pipes in the system?

● Are there drain-valves at low points in the central heating circuit?

Draining down for simple repairs

Once you are thoroughly familiar with the contents and layout of your own plumbing and central heating systems, you will be able to work out for yourself how much draining-down will be necessary before you undertake any particular item of maintenance or any particular project. If, for instance, you wish to rewasher the cold tap over the kitchen sink (this is supplied direct from the rising main) or to tee into the rising main to provide a garden water supply, all that you need to do is to turn off the main stop-valve and to turn on the kitchen cold tap until water ceases to flow from it. You will then have drained the rising main to the level of the cold tap. In many modern homes a drain-valve is provided immediately above the main stop-valve to permit the rising main to be completely drained.

Rather more drainage is necessary when you wish to renew the washer on a hot tap, or on a cold tap supplied from a storage cistern, or to renew a ball-valve in a WC cistern that is supplied with water from a storage cistern. First of all, see if there are any stop-valves or gate-valves on the distribution pipes leading to the particular tap or ball-valve. There could be gate-valves on the main hot and cold distribution pipes just below the level of the main cold water storage cistern. There could even be a mini-stop-valve on the distribution pipe immediately before its connection to the tail of the tap or ball-valve.

In either of these circumstances you're in luck! All you have to do is to turn off the appropriate gate-valve or mini-stop-valve and then to turn on the tap or flush the lavatory cistern. You can then carry out the necessary repairs.

Avoiding unnecessary drainage

The chances are, though, that the main stop-valve will be the only one in the system, and that you'll have to contemplate draining the main cold water storage cistern and the appropriate distribution pipes before you can get on with your task, by turning off the main stop-valve and draining the cistern and pipes from the taps supplied by the cistern. This, however, will mean that the whole of the plumbing system is out of action for as long as it takes you to complete the job. It is generally better to go up into the roof space and lay a slat of wood across the top of the cold water storage cistern. You can then tie the float arm of the ball-valve up to it, so that water cannot flow into the cistern. Then drain the cistern by opening the bathroom taps. In this way the cold tap over the sink will not be put out of action.

Here's another useful money-saving tip: even if you are draining down to rewasher a hot tap, there is no need to run to waste all that hot water stored in the hot water cylinder, *provided that your bathroom cold taps are supplied from the cold water storage cistern.* Having tied up the ball-valve, run the bathroom *cold* taps until they cease to flow and only then turn on the hot tap you want to work on. Because the hot water distribution pipe is taken from above the hot water storage cylinder, only a little hot water – from the pipe itself – will flow away to waste and the cylinder will remain full of hot water.

For the same reason, unless you expect to have the hot water system out of action for a

WHERE TO DRAIN THE SYSTEM

On a well-designed plumbing system you should find that drain-valves have been installed at several points, so that partial draining-down is possible.

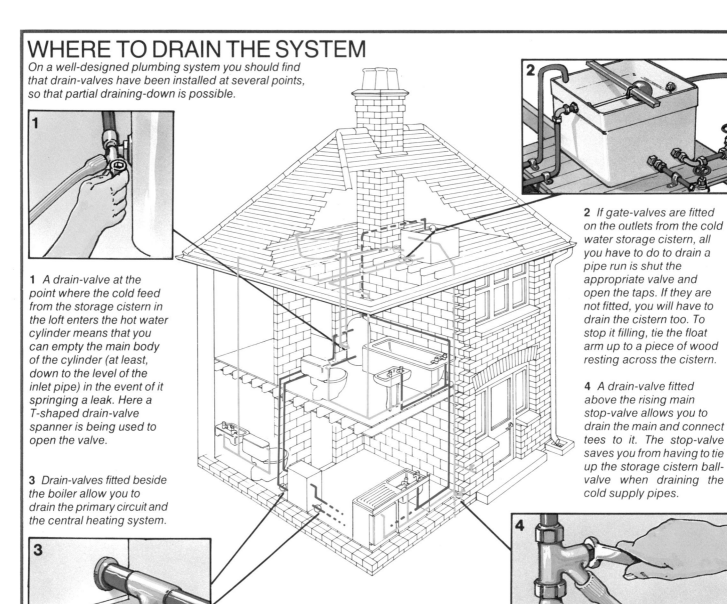

1 *A drain-valve at the point where the cold feed from the storage cistern in the loft enters the hot water cylinder means that you can empty the main body of the cylinder (at least, down to the level of the inlet pipe) in the event of it springing a leak. Here a T-shaped drain-valve spanner is being used to open the valve.*

3 *Drain-valves fitted beside the boiler allow you to drain the primary circuit and the central heating system.*

2 *If gate-valves are fitted on the outlets from the cold water storage cistern, all you have to do to drain a pipe run is shut the appropriate valve and open the taps. If they are not fitted, you will have to drain the cistern too. To stop it filling, tie the float arm up to a piece of wood resting across the cistern.*

4 *A drain-valve fitted above the rising main stop-valve allows you to drain the main and connect tees to it. The stop-valve saves you from having to tie up the storage cistern ball-valve when draining the cold supply pipes.*

Action checklist

Which part of the system you drain, and how you go about it, depends on the job you're doing. Here's a brief checklist of the sequence of operations in each case.

Job: *to rewasher/replace kitchen cold tap, tee off rising main for new supply pipe;*
● *turn off rising main stop-valve and drain rising main via drain-valve*
● *if no drain-valve fitted, open kitchen cold tap to drain main down to level of tee to kitchen sink.*

Job: *to rewasher/replace other cold tap, renew WC ball-valve, extend cold supply;*
● *if gate-valve fitted to outlet at cold cistern, close valve and open lowest appropriate cold tap; otherwise*
● *tie up arm of cold cistern ball-valve and drain cistern by opening cold taps.*

Job: *to rewasher/replace hot tap, extend existing hot supply;*
● *close gate-valve on outlet at cistern or tie up cistern ball-valve*
● *open <u>cold</u> tap until flow stops*
● *<u>only then</u> open hot tap.*

Job: *to replace hot cylinder;*
● *close gate-valve or tie up ball-valve arm*
● *turn off boiler or immersion heater*
● *empty cylinder via cylinder drain-valve*
● *close gate-valve on outlet from feed/expansion tank, or tie up ball-valve*
● *drain primary circuit via drain-valve at boiler.*

Job: *to replace cold cistern;*
● *close rising main stop-valve*
● *drain cistern by opening cold taps (hot water will still run from cylinder).*

Job: *to replace boiler;*
● *on **direct systems,** turn off boiler or immersion heater and also heating system*
● *close rising main stop-valve*
● *open all taps, and drain boiler from drain-valve nearby*
● *on **indirect systems,** turn off boiler*
● *close feed/expansion tank gate-valve*
● *drain primary and central heating systems from drain-valves at boiler.*

prolonged period there is no need to switch off the immersion heater or to let out the boiler when carrying out a maintenance operation on the bathroom hot tap.

Problems with air locks

If your hot and cold water distribution systems are properly designed – with 'horizontal' runs of pipe actually having a slight fall away from the storage cistern or the vent pipe to permit air to escape – then the system should fill up with little or no trouble when you untie the ball-valve and permit water to flow into the cistern again. Should an air-lock prevent complete filling, try connecting one end of a length of hose to the cold tap over the kitchen sink and the other end to one of the taps giving trouble. Turn on first the tap giving trouble and then the one over the kitchen sink. Mains pressure from this cold tap should blow the air bubble out of the system.

Draining the whole system

Very occasionally – perhaps because of a major reconstruction of the system or because of that most traumatic of all plumbing emergencies, a leaking boiler – it may be necessary to drain the whole system. Let's assume, first of all, that you have either a direct hot water system or a self-priming indirect one.

Switch off the immersion heater and let out or switch off the boiler. Turn off the central heating system if this is operated from the self-priming cylinder. Close the main stop-valve and open up every tap in the house – hot as well as cold. Connect one end of a length of hose to the drain-valve beside the boiler or, if the cylinder is heated by an immersion heater only, at the base of the cold supply pipe entering the cylinder, and take the other end of the hose to an outside gully. Open up the drain-valve and allow the system to drain.

If you have an indirect system you should again turn off the boiler and central heating system. Then close the gate-valve leading from the feed-and-expansion tank, or tie up it's ball-valve, and drain the system from the boiler drain-valves.

How you proceed depends upon the reason for which you have carried out the draining-down. Your aim should be to get as much of the plumbing system as possible back into operation quickly.

Restoring partial supplies

The first step is to go up into the roof space and tie up the ball-valve on the main storage cistern as already described. Open up the main stop-valve and water supply will be restored to the cold tap over the kitchen sink.

It should also be possible to restore the bathroom cold water supplies. Trace the distribution pipe that takes water from the cold water storage cistern to the hot water cylinder.

COPING WITH AIRLOCKS

Clear supply-pipe airlocks by linking the affected tap to the kitchen cold tap with hose secured by worm-drive clips. Open the affected tap first, then the kitchen tap.

Avoid airlocks in primary or heating circuits by filling them upwards via a hose linking the kitchen cold tap and the boiler drain-valve. Close vents as radiators fill.

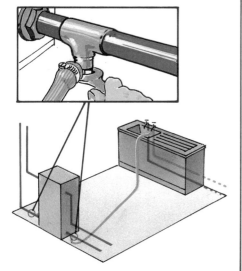

Find a cork of the correct size, lean into the cistern and push it into the pipe's inlet. Before doing so, it is a good idea to screw a substantial woodscrew part of the way into the cork to facilitate removal. You can then untie the ball-valve and allow the cistern to refill; no water will flow to the hot cylinder.

Draining heating systems

If you have a conventional indirect hot water system – perhaps installed in conjunction with a central heating system – you can drain the primary circuit, together with the radiator circuit if there is one, without draining the water from the outer part of the storage cylinder. Because of the increased risk of corrosion that arises from water and air coming into contact with steel surfaces, a radiator circuit should be drained only when absolutely essential. When this has to be done – to add additional radiators, perhaps – you should tie up the ball-valve serving the feed-and-expansion tank and drain from both the drain-valve beside the boiler and from any drain-valves provided at low points of the system. You must, of course, let out or switch off the boiler before attempting this.

When refilling the primary circuit (or when refilling a direct system with boiler) it may help to prevent the formation of air-locks if you connect one end of your garden hose to the boiler drain-valve and the other end to the cold tap over the kitchen sink. Open them both up and the system will fill upwards, with air being driven out in front of the rising water. As the central heating circuit refills,

open up all the radiator vents – and any other air vents that there may be in the system – and leave them open until water begins to flow through them. It is a good idea, when refilling a central heating system, to introduce a reliable corrosion-proofer into the feed-and-expansion tank to prevent future internal corrosion, but you can do this only if you fill the system from the top, not from the bottom.

Winter precautions

One final point: if you are leaving your home empty during the winter months, you should drain the main cold water storage cistern and, if you have a direct hot water system and will be away for more than two or three days, you should drain the hot cylinder, the boiler and its circulation pipes as well. Human memory is fallible. Having done so, leave a conspicuous notice on the boiler and by the immersion heater switch saying 'SYSTEM DRAINED – DO NOT LIGHT BOILER OR SWITCH ON HEATER UNTIL IT HAS BEEN REFILLED'.

Because of the risk of corrosion already referred to, the primary circuit and any central heating system connected to it should not be drained in these circumstances. If you have a central heating system that is capable of automatic control, leave it switched on under the control of a frost-stat. This is a thermostatic control, usually positioned in a garage or in the roof space, that will bring the heating into operation when a predetermined, near-freezing-point temperature, is reached.

INSTALLING A SINK UNIT

The sink is a highly important item of kitchen equipment, and replacing an old model is usually one of the first priorities for anyone modernising their kitchen. In this article we consider the range available and how to fit them.

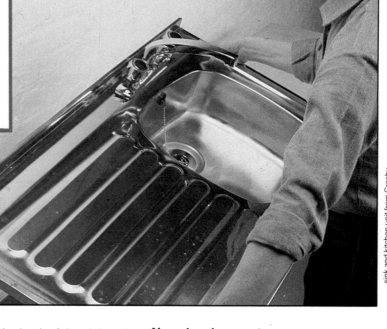

sink and kitchen unit from Crosby

If your house was built in the 1930s or 1940s, and the kitchen has never been modernised, the chances are that it contains the original deep white glazed stoneware 'Belfast pattern' sink, supported by heavy cast-iron brackets built into the wall. It will incorporate a weir overflow and will probably have a detachable wooden draining board. A deep sink of this kind was regarded as the height of domestic luxury in the pre-war and early post-war years. An even older property might have a shallow yellow 'London pattern' sink, probably supported by brick pillars. In either case the water will very likely come from brass bib-taps (taps with horizontal inlets) projecting from a tiled splash-back fixed to the wall behind the sink. Old London pattern sinks were sometimes installed with an untrapped waste that passed through the kitchen wall to discharge over an outside gully drain. More recent sinks would have a lead or brass U-trap screwed to the waste outlet from which a branch waste pipe would discharge over the gully.

Sink units
Because these old stoneware sinks were certain death to crockery dropped into them, and looked increasingly dated, they were gradually replaced by sink units with one-piece sink tops. The sink tops were made of enamelled pressed steel or stainless steel, and the units into which they were fixed became the starting point for complete kitchen ranges incorporating continuous work surfaces. The early enamelled pressed steel sink tops had the disadvantage that the enamel was vulnerable to accidental damage. Dropping any hard object onto them could easily chip or crack the enamel. The stainless steel sink therefore became the most important innovation.

Taps and traps
It was usual, when replacing an old stoneware sink with a stainless steel or an enamelled pressed-steel sink, to get rid of the old bib-taps projecting from the wall, and to replace them with chromium-plated brass pillar taps or a mixer fitted into the

holes provided at the back of the sink and connected to the hot and cold water distribution pipes concealed within the unit.

Early sinks of this kind were provided with traps, also concealed within the unit. The trap might still be of brass with a copper waste pipe, but plastic was soon introduced, connected to a plastic waste pipe by means of ring-seal push-fit connectors. Bottle traps, as distinct from the traditional U-traps, became increasingly popular. They were neater in appearance, space saving and easy to dismantle in case of a blockage, although their discharge rate was not as great. Modern ground floor sinks often still discharge over a yard gully, but the waste pipe outlet should be taken to below the gully grid either through a slotted grid or by the use of a back or side-inlet gully.

Overflows
Early sink tops had a built-in overflow consisting of a unit welded to the back of the sink. But these inevitably leaked after a time, and nowadays they have been replaced by a flexible overflow pipe. This is like the overflow pipe from a bath which is taken from the sink's overflow outlet to connect, by means of a sleeve or 'banjo' fitting, to the slotted waste pipe, before its connection to the trap. Householders who possess a sink of the older pattern with a leaking built-in overflow, will find that if the sink is dismounted and turned upside down, the overflow unit can be sawn off and replaced with one of the more modern waste and overflow fittings. But, of course, it may be better to replace the the sink.

New developments
Nowadays, there is no question of being restricted to a single sink with either right or left-hand drainer. Double sinks, one for washing the crockery and cutlery and the other for a hot rinse before air drying, have become more and more popular. The two sinks may be of equal size, around 450mm (18in) in width, or one may be smaller than the other for use in food preparation. A second sink like this might be only 240mm (10in) in width. There are also sinks with double drainers, though these are rather less in demand as they take up a lot of space; they are usually around 2m (6ft 8in) long. Overall sizes of rectangular sinks and drainer units range from about 900mm (3ft) to 1500mm (5ft) in length, and usually measure 500 or 600mm (20 to 24in) deep, to fit metric base units. Some sink tops are still available in the 21in (533mm) size to match old imperial base units. There are also many intermediate sizes, and bowl depths may range between 130 and 180mm (5 and 7in).

Early glass-reinforced plastic sink tops and drainers proved to be a complete disaster. They were incapable of standing up to the very heavy use to which sinks are subjected, their colours faded and they cracked, and crazed. Considerable advances have since been made, and modern plastic sinks and sink tops seem well able to stand up to everything that is required of them.

Ceramic sinks are making a come back, though they are very different from the old Belfast and London pattern sinks. Modern ranges include tough inset sinks and tops in an attractive range of colours. There are inset round bowls 450mm (18in) in diameter with an accompanying but separate round drainer 380mm (14in) in diameter. Then there is a conventional rectangular double sink and drainer – all of ceramic ware – an overall size of 1125 x 505mm (45 x 20in). There is also a conventional rectangular single sink and drainer and round double sinks and drainer in one unit. A feature of these new ceramic units is their extreme toughness.

The waste and overflow of the new ceramic sinks are arranged in exactly the same way as those of the old Belfast models. A built-in overflow connects to the slot in a slotted waste outlet that is bedded on mastic in the outlet hole. Stainless steel sinks are provided with the flexible overflow already referred to, which connects to the slotted waste below the sink but above the trap. Double sinks have only one trap. This is fitted into the outlet of the sink nearest to the drain outlet, the waste from the other sink being connected to it above the level of the single trap.

Mixers
Individual sink pillar taps are still freely available, but the choice nowadays is more likely to be a sink mixer. A mixer with a swivel spout is an essential where a double sink is installed.

Sink mixers differ from bath and basin mixers in one important respect. The latter are simply two taps with a single spout. The hot and cold streams of water mix within the body of the mixer unit. Sink mixers have

separate channels for the hot and cold streams of water which mix in the air as they leave the spout. The reason for this is that the cold water supply to the kitchen sink (the household's supply of water for drinking and cooking) comes direct from the rising main. The hot supply usually comes from a cylinder storage hot water system, fed with water from a main cold water storage cistern. It is illegal to mix, in one fitting, water from the main and water from a storage cistern.

Everybody is familiar with the conventional sink mixer, made of chromium-plated brass with 'shrouded' cross-top handles of plastic and a long swivel spout. Nowadays, though, there are some exciting new designs available. With some the mixer unit is fitted into just one hole at the back of the sink. The other hole may be blanked off or may be used to accommodate a rinsing brush, supplied with hot water by a flexible tube connected to the hot water supply pipe.

Putting in the sink top
When you come to install your new sink it's a good idea to make the first job fitting the taps or mixer, waste and overflow to it. This will avoid unnecessary interruption to the rest of the plumbing services. Start by putting in the combined waste and overflow unit, then attach the taps or mixer. If the sink is made of stainless steel the shanks of the taps will protrude through the holes so you won't be able to screw up the back-nuts tight. Use 'top hat' or spaces to accommodate the shanks.

When the sink is in position the tap tails will usually be fairly inaccessible, so it may be a

good idea to attach purpose-made extension pieces to bring them to a level below the sink basin where they will be accessible.

When you've got the new sink top ready, you'll have to turn off the main stop-valve and drain the hot and cold water pipes which supply the existing sink. Then you can disconnect the waste outlet, and use a cold chisel and hammer to chip away any seal between the back of the sink and the wall. You can remove the old sink (remember, it's going to be very heavy) and saw off the heavy cantilevered brackets that supported the old sink flush with the wall.

The hot and cold water supply pipes to the bib-taps over the old sink will probably be chased (inset) into the wall, so you'll have to unscrew and remove the old taps, excavate the pipes from the wall and pull them forward so that they can be connected to the tails of new taps.

With the new sink unit in position, the next job is to cut the water supply pipes to the correct length to connect to the tails of the taps. The sink top simply rests on the sink unit, so the tails of the taps can now be connected to the water supply pipes. If the trap of the old sink will connect to the new waste it can be reused.

THE PLUMBING CONNECTIONS

mixer, gasket, tail, sink top, back-nut, connector, supply pipe, overflow, plumber's putty, nylon washer, back-nut, trap, tail, top hat washer

INSTALLING A SINK TOP

1 Take out your old sink top and check that the existing plumbing connections are undamaged. Replace as necessary.

2 Place your new sink top downwards on the floor. Take the waste outlet and press plumber's putty around the top of the screw.

3 Press the outlet firmly into position in the sink outlet aperture, at the same time squeezing out excess putty. Then put on the plastic washer.

6 Place the outlet collar of the banjo unit firmly on top of the plastic washer and support it with one hand before putting on the back-nut.

7 Put on the back-nut and screw it up tightly against the banjo unit collar, making sure it runs straight towards the sink outlet hole.

8 Screw up the overflow rose to the banjo unit overflow pipe. To help get it tight, hold the back of the outlet with a pair of pliers.

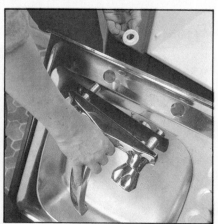

11 Take the mixer unit and ensure that the rubber gasket has no grit on it; then place the inlet tails into the holes and press the unit into position.

12 Screw on the inlet tail back-nuts and tighten them making sure the gasket remains flat. You don't need to use any plumber's putty.

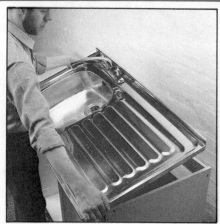

13 When the outlet and mixer installation is complete, lift the sink top into its correct position and screw it to the kitchen unit.

4 With the plastic washer pushed firmly home, take a roll of PTFE tape and run it around the thread right up to the end of the outlet.

5 Before putting on the banjo unit run a thick film of pipe-jointing compound around the uppermost surface of the plastic washer.

9 Run a knife around the edge of the plumber's putty squeezed out from around the outlet flange. Be careful not to score the metal.

10 Peel away the surplus putty and check that the outlet flange is tightly held into the sink. If not, tighten the back-nut further.

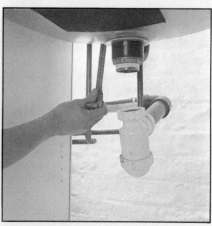

14 Attach the inlet pipes to the mixer tails and tighten the nuts with a crowsfoot spanner, which helps you reach them.

15 Check that the old trap is clear and screw it up tightly to the outlet pipe; then turn on the taps to check that there are no leaks.

Ready Reference

SINK DESIGNS

Sink designs come in several different variations particularly in the inset range. Think carefully about what you use your sink for, and what space you have available before deciding on size and design.

TYPICAL SINK SIZES

S=single, D=double, Si=sink, Dr=drainer

	Tops	Inset
SDrSSi	42x31in	37x19in
	1000x500mm	940x485mm
	1000x600mm	
	1200x600mm	
DDrSSi	63x21in	55x19in
	1500x500mm	1395x485mm
	1500x600mm	
SDrDSi	63x21in	55x19in
	1500x600mm	1395x485mm
DDrDSi	84x21in	74x19in
	2000x600mm	1850x485mm

TYPICAL DESIGNS

If you don't have a dishwasher a double bowl is useful – one for washing and one for rinsing.

double bowl

A double drainer will give you a greater working area at the sink but will cut down on the remainder of your work surface.

double drainer

If you're short of space you may dispense with the drainer altogether and use an inset bowl only. There are also units with small subsidiary bowls specially incorporated to house a waste disposal unit. These may also be supplied with trays which fit in or over the bowl, facilitating such tasks as salad preparation.

disposal sink and trays

PLUMBING IN KITCHEN APPLIANCES

Washing machines and dishwashers can be a great boon in the house. They are best plumbed into a water supply and the waste outlet, otherwise you'll find they don't save as much time as they should.

These days you'll probably opt for an automatic washing machine that fills and empties itself according to a pre-set programme, and so can be left unattended. There is a choice between top loaders and front loaders, although the latter are by far the more common. Obviously top loaders can't fit under a work surface, but drum-type top loaders tend to be narrower and this may suit your particular space requirements.

Dishwashers are almost always automatic, except for some small, cheaper sink-top models. They, too, are available as top or front loaders, though again front loaders are by far the more popular. They are also easier to load and unload, as with top loaders it's easy for crockery and cutlery to slip to the bottom of the machines.

Washing machines have become almost a necessity in busy family homes, especially where there are young children. Dishwashers are far less common, but sales are developing rapidly as more and more people wake up to their advantages. It's a simple matter to stack a dishwasher with dirty crockery direct from the meal table and then turn it on before going to bed at night. Again, for a family the labour saving is considerable.

Some washing machines don't have to be plumbed in. The inlets can be attached to the kitchen taps when the sink isn't being used, and the outlet can be hooked over the edge of the sink. The same goes for dishwashers, which usually require only a cold water feed. But to keep things really neat and tidy as well as more practical, it is best to create permanent connections for both the water supply and the waste outlet. In most kitchens this should be a fairly easy task, provided you have room for the machines in the first place.

As far as the capacities of washing machines and dishwashers go, you don't really have much choice. Washing machines have a capacity of about 4-5kg (9-11lb) and dishwashers will function quite happily provided you stack them up within the obvious tray limitations. It's important to follow the manufacturers' instructions for day-to-day maintenance. Many washing machines need their outlet filter cleaned regularly, as

do dishwashers. They may also need regular doses of salts, not to mention rinse aids.

Water supply

There are a number of ways in which you can arrange the water supply. One of them is sure to suit your plumbing system or the layout of your kitchen or utility room. A washing machine may need a hot and cold supply; dishwashers and some cheaper washing machines need only a cold supply.

Let's first consider the conventional means of plumbing in – the means that a professional plumber would almost certainly adopt if you called him in to do the job for you. It is likely to be most satisfactory where the machine is to be positioned in the immediate vicinity of the kitchen sink and the 15mm (½in) hot and cold supply pipes to the sink taps are readily accessible and in close proximity to each other.

The technique is to cut into these two pipes

at a convenient level, after cutting off the water supply and draining the pipes, and to insert into them 15mm compression tees. From the outlets of the tees lengths of 15mm (½in) copper tube are run to terminate, against the wall, in a position immediately adjacent to the machine. Onto the ends of these lengths of pipe are fitted purpose-made stop-cocks. These are usually provided with back-plates that can be screwed to the wall after it has been drilled and plugged. The outlets of the stop-cocks are designed for connection to the machine's inlet hose or hoses.

As an alternative, which is best used where the hot and cold water pipes in the kitchen are in close proximity to the position of the machine, you can use a special patent valve. This is a 'tee' with a valve outlet designed for direct connection to the washing machine hose. There are compression joints at each end of the tee and the valve is particularly

PLUMBING IN A WASHING MACHINE

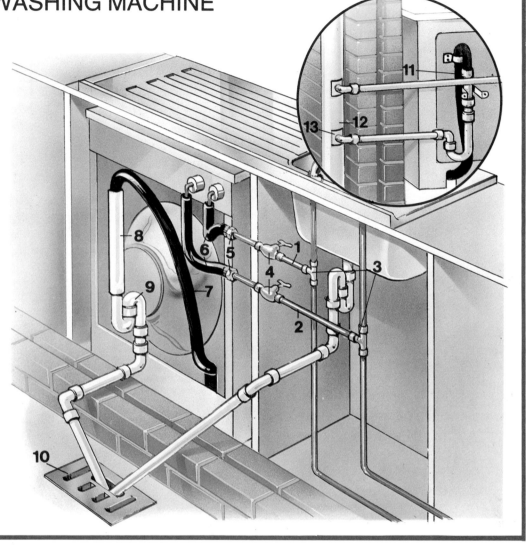

Plumbing in a washing machine shouldn't present too many problems. Normally it's sited next to an existing sink, so you'll know that the water supply pipes and drainage facilities are close at hand.

Most machines are run off separate 15mm (½in) hot and cold supplies (1 & 2) taken from tees (3) inserted in the pipe runs to the sink. You should also insert some form of stop-valve (4) into the pipes so the machine can be isolated for repairs. You'll have to use female/male connections (5) to join the copper pipes to the machine's rubber inlet hoses (6).

When the water has been used, it's fed into a rubber drain hose (7) which should be loosely inserted into the top of the stand-pipe (8). This in turn connects to a 75mm (3in) trap (9) and from here the waste water is taken in 38mm (1½in) pipe to discharge in the gully outside below the grille.

Dealing with single-stack drainage

From the trap at the bottom of the stand-pipe (11) the waste water is conducted to the main drainage stack (12) where the pipe is connected via a fitting known as a strap boss(13).

easily fitted because there is no tube-stop in one of these joints. This cuts out the difficult business of 'springing' the cut ends of the pipe into the tee.

Then there are valves which can be connected without cutting a section out of the water supply pipes. With one such valve the pipe is drained and is then drilled with a 8mm (⁵⁄₁₆in) bit. A back-plate is then fitted to the wall behind it and a front-plate, with a short projecting pipe and a rubber seal that fits into the hole in the pipe, is clamped to it. The washing machine valve then screws into this front-plate.

Yet another valve is self-tapping and screws its own hole in the water pipe. This, so the makers claim, can be done without cutting off the water supply and draining the pipe.

A valve which depends upon drilling the water supply pipe will not permit the same flow of water as one in which the pipe is cut and a tee inserted. It must be said, though,

that this seems to make very little difference in practice, but obviously in the former case the tightening of the connection must be more than sufficient for it to work properly.

Putting in drainage

The simplest method is undoubtedly to hook the machine's outlet hose over the rim of the kitchen or utility room sink when required. However, this method isn't always convenient and is certainly untidy. An alternative is to provide an open-ended stand-pipe fixed to the kitchen wall into which the outlet hose of the machine can be permanently hooked. The open end of the stand-pipe should be at least 600mm (24in) above floor level and should have an internal diameter of at least 35mm (1⅜in). A deep seal (75mm or 3in) trap should be provided at its base and a branch waste pipe taken from its outlet to an exterior gully, if on the ground floor, or to the main soil and waste stack of a single stack

system if on an upper floor. As with all connections to a single soil and waste stack this should be done only under the supervision of the district or borough council's Building Control Officer. Manufacturers of plastic drainage systems include suitable drainage stand-pipes and accessories in their range of equipment (the trap and pipe being sold as one unit).

It is sometimes possible to deal with washing machine or dishwasher drainage by taking the waste pipe to connect directly to the trap of the kitchen sink and this course of action may be suggested at DIY centres and by builders' merchants staff. But it must be stressed that this is not recommended by the manufacturers of washing machines, who consider that it involves a considerable risk of back-siphonage. This could lead to waste water from the sink siphoning back into the machine. In the case of a washing machine this could mean considerable problems.

PLUMBING IN A DISHWASHER

1 Start by working out how to run the waste outlet. This will often mean making a hole in the wall using a club hammer and cold chisel.

2 Measure up the run on the inside, then cut a suitable length of 38mm (1½in) PVC plastic waste pipe and push it through the hole you have made.

3 Make up the outside pipe run dry, to ensure it all fits, then solvent weld it. It's useful to put in an inspection elbow in case of blockages.

6 Carry on assembling the run on the inside using standard waste pipe fittings. Try to keep the run close to the wall for a neat appearance.

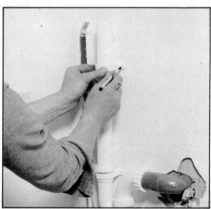

7 Take the trap and stand-pipe, which you can buy as a standard fitting or make up yourself, and mark the bracket positions on the wall.

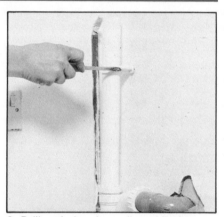

8 Drill and plug the wall, and fix the stand-pipe in position. Make sure that it is fully supported and vertical and the trap is screwed tight.

11 Make good the damage to the wall both on the inside and out; the plastic pipe will be held firmly in place by the mortar and plaster.

12 You can now move the machine into position and connect it up. The inlet hose has a female screwed connector, which must have a washer in it.

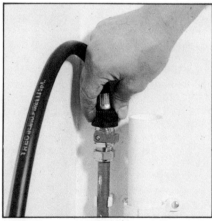

13 With the washer in place, screw up the connector to the tap on the inlet pipe; it's enough to hand-tighten this connection.

4 If the run terminates in a gully drain, then make sure that you fit the pipe so that the end is situated below the level of the water.

5 When you have completed the outside waste run, replace the grid. Cut away as much of it as necessary to fit round the pipe, using a hacksaw.

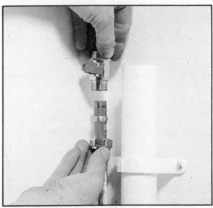

9 Run the cold water supply using 15mm (¹/₂in) pipe via a tee cut into the domestic cold supply, and attach a running tap to the end.

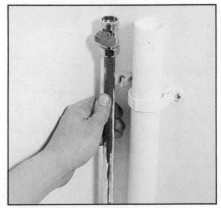

10 Secure the supply pipe to the wall using pipe brackets, then go back and make sure that all your connections are sound.

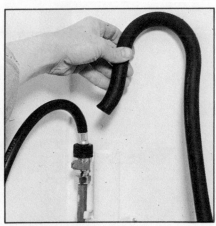

14 Take the outlet hose from the machine and place it in the top of the stand-pipe.You should not attempt to make the connection airtight.

15 Move the machine exactly into position and check that it is level; if not, adjust the feet. Then turn on the water and test the machine.

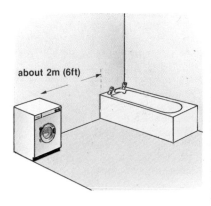
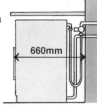
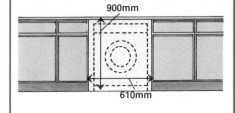

REPLACING A WASHBASIN

Replacing a washbasin is fairly straightforward. It's a job you'll have to undertake if the basin is cracked – but you may also want to change the basin if you're redesigning your bathroom and adding some up-to-date fittings.

A part from replacing a cracked basin, which you should do immediately, the most common time to install a new basin is when you're improving a bathroom or decorating a separate WC. The chances are that the basin you'll be removing will be one of the older ceramic types, wall-hung, a pedestal model or built into a vanity unit.

The main advantage of a wall-hung basin is that it doesn't take up any floor space and because of this it is very useful in a small bathroom, WC or cloakroom. You can also set the basin at a comfortable height, unlike a pedestal basin whose height is fixed by the height of the pedestal. However, it's usual to fit a wall-hung basin with the rim 800mm (32in) above the floor.

Vanity units are now increasing in popularity. In fact they're the descendents of the Edwardian wash-stand, with its marble top, bowl and large water jug. The unit is simply a storage cupboard with a ceramic, enamelled pressed steel or plastic basin set flush in the top. The advantage of vanity units is that you have a counter surface round the basin on which to stand toiletries. There is rarely, if ever, sufficient room for these items behind or above conventional wall-hung or pedestal basins. Usually the top has some form of plastic covering or can be tiled for easy cleaning.

Fittings for basins
It's a good idea to choose the taps and waste fittings at the same time you select the basin, so everything matches. You could perhaps re-use the taps from the old basin, but it's doubtful if these will be in keeping with the design of the new appliance. As an alternative to shrouded head or pillar taps, you could fit a mixer, provided the holes at the back of the basin are suitably spaced to take the tap tails. But remember that because of the design of most basin mixers, you shouldn't use them if the cold water supply is directly from the mains.

Ceramic basins normally have a built-in overflow channel which in most appliances connects into the main outlet above the trap. So if you accidentally let the basin overfill you reduce the risk of water spillage.

Basin and fittings from Royal Doulton

PUTTING IN A NEW BASIN

You should have little trouble installing a new washbasin in the same place as the old one. It's also a good opportunity to check the pipe runs. If they're made of lead it's a good idea to replace them.

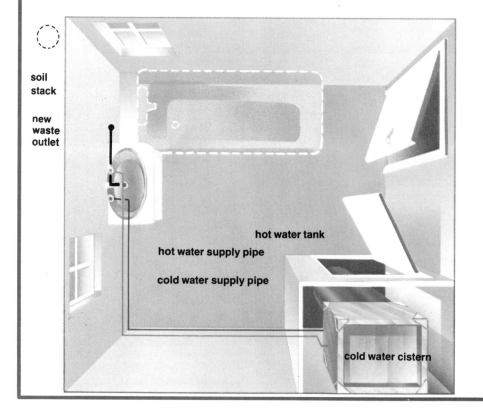

soil stack

new waste outlet

hot water tank

hot water supply pipe

cold water supply pipe

cold water cistern

Vanity unit basins are usually sold complete with a waste and overflow unit which resembles that of a modern stainless steel sink. A flexible tube connects the overflow outlet of the basin with a sleeve or 'banjo' unit which fits tightly round a slotted waste fitting.

With both types of basin the flange of the waste outlet has to be bedded into the hole provided for it in the basin on a layer of plumber's putty. The thread of the screwed waste must also be smeared with jointing compound to ensure a watertight seal where the 'banjo' connects to it.

Traps

The outlet of the waste must, of course, connect to a trap and branch waste pipe. At one time it was the practice to use 'shallow seal' traps with a 50mm (2in) depth of seal for two-pipe drainage systems, and 'deep seal' traps with a 75mm (3in) depth of seal for single stack systems. Today, however, deep seal traps are always fitted.

Of course, the modern bottle trap is one of the most common types used. It's neater looking and requires less space than a traditional U-trap. Where it's concealed behind a pedestal or in a vanity unit you can use one made of plastic, but there are chromium-plated and brass types if you have a wall-hung basin where trap and waste will be clearly visible. The one drawback with bottle traps is that they discharge water more slowly then a U-trap. You can now also buy traps with telescopic inlets that make it easy to provide a push-fit connection to an existing copper or plastic branch waste pipe (see pages 296-300).

Connecting up the water supply

It's unlikely that you'll be able to take out the old basin and install a new one without making some modification to the pipework. It's almost certain that the tap holes will be in a different position. To complicate matters further, taps are now made with shorter tails so you'll probably have to extend the supply pipes by a short length.

If you're installing new supply pipes, how you run them will depend on the type of basin you're putting in. With a wall-hung basin or the pedestal type, the hot and cold pipes are usually run neatly together up the back wall and then bent round to the tap tails. But as a vanity unit will conceal the plumbing there's no need to run the pipes together.

You might find it difficult to bend the required angles, so an easy way round the problem is to use flexible corrugated copper pipe which you can bend by hand to the shape you need. You can buy the pipe with a swivel tap connector at one end and a plain connector, on which you can use capillary or

FITTING A VANITY UNIT

1 *Cut a hole in the vanity unit with the help of the template provided or, if the hole is precut, check the measurement against that of the sink.*

2 *Prop the basin up while you install the mixer unit. Start with the outlet spout which is fixed with a brass nut and packing washers.*

3 *Now take the water inlet assembly and check that the hot and cold spur pipes are the right length so that the tap sub-assemblies are correctly positioned.*

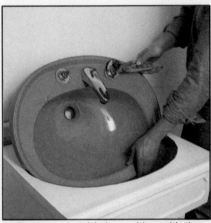
4 *Fix the assembly in position with the brass nuts supplied by the manufacturer. Make sure that all the washers are included otherwise the fitting won't be secure.*

5 *Now complete the tap heads by first sliding on the flange which covers up the securing nut; next put on the headwork and tighten the retaining nut.*

6 *Finish off the tap assembly by fitting the coloured markers into place (red for hot is usually on the left), and gently pressing home the chrome cap.*

7 Now insert the waste outlet. Make sure the rubber flange is fitted properly and seats comfortably into the basin surround.

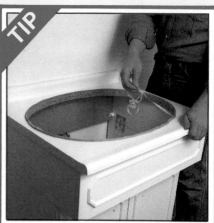

9 Before you put the basin into its final position put a strip of mastic around the opening in the vanity unit to ensure a watertight seal.

11 Now fix the inlet pipes to the two mixer connections and screw on the waste trap. Take the doors off the vanity unit to make access easier.

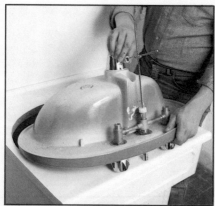

8 Turn the basin over; secure the outlet and the pop-up waste control rods. These may need shortening depending on clearance inside the vanity unit.

10 Press the basin gently into position and fix it to the underside of the top of the vanity unit. Attach the waste plug to its keeper.

12 Turn the water back on and check for leaks. Check the pop-up waste system works, then put the doors of the vanity unit back on.

Ready Reference

BASIN SIZES

On basins, the dimension from side to side is specified as the length, and that from back to front as the width.

Most standard sized basins are between 550 and 700mm (22 and 28in) long, and 450 to 500mm (18 to 20in) wide.

BASIN COMPONENTS

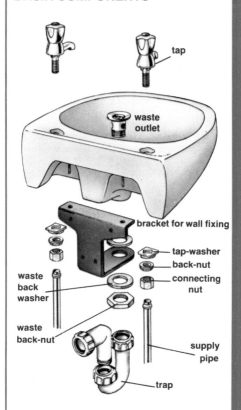

tap

waste outlet

bracket for wall fixing

tap-washer
back-nut
connecting nut

waste back washer

waste back-nut

supply pipe

trap

THE SPACE YOU'LL NEED

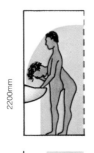

2200mm

1000mm

400mm   700mm

Think about the space around your basin particularly if you are installing a new one. You not only need elbow room when you are bending over it, such as when you are washing your hair, but also room in front to stand back – especially if you put a mirror above it. Here are the recommended dimensions for the area around your basin.

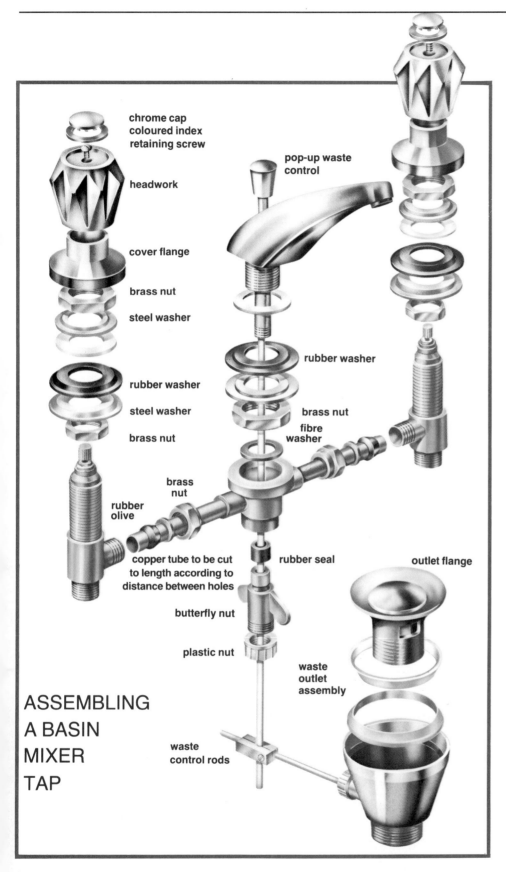

chrome cap
coloured index
retaining screw

headwork

cover flange

brass nut

steel washer

rubber washer

steel washer

brass nut

rubber olive

brass nut

pop-up waste control

rubber washer

brass nut
fibre washer

copper tube to be cut to length according to distance between holes

butterfly nut

plastic nut

rubber seal

outlet flange

waste outlet assembly

waste control rods

ASSEMBLING A BASIN MIXER TAP

When fitting the taps all you have to do is to remove the back-nuts and slip flat plastic washers over the tails (if they aren't there already). The taps can then be positioned in the holes in the basin. When this has been done more plastic washers (or top hat washers) have to be slipped over the tails before the back-nuts are replaced. It's important not to overtighten these as it's quite easy to damage a ceramic basin.

Because some vanity unit basins are made of a thinner material, you may find that the shanks of the taps fitted into them will protrude below the under-surface of the basin. The result is that when the back-nut is fully tightened, it still isn't tight against the underside of the basin. To get round the problem you have to fit a top hat washer over the shank so the back-nut can be screwed up against it.

Mixers usually have one large washer or gasket between the base of the mixer and the top of the basin and you fix them in exactly the same way.

When you've fitted the taps you can then fit the waste. With a ceramic basin you'll have to use a slotted waste to enable water from the overlfow to escape into the drainage pipe. Getting this in place means first removing the back-nut so you can slip it through the outlet hole in the basin – which itself should be coated with a generous layer of plumber's putty. It's essential to make sure that the slot in the waste fitting coincides with the outlet of the basin's built-in overflow. You'll then have to smear jointing compound on the protruding screw thread of the tail, slip on a plastic washer and replace and tighten the back-nut. As you do this the waste flange will probably try to turn on its seating, but you can prevent this by holding the grid with pliers as you tighten the back-nut.

Finally, any excess putty that is squeezed out as the flange is tightened against the basin should be wiped away.

A vanity unit will probably be supplied with a combined waste and overflow unit. This is a flexible hose that has to be fitted (unlike a ceramic basin, where it's an integral part of the appliance). The slotted waste is bedded in in exactly the same way as a waste on a ceramic basin. You then have to fit one end of the overflow to the basin outlet and slip the 'banjo' outlet on the other end over the tail of the waste to cover the slot. It's held in position by a washer and back-nut.

Fitting the basin
Once the taps and waste have been fixed in position on the new basin, you should be ready to remove the old basin and fit the new one in its place. First you need to cut off the water supply to the basin, either by turning off the main stop-valve (or any gate valve on

compression fittings at the other. If you're using ordinary copper pipe, the easiest way to start is by bending the pipe to the correct angle first, and then cutting the pipe to the right length at each end afterwards.

Preparing the basin
Before you fix the basin in position, you'll need to fit the taps (or mixer) and the waste. It's much easier to do this at this stage than later when the basin is against the wall because you will have more room to manoeuvre in.

the distribution pipes) or by tying up the ball-valve supplying the main cold water storage cistern. Then open the taps and leave them until the water ceases to flow. If the existing basin is a pedestal model you'll have to remove the pedestal which may be screwed to the floor. Take off the nut that connects the basin trap to the threaded waste outlet and unscrew the nuts that connect the water supply pipes to the tails of the taps. These will either be swivel tap connectors or cap and lining joints. You'll need to be able to lift the basin clear and then remove the brackets or hangers on which it rests.

You'll probably need some help when installing the new basin as it's much easier to mark the fixing holes if someone else is holding the basin against the wall. With a pedestal basin, the pedestal will determine the level of the basin. The same applies with

a vanity unit. But if the basin is set on hangers or brackets, you can adjust the height for convenience.

Once the fixing holes have been drilled and plugged, the basin can be screwed into position and you can deal with the plumbing. Before you make the connections to the water supply pipes you may have to cut or lengthen them to meet the tap tails. If you need to lengthen them you'll find it easier to use corrugated copper pipe. The actual connection between pipe and tail is made with a swivel tap connector – a form of compression fitting.

Finally you have to connect the trap. You may be able to re-use the old one, but it's more likely you'll want to fit a new one. And if its position doesn't coincide with the old one, you can use a bottle trap with an adjustable telescopic inlet.

FITTING A PEDESTAL BASIN

1 *Stand the basin on the pedestal to check the height of the water supply pipe runs and the outlet. Measure the height of the wall fixing points.*

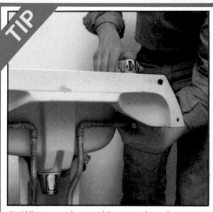

2 *When you're making up the pipe run to connect to the tap tails, plan it so the pipes are neatly concealed within the body of the pedestal.*

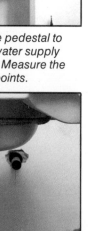

3 *Line up the piped waste outlet and fix the trap to the basin outlet. A telescopic trap may be useful here to adjust for a varying level.*

4 *Move the whole unit into its final position, screw the basin to the wall, connect the waste trap to the outlet, and connect up the supply pipes.*

Ready Reference

TYPES OF BASIN

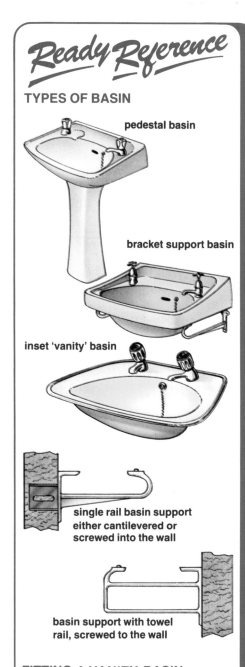

pedestal basin

bracket support basin

inset 'vanity' basin

single rail basin support either cantilevered or screwed into the wall

basin support with towel rail, screwed to the wall

FITTING A VANITY BASIN

When you buy a vanity basin it should be supplied with a template to guide you in cutting your work surface or vanity unit. This should also include fitting instructions, and necessary fixing screws and mastic strip. It may look like this.

REPLACING TAPS

Changing the old taps on your basin is a bright and practical way of making your bathroom more attractive. It may also be a good idea if they are old and inefficient. Here's what is involved.

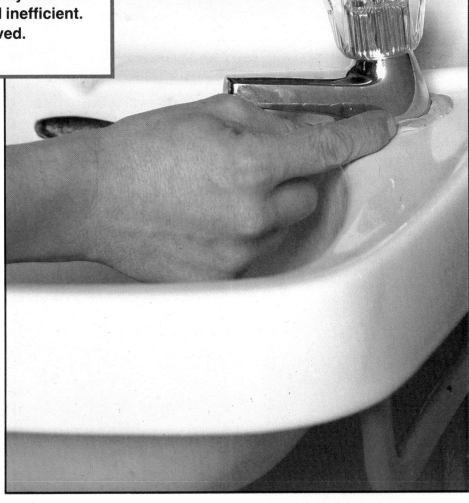

There may be a number of reasons why you wish to replace the taps supplying your sink, basin or bath. They may continually drip or leak, where new taps would give efficient, trouble-free service. Perhaps you want the advantages that mixers have over individual taps or perhaps it is simply that the chromium plating has worn off leaving the taps looking incurably shabby.

It is more likely, however, that appearance, rather than malfunction, will be your reason for changing. There are fashions in plumbing fittings as in clothing and furniture. Taps of the 1950s or 60s are instantly recognisable as out-of-date in a bathroom or kitchen of the 1980s. Fortunately, fashions in sinks, basins and baths have changed rather less dramatically over the past three decades. There is probably no more cost-effective way of improving bathroom and kitchen appearance than by the provision of sparkling new taps or mixers.

Choosing taps

When you come to select your new taps you may feel that you are faced with a bewildering choice. Tap size, appearance, the material of which the tap is made, whether to choose individual taps or mixers and – for the bath – whether to provide for an over-bath shower by fitting a bath/shower mixer: all these things need to be considered.

Size is easily enough dealt with. Taps and mixers are still in imperial sizes. Bath tap tails are ¾in in diameter, and basin and sink taps ½in in diameter. There are, however, a few suppliers who are beginning to designate taps by the metric size, not of the taps themselves, but of the copper supply pipes to which they will probably be connected. Such a supplier might refer to bath taps as 22mm and sink and basin taps as 15mm.

Most taps are made of chromium-plated brass, though there are also ranges of enamelled and even gold-plated taps and mixers. Although taps and mixers are still manufactured with conventional crutch or capstan handles, most people nowadays prefer to choose taps with 'shrouded'

heads made of acrylic or other plastic. In effect, these combine the functions of handle and easy-clean cover, completely concealing the tap's headgear. A still popular alternative is the functional 'Supatap', nowadays provided with plastic rather than metal 'ears' for quick and comfortable turning on and off.

There is also a very competitively priced range of all-plastic taps. These usually give satisfactory enough service in the home, but they cannot be regarded as being as sturdy as conventional metal taps, and they can be damaged by very hot water.

So far as design is concerned the big difference is between 'bib taps' and 'pillar taps'. Bib taps have a horizontal inlet and are usually wall-mounted while pillar taps have a vertical inlet and are mounted on the bath, basin or sink they serve.

Taking out old basin taps

When replacing old taps with new ones the most difficult part of the job is likely to be – as with so many plumbing operations – removing the old fittings. Let's first consider wash basin taps.

You must, of course, cut off the hot and cold water supplies to the basin. The best way of doing this will usually be to tie up the float arm of the ball valve supplying the cold water storage cistern so as to prevent water flowing in. Then run the bathroom cold taps until water ceases to flow. Only then open up the hot taps. This will conserve most of the expensively heated water in the hot water storage cylinder.

If you look under the basin you will find that the tails of the taps are connected to the water supply pipes with small, fairly accessible nuts, and that a larger – often

REMOVING OLD TAPS

1 *It's best to change taps by removing the basin completely. Loosen the two tap connectors carefully with an adjustable spanner.*

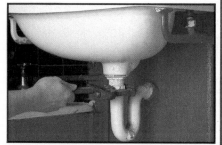

2 *Disconnect the waste trap connector using an adjustable wrench. Take care not to damage the trap, particularly if it is lead or copper.*

3 *Undo any screws holding the basin to its brackets on the wall, and lift it clear of the brackets before lowering it carefully to the floor.*

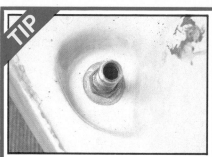

4 *Check the condition of the back-nuts, which may be badly corroded. It's a good idea to apply penetrating oil and leave this to work for a while.*

5 *Use the crowsfoot (with extra leverage if necessary) to undo the back-nut. If more force is needed, grip the tap itself with a wrench to stop it turning.*

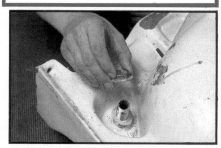

6 *Remove the back-nut and any washers beneath it and the basin. Old washers like these should always be replaced with new washers.*

inaccessible – back-nut secures the tap to the basin. The nuts of the swivel tap connectors joining the pipes to the taps are usually easily undone with a wrench or spanner of the appropriate size. The back-nuts can be extremely difficult – even for professional plumbers!

There are special wrenches and basin or 'crows foot' spanners that may help, but they won't perform miracles and ceramic basins can be very easily damaged by heavy handedness. The best course of action is to disconnect the swivel tap connectors and to disconnect the trap from the waste outlet. These are secured by nuts and are easily

undone. Then lift the basin off its brackets or hanger and place it upside down on the floor. Apply some penetrating oil to the tap tails and, after allowing a few minutes for it to soak in, tackle the nuts with your wrench or crowsfoot spanner. You'll find they are much more accessible. Hold the tap while you do this to stop it swivelling and damaging the basin.

Fitting the new taps

When fitting the new taps or mixer, unscrew the back-nuts, press some plumber's putty round the tail directly below the tap body or fit a plastic washer onto the top tail.

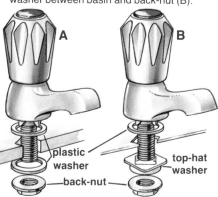

FITTING NEW TAPS

1 Remove the tap and clean up the basin surround, chipping away scale and any old putty remaining from when the tap was originally installed.

2 Now take one of the new taps and fit a washer or plumber's putty around the top of the tail before pushing it into the hole in the basin.

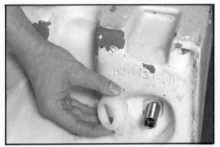

3 Twist the tap so that it's at the correct angle to the basin and is firmly bedded on the putty. Then push a top-hat washer onto the tail.

4 With the top-hat washer firmly in place, take the new back-nut and screw it up the tail of the tap by hand.

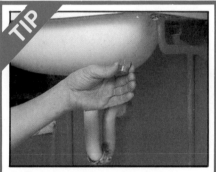

5 Tighten up the back-nut until the tap assembly is completely firm, using the crowsfoot or an adjustable spanner. Repeat the process for the other tap.

TIP

6 Reconnect all the pipework. Use tap-tail adaptors if the new taps have shorter tails than the old ones.

7 When all is secure, remove any surplus putty from around the base of the taps, wiping it over with a finger to leave a smooth, neat finish.

8 Turn the water back on. Check that the flow from the taps is regular and that the waste trap is not leaking. If it is, tighten up its connectors slightly.

Push the tails through the holes in the basin. Slip flat plastic washers over the tails where they protrude from beneath the basin, screw on the back-nuts and tighten them up. Make sure that the taps or mixer are secure, but don't overtighten them. To make tightening easier, (and undoing, if ever necessary) use top-hat washers.

All that remains to be done is to connect the swivel tap connectors to the tails of the new taps or mixer. You will see that a tap connector consists of a lining – with a flange – that is inserted into the tap tail and is then secured by the coupling nut. This nut is provided with a washer to ensure a watertight connection. When renewing taps you may well need to renew this small washer.

It is possible that when you come to connect the water supply pipes to the taps you will get an unpleasant surprise. The tails of modern taps are slightly shorter than those of older ones and the tap connectors may not reach. If the water supply pipes are of lead or of copper it is quite likely that they will have enough 'give' to enable you to make the connection but, if not, there are extension pieces specially made to bridge the gap.

Bib taps
If you're replacing existing bib taps with those of a more modern design, it's a relatively simple matter of disconnecting and unscrewing the old ones and fitting the new taps in their place. However, it's quite possible that you'll want to remove the bib taps altogether and fit a new sink with some pillar taps. This will involve a little more plumbing work. To start with, turn off the water supply and remove the taps and old sink. If the pipework comes up from the floor, you'll need to uncover the run in the wall to below where the new sink will go. You should then be able to ease the pipes away from the wall and cut off the exposed sections. This will allow you to join short lengths of new pipe, bent slightly if necessary, to link the pipe ends and the tap tails. Alternatively, if the pipes come down the wall you'll have to extend the run to below the level of the new sink and use elbow fittings to link the pipe to the tap tails. In either case it's a good idea to fit the taps to the new sink first and to make up the pipework runs slightly overlong, so that when the new sink is offered up to the wall you can measure up accurately and avoid the risk of cutting off too much pipe. Rather than having to make difficult bends you can use lengths of corrugated copper pipe. One end of the pipe is plain so that it can be fitted to the 15mm supply pipes with either a soldered capillary or compression fitting; the other end has a swivel tap connector.

INSTALLING A SHOWER

Showers have become a part of the modern home, whether fitted over the bath or in a separate cubicle. They save time, space and energy and are quite easy to install once the design is right.

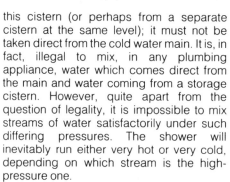

It is possible for four or five members of a family to have showers in the same time – and with the same amount of hot water – that would be needed for just one of them to have a bath. Showers, if properly installed, are safer for use by the elderly and the very young than a sit-down bath and need less cleaning. They are also more hygienic to use than a bath, as the bather isn't sitting in his own soapy and dirty water, and can rinse thoroughly in fresh water.

Where a shower is provided in its own cubicle, as distinct from over a bath, it takes up very little extra space. One can be provided in any space which is at least 900mm (36in) square, and can be put in a variety of locations such as a bedroom, on a landing, in a lobby or even in the cupboard under the stairs.

Yet shower installation can all too often prove to be a disappointment. Poorly designed systems may provide only a trickle of water at the sprinkler, or may run icy cold until the cold tap is almost turned off, and will then run scalding hot.

So, although it is possible to provide a shower in virtually any household, it is important that you match the shower equipment and your existing hot and cold water systems. If you have a cylinder storage hot water system, which is by far the commonest kind of hot water supply to be found in British homes, a conventional shower connected to the household's hot and cold water supplies is likely to be the most satisfactory and the easiest to install. But the hot and cold water systems must comply with certain quite definite design requirements if the shower is to operate safely and satisfactorily.

Pressure

The most important requirement is that the hot and cold supply pipes to the shower must be under equal water pressure. With a cylinder storage hot water system, whether direct or indirect (see pages 140–143 for the distinction), hot water pressure comes from the cold water storage cistern supplying the cylinder with water. The cold water supply to the shower must therefore also come from

this cistern (or perhaps from a separate cistern at the same level); it must not be taken direct from the cold water main. It is, in fact, illegal to mix, in any plumbing appliance, water which comes direct from the main and water coming from a storage cistern. However, quite apart from the question of legality, it is impossible to mix streams of water satisfactorily under such differing pressures. The shower will inevitably run either very hot or very cold, depending on which stream is the high-pressure one.

The cold water storage cistern must also be high enough above the shower sprinkler to provide a satisfactory operating pressure. Best results will be obtained if the base of the cold water storage cistern is 1.5m (5ft) or more above the sprinkler. However, provided that pipe runs are short and have only slight changes of direction, a reasonable shower can be obtained when the vertical distance between the base of the cistern and the shower sprinkler is as little as 1m (39in). The level of the hot water storage tank in relation to the shower doesn't matter in the least. It can be above, below or at the same level as the shower. It is the level of the cold water storage cistern that matters.

There is yet another design requirement for conventional shower installation which sometimes applies. This is that the cold water supply to the shower should be a separate 15mm (½in) branch direct from the cold water storage cistern, and not taken from the main bathroom distribution pipe. This is a safety precaution. If the cold supply were

taken as a branch from a main distribution pipe, then flushing a lavatory cistern would reduce the pressure on the cold side of the shower causing it to run dangerously hot. For the same reason it is best for the hot supply to be taken direct from the vent pipe immediately above the hot water storage cylinder and not as a branch from another distribution pipe, though this is rather less important. A reduction in the hot water pressure would result in the shower running cold. This would be highly unpleasant, although not dangerous.

Mixers

Showers must have some kind of mixing valve to mix the streams of hot and cold water and thus to produce a shower at the required temperature. The two handles of the bath taps provide the very simplest mixing valve, and push-on shower attachments can be cheaply obtained. Opening the bath taps then mixes the two streams of water and diverts them upwards to a wall-hung shower rose. These very simple attachments work quite satisfactorily – provided that the design requirements already referred to are met. However, it isn't always easy to adjust the tap handles to provide water at exactly the temperature required.

A bath/shower mixer provides a slightly more sophisticated alternative operating on the same principle. With one of these, the tap handles are adjusted until water is flowing through the mixer spout into the bath at the required temperature. The water is then

CHOOSING THE RIGHT SHOWER TYPE

The type of shower you can install depends on the sort of water supply you have in your home. This chart will help you make the right selection.

Flowchart:

- Hot and cold water stored → Is there 1m (3ft) between cistern base and shower rose?
- Cold taps from mains hot water stored → Can new cold water cistern be installed?
- No water storage → Consider instantaneous water heater shower
- Can new cold water cistern be installed? — YES → Is there 1m (3ft) between cistern base and shower rose?; NO → Consider instantaneous water heater shower
- Is there 1m between cistern base and shower rose? — YES → Consider mixer-type shower; NO → Can cistern be raised or a pump be fitted?
- Can cistern be raised or a pump be fitted? — YES → Consider mixer-type shower; NO → How is domestic hot water heated?
- Consider mixer-type shower → Will children or the old use the shower?
- Will children or the old use the shower? — YES → Use thermostatic mixer-type shower; NO → Use manual or thermostatic mixer-type shower
- How is domestic hot water heated? → Instantaneous gas water heater; Non-storage electric water heater
- Instantaneous gas water heater → Mixer-type shower can be used with some gas water heaters → If heater suitable, use mixer-type shower
- Non-storage electric water heater → Is there a gas supply in the house? — YES → Mixer-type shower can be used with some gas water heaters; NO → Install instantaneous electric shower

diverted up to the head by turning a valve.

Then there are manual shower mixers. These are standard equipment in independent shower cubicles and may also be used over a bath. With a manual mixer the hot and cold streams of water are mixed in a single valve. Temperature, and sometimes flow control, are obtained by turning large knurled control knobs.

Finally, there are thermostatic shower mixing valves. These may resemble manual mixers in appearance but are designed to accommodate small pressure fluctuations in either the hot or cold water supplies to the shower. They are thus very useful safety devices. But thermostatic valves cannot, even if it were legal, compensate for the very great difference of pressure between mains supply and a supply from a cold water storage cistern. Nor can they add pressure to either the hot or cold supply. If pressure falls on one side of the valve the thermostatic device will reduce flow on the other side to match it.

Thermostatic valves are more expensive but they eliminate the need to take an independent cold water supply pipe from the storage cistern to the shower and can possibly reduce the total cost of installation.

Where a shower is provided over an existing bath, steps must be taken to protect the bathroom floor from splashed water. A plastic shower curtain provides the cheapest means of doing this but a folding, glass shower screen has a much more attractive appearance and is more effective.

Electric showers

You can run your shower independently of the existing domestic hot water system by fitting an instantaneously heated electric one. There are a number of these on the market nowadays. They need only to be connected to the rising main and to a suitable source of electricity to provide an 'instant shower'.

Installing a bath/shower mixer

To install a shower above a bath, first disconnect the water supply, and drain the cistern if no gate-valve is fitted to its outlet. Remove the bath panel, if there is one, and disconnect the tap tails from the supply pipes. Then unscrew and remove the tap back-nuts and take the taps off.

You can now fix the new mixer in place. Finally, decide on the position for the shower spray bracket and fix it in place on the bathroom wall.

Ready Reference

WHY HAVE A SHOWER?

Showers have many advantages over baths:
● they are hygienic as you don't sit in dirty, soapy water and you get continually rinsed
● they are pleasant to use. Standing under jets of water can be immensely stimulating, especially first thing in the morning
● they use a lot less water per 'wash' than a bath, which saves energy and is also an advantage where water softeners are in use
● economy of hot water usage means that at peak traffic times there is more water to go round
● showers take less time, they don't have to be 'run', and users can't lay back and bask, monopolizing the bathroom
● easy temperature adjustment of a shower gives greater comfort for the user and lessens the risk of catching cold in a cold bathroom.

SHOWER LOCATION

You don't have to install a shower over a bath or even in the bathroom. A bedroom is one alternative site, but landings and utility rooms are another possibility. Provided a supply of water is available, the pressure head satisfactory, and the disposal of waste water possible, a shower can provide a compact and very useful house improvement in many parts of the home.

In a bathroom a shower will usually go over a bath, which is the easiest and most popular position. In a larger bathroom a cubicle is a good idea.

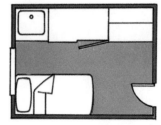

In a bedroom a shower can be easily fitted at the end of built-in wardrobes.

HOW TO ADAPT YOUR SYSTEM

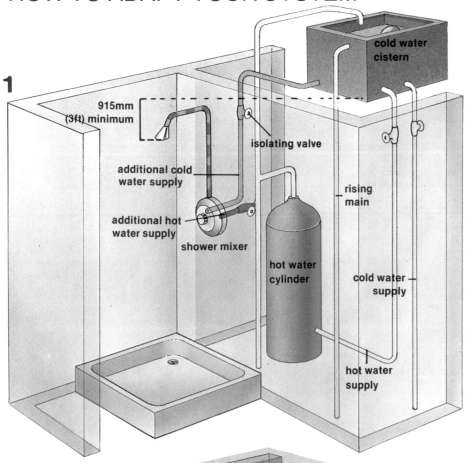

1 : Just add pipework

◁ The most common domestic plumbing system has a cold water cistern in the loft which feeds a hot water tank. In this case you must check that the vertical distance from the bottom of the cold cistern to the shower outlet head is at least 915mm (3ft). To install a shower you must take a 15mm cold water supply direct from the cistern to the cold inlet of the mixer, and a 15mm hot water supply from the vent and draw-off pipe, which emerges from the hot water tank, to the hot water inlet of the mixer.

2 : Raise the cistern

▷ In many older houses the cold water cistern may be in the airing cupboard immediately above the hot water tank, or in another position but still beneath ceiling height. This will usually mean that there is insufficient pressure for a mixer-type shower on the same floor. To get round this problem the cistern can be raised into the loft by extending the pipework upwards. Moving an old galvanised cistern will be rather arduous so this is a good opportunity to replace it with a modern plastic one, (see a future issue).

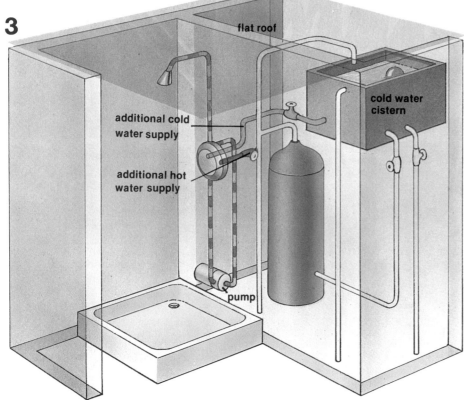

3 : Install a pump

◁ In some homes which have flat roofs it is impossible to raise the cistern indoors to provide a sufficient pressure head for a shower on the same floor. While you could consider putting the cistern on top of the roof this would involve providing extensive insulation and is an unsatisfactory solution. Pump-assisted mixer showers are available which will artificially increase the pressure head when the shower is turned on and these are fairly simple to install. As they are electrically operated they should be situated outside the bathroom area.

4 : Add a new cistern

▷ Many modern houses have combination hot and cold water storage units which are supplied and installed as one unit. They have a disadvantage in that cold water capacity is about one-third of the hot water cylinder and would provide an insufficient supply for a shower. This problem can be overcome by installing a pump and a supplementary cold water storage cistern. To ensure similar hot and cold pressures at the shower the supplementary cistern must be at a comparable level with the combination unit's cold water storage.

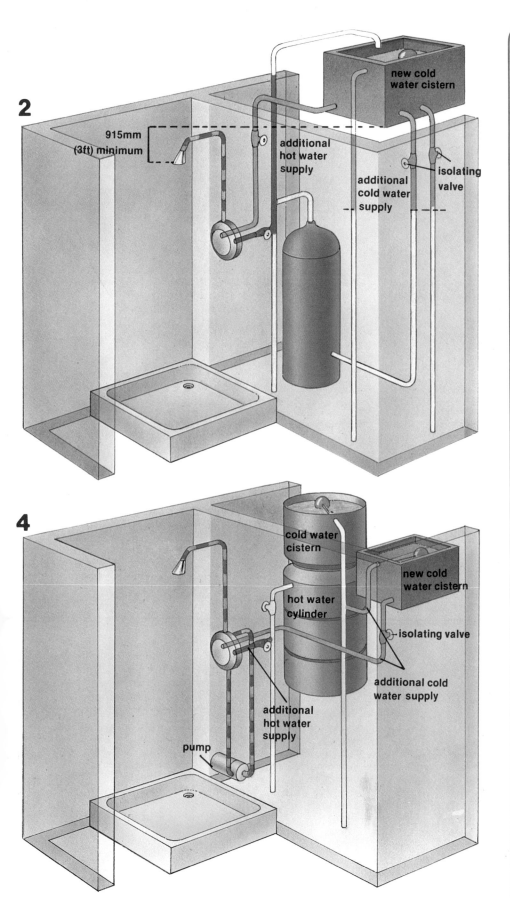

2

915mm
(3ft) minimum

new cold
water cistern

additional
hot water
supply

additional
cold water
supply

isolating
valve

4

cold water
cistern

new cold
water cistern

hot water
cylinder

isolating valve

additional cold
water supply

additional
hot water
supply

pump

Ready Reference

TYPES OF SHOWER

There are two basic types of shower:
● those attached to a mixer on a bath
● those independent of the bath, discharging over their own bases, in their own cubicles.

Bath showers may be attached to a mixer head on which you have to adjust both taps, or they may simply fit over the tap outlets. The shower head in either case is detachable and may be mounted at whatever height you require.

Independent showers have fixed position heads or are adjustable. They may have a single control mixer, or a dual control which means that you can adjust the flow as well as the temperature. Thermostatic mixing valves are also available which can cope with small pressure fluctuations in the hot and cold water supply. These only reduce pressure on one side of the valve if that on the other side falls; they cannot increase the pressure unless they have already decreased it.

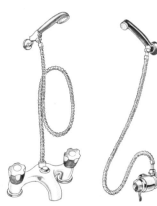

bath/shower mixer

single control mixer

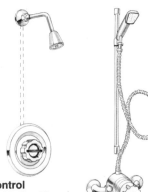

dual control
mixer with fixed head

thermostatic mixer
with adjustable head

BUILDING A SHOWER CUBICLE

The simplest way to add showering facilities to your bathroom is to install the shower over the bath. However, building a separate cubicle is a better solution.

When you come to install a shower in your home, the most obvious place for it is over the bath because you can make use of the bath's water supply and waste facilities. But this isn't the most advantageous site: putting a shower there does not increase your bathing facilities, it merely improves the existing ones. It's far better to have your shower as a separate cubicle, even if the cubicle is in the bathroom itself. If you can put the cubicle in another part of the home, you have as good as provided an extra bathroom.

You may think that you have no room in your home for a shower outside the bathroom, but that is not necessarily true. A shower does not require all that much space and you can make do with an area about 750mm (2ft 6in) square. But you've got to think about how much space you need to get into and out of the shower. It isn't usually that easy or efficient to dry off inside, so you need some space to dry off at the point of exit. You will also have to take into consideration the relationship of the drying area with bathroom fittings.

You can buy a ready-made shower cubicle, or build your own from scratch. The latter course will save a lot of money, and is easier than you might think, but you've got to take care to ensure that it is properly waterproofed.

Putting in the tray

To build a shower cubicle you start with the shower tray. Many people attempt to make one of these themselves by building a box that they cover with some impervious material – usually tiles. However, the construction is not easy because making the box absolutely waterproof can present problems, and then it is difficult to get the right gradient from every part of the tray to carry water to the waste outlet. On the whole, you would do better to buy a tray.

Normally, trays are made in acrylic plastic or glazed ceramics. The latter are dearer, but much longer-lasting, as acrylics can crack. Both types are available in standard sanitary-ware colours, so if you have a modern coloured bathroom suite, you should be able to match it. Trays come in a range of sizes, so be sure to choose one to fit

the space you have, since obviously the size of tray governs the area your installation will take up. Ceramic trays can also be very heavy so it's likely you'll need help to get one into position.

The tray will have a waste outlet, and this may be in one corner, or in the middle of one side. It must be sited so that its waste pipe can discharge conveniently into a hopper of a two-pipe system, or be connected up to an existing waste pipe, or to the main stack of a single-pipe system. The waste pipe must slope downwards all the way, and it is important to get the fall right in order to drain water away efficiently. In general, the fall should be between 6 and 50mm per 300mm run of pipe (¼ to 2in per ft) depending on the length of the run (measured from the actual waste outlet). Too steep a run can produce a siphonage effect that will drain the water out of the trap, thus depriving your home of its protection from drain smells (see pages 144–148 for more details). It's a good idea to set a fall of 25mm (1in) per 300mm for a short run of say 600 to 900mm (2 to 3ft), but only a 12mm (½in) fall where the run will be 3 to 4.5m (10 to 15ft).

Most shower trays are square, and obviously these can be turned round to place the outlet in the most convenient position. However, for installation in a corner, triangular shaped trays, or quadrants – with two straight

sides at right angles and a curved front – are on sale, but they're quite expensive.

The outlet does not have a plug, because it is never the intention that the tray should be filled up. Since there is no plug, no overflow is required. However, like all your bathroom fittings, it must have a trap. This should be 38mm (1½in) in diameter but, like a bath, does not have to be of the deep-seal variety.

Some trays are designed to have enough depth to enable the trap to be installed above floor level. Others are quite shallow, and the trap must go under the floor, a point to bear in mind if you have a concrete floor. Yet another possibility is to mount the tray on supports, to raise its height, and some manufacturers sell special supports to raise the tray off the ground. Otherwise you can use bricks or timber, suitably disguised by a plinth. It's a good idea to provide an inspection panel should you ever want to get access to the plumbing. Whatever the case, you will never have good access to the outlet plumbing after it's been installed – so be sure to make a good job of it.

Providing a cubicle

A shower tray is best positioned in a corner, so that two sides of the shower enclosure are already provided by the shower tray itself; you can bridge the gap with timber covered with tiles set flush with the top of the tray.

INSTALLING THE SHOWER TRAY

1 Press a sausage of plumber's putty around the underside of the outlet flange, then wind PTFE tape along the length of the thread.

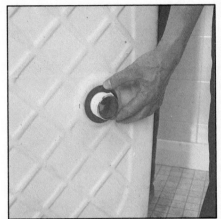

2 Push the flange into the waste hole in the tray, press it home until the putty squeezes out round the edge, and put on the metal washer.

3 Screw on the back-nut by hand and tighten it with an adjustabale wrench. This will squeeze more putty out; remove the excess neatly.

4 Take the special low-seal shower trap and screw it onto the outlet flange, after first making sure that the O ring is in place.

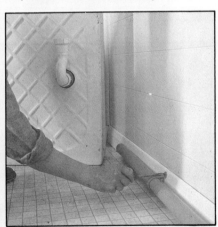

5 Measure up the position needed for the waste run, and install the plastic waste pipe in position ready to be connected up to the trap.

6 Lower the tray into place and connect up the trap to the waste pipe. Check that it is level on your prepared base.

Ready Reference

WASTE OUTLET RUNS
You must provide sufficient depth underneath the shower tray to accommodate the waste trap and the outlet pipe. You can:
● support the tray on timber or bricks and face the elevation with panels

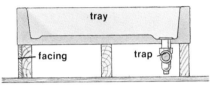

● support the tray with special supporting brackets which are usually available from shower tray manufacturers, and face the elevation with panels

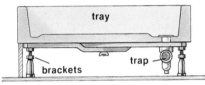

● cut a hole in the floor – if it's made of wood – and run the trap and waste above the ceiling of the room underneath. You can do this only if the joists run in the same direction as the waste pipe.

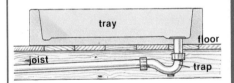

HOW MUCH SPACE?
It's very easy to think of a shower as only occupying the same space as the tray itself. But don't forget that you will usually step out of it soaking wet and so will need sufficient area in which to dry off. If the shower is enclosed on three sides you will need more space than if it's enclosed on one side and curtained on the others.

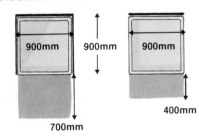

PUTTING UP A SURROUND KIT

1 Mark the position of the wall uprights; use a spirit level to make sure that they will be truly vertical when fixed in position.

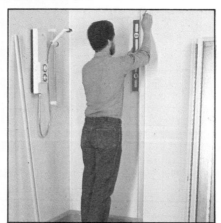

2 Drill holes for the upright fixings, then plug them with plastic wall plugs and screw on the uprights with the screws supplied.

3 Slide the first panel into position on the wall upright and fix it; again check that the structure is in a properly vertical position.

4 Adjust the length of the panel to fit the size of the shower tray and tighten up the screws carefully. Attach the corner bracket.

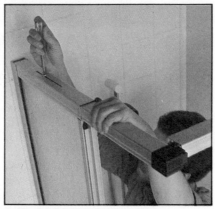

5 Fix the other panel in position and adjust its length so that it mates up accurately and squarely with the corner bracket.

6 Adjust the bottom runners to the correct size so that they match up with the bottom corner bracket; check they are square to the tray.

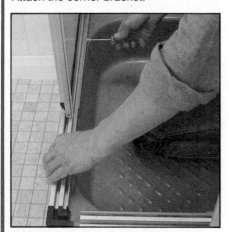

7 Screw up the bottom corner bracket, then check that the whole structure is firm and square and that the door opens and closes smoothly.

8 Loosen the wall upright fixings and wedge up each side in turn. Squeeze sealant between the frame and the tray and refix the frame.

9 Check again for alignment, then finish off the base by firmly fixing the supports in position and finally boarding in the sides of the shower.

Existing walls forming part of the cubicle will also need tiling or covering with some laminated material – commonly waterproofed decorative wallboard, or even glass or sheet plastic over paint or wallpaper. It is obviously very important to make sure that all gaps are sealed, otherwise gradual water seepage will occur which will damage the fabric of your house.

The sides of the cubicle you have to install can be home-made or bought as kits. The simplest way to fill one or two sides is with a curtain rail and shower curtain. This works quite well with a shower in the bath, but the sides of a shower tray are much shallower than those of a bath and water is therefore quite likely to splash onto the floor. This means that curtains are really only at all suitable for the entry side of the cubicle where you might protect the floor with a bath mat, or where the floor of your bathroom is tiled and fully sealed.

You can construct any solid sides of the cubicle using a timber framework, but you will have to buy a suitable proprietary door unless you use a curtain. These doors are usually made of aluminium frames with opaque safety glass or plastic panels. They come in a wide variety of designs and colours. You can have, for example, a plain aluminium frame with clear glass, or a gold satin frame with dark smoked glass. If you plan to buy a door, check that you have calculated the size of your cubicle to fit it, and that the door comes with suitable rust-proof fittings to hang it.

The easiest (though most expensive) solution is to buy the complete surround, including a sliding or ordinary door, which will be supplied in kit form. These surrounds are made by the same manufacturers as shower doors and usually come complete with fixing instructions. They are usually adjustable to fit different shower tray sizes, and are simply fitted to the wall at each end to provide a rigid frame. Before finishing they have to be sealed where they meet the tray using a proprietary sealant, to ensure a waterproof joint. If this isn't done perfectly, water will gradually seep in and cause damp on the floor and walls of your bathroom.

Home-made surrounds

Making your own surround will save money, and it has the advantage that you can tailor it exactly to your needs. You might, for example, want a surround which is larger than the tray itself; in which case you can install a shelf or seat next to the tray.

Begin by making a framework of 50mm (2in) square timber. You need a length on every edge, plus extra horizontal ones at 450mm (18in) centres. All should be joined with halving joints. In addition, fit any extra length needed to provide a fixing point (for

the shower rose, for instance). The inside face of the partition should then be clad with 6mm (¼in) plywood. Use an exterior-grade board if the cubicle is to be tiled.

Another possibility is to use 10mm (⅜in) thick plasterboard. The framework for this should consist of a 50mm (2in) sq batten on every edge, plus one extra vertical and horizontal in the middle, and any additional member needed to provide a fixing point. Fix the board with galvanised plasterboard nails driven in until the head slightly dimples the surface of the board, but without fracturing the paper liner. You can use 3mm (⅛in) hardboard to cover the outside of the cubicle framework.

Do not fix the exterior cladding for the time being. You should first clad the inside face, then fix the half-completed partition in place by driving screws through the frame members into the floor below, the wall behind and the ceiling too if it is to be a room height job.

The interior of this partition is a good place in which to conceal the supply pipes to the shower. You would then need an inspection panel, held by screws (not glued and nailed) to allow easy access to the pipework should maintenance ever be needed.

If the cubicle is not a floor-to-ceiling one, you will also need extra support at the top as you cannot leave the front top edge flapping free. This can take the form of a 75x25mm (3x1in) batten, decoratively moulded if you wish, spanning the two sides of the cubicle or fixed at one end to a block screwed to the wall, should there be only one side.

The whole interior of the shower cubicle needs to be clad with an impervious material to make sure it is waterproof. The most obvious choice is tiles, and these can be fixed to both the plywood or plasterboard cladding and the plaster of a wall. Make sure that the latter is clean and sound before tiling. Do not, however, fix the tiles direct to the timber part of the framing.

As an alternative to tiles you could use a special plastic-faced hardboard, with a tile pattern and a backing of plain hardboard. Fix the plastic-faced board by glueing and pinning with rustproof nails (if these can be lost somewhere in the pattern). Otherwise use a contact adhesive. This does not need to be spread all over the meeting surfaces. Apply it in a pattern similar to that detailed for the framework of the partitions. Adhesives applied by gun are available for this sort of work. The board on the back wall should be fixed in a similar manner.

Whatever material you use, all joins – where partitions meet the wall, or the tray – should be sealed with a silicone bath sealant. Any parts not clad with impervious material should be well painted with a three-coat system of primer, undercoat and one or two top coats.

Ready Reference

SHOWER SURROUNDS

Buying a ready-made shower surround and door in kit form is the easy, but expensive, solution to enclosing the shower tray. You can use a curtain, which is less efficient, but cheaper. Surrounds can fill one, two or three sides; some of the options are illustrated below.

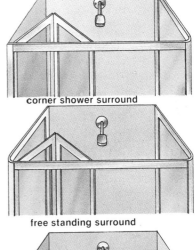

corner shower surround

free standing surround

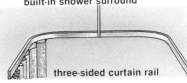

built-in shower surround

three-sided curtain rail

TIP: WATERPROOF SEALS

There's no point in fitting a surround if it's not watertight, and it is most likely to leak where the surround meets the tray. Fill this gap with non-setting mastic and then seal with any acrylic or silicone sealant to match the tray colour.

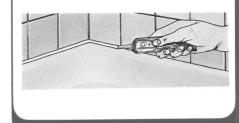

REPLACING A RADIATOR

If one of your existing radiators is malfunctioning in some way, or else just out of character with the decor of your home why not replace it with a brand new one? You'll find this job straightforward if you follow our instructions.

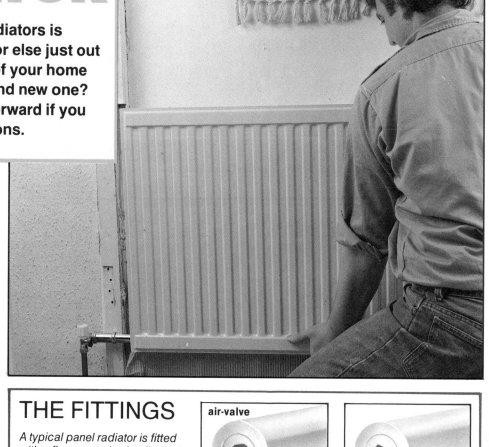

There are a number of reasons why you may want to replace an existing radiator in your home's central heating system. These can range from the aesthetic to the purely practical. At one time radiators were ugly and cumbersome, and if you have any still in use like this it's quite likely that they'll clash with the decor of your home. On the practical side, you may well find that a radiator in your system has developed leaks. This will mean both water and heat loss, as well as the inconvenience of cleaning up the mess. And, of course, you may simply feel that a modern radiator would produce more heat, and so improve the comfort in your home. Whatever your reasons for replacing a radiator, you'll have to choose a new one to go in its place, before actually removing the existing one.

Choosing a new radiator

Modern radiators are usually made of 1.25mm (about 1/16in) thick pressed steel, and are designed to be space-saving, neat and attractive. For a simple replacement job, size will be among the most important considerations. If the new radiator can be successfully connected to the existing fittings, you won't need to alter or modify the circulating pipes. Consequently, the job will be that much easier. Radiators are available in a wide variety of sizes, ranging in height from 300mm (12in) to 800mm (30in) and in length from 480mm (19in) to 3200mm (10ft 6in) – so you shouldn't have too much difficulty in finding one that will fit into the space left by the old one. Special low, finned radiators are also available. These are usually fitted along the skirting and are both neat and unobtrusive – yet can be turned into decorative features in their own right.

But size isn't the only important consideration. After all, a radiator's job is to provide heat, so you'll have to shop around and find the one which, for its size, will produce most heat. A radiator's heat output is measured in Btu – British Thermal units – so you should look for the one with the highest Btu rating for its size. Remember, it's always possible to turn off a radiator that makes a room too warm; it's far less easy to increase heat output in a room which, with the radiator

THE FITTINGS

A typical panel radiator is fitted with a flow control valve (below), a lock-shield valve (bottom right), an air-bleed valve (right) and a blanking-off plate (far right).

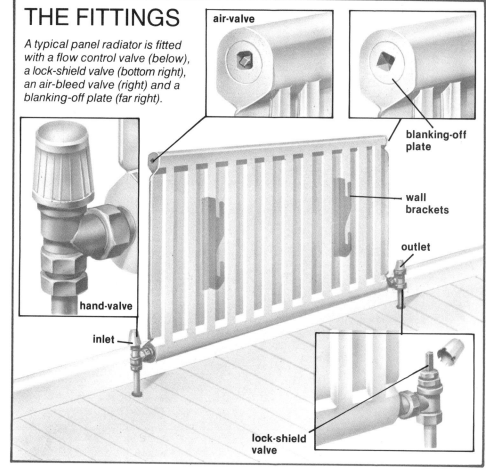

air-valve

blanking-off plate

wall brackets

outlet

hand-valve

inlet

lock-shield valve

REMOVING THE OLD RADIATOR

1 *Turn off the flow control valve by hand, and the lock-shield valve by turning its spindle with pliers. Note how many turns are needed to close it completely.*

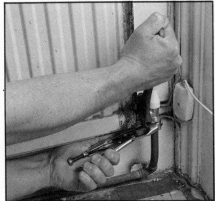

2 *Hold the lock-shield valve body with a wrench so you don't bend the pipework, and undo the valve coupling carefully with an adjustable spanner.*

3 *Open the air-bleed valve, pull the coupling away and allow the radiator to drain into a convenient container. Have rags and a larger bowl handy too.*

4 *Having drained most of the water, undo the other coupling, lift the radiator off its brackets and drain out the dregs. Then remove the old brackets.*

turned fully on, remains uncomfortably chilly.

However, one way of increasing heat output, while retaining the same sized radiator, is to install a double-panel radiator. This is, literally, an ordinary radiator with two panels for the hot water to fill instead of the usual one and therefore has virtually double the heat output. So, while a single panel radiator 685mm x 1150mm (27in x 45in) will have a heat output of 3575Btu, a double panel one of the same size will be rated at 5990Btu.

Although modern radiators are likely to provide more heat than the older variety, they do have one drawback. Because of the thinness of their metal, they are more prone to internal corrosion and this will ultimately produce leaks.

Dealing with internal corrosion

Internal corrosion in modern radiators arises from an electrolytic reaction between the steel of the radiators and the copper circulating pipes of the central heating system. This results in the production of a corrosive black iron oxide sludge (magnetite) and hydrogen gas. In a similar fashion, if the original installation of your heating system was somewhat messily done, then copper swarf, produced when the pipes were cut, could have been retained within the circulating pipes. This will also corrode the steel at any point where the two come in contact – usually within a radiator. Because the raw material from which the sludge is produced is the metal of the radiators, eventually they will leak and need to be replaced. And as the sludge is also attracted by the magnetic field of the circulating pump, its abrasive qualities are a common cause of early pump failure.

Early indications of serious internal corrosion are a need to vent one or more radiators at regular intervals, and cold spots on their

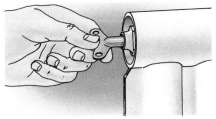

surfaces. If in doubt, the diagnosis can be confirmed by applying a flame to the escaping gas when the radiator is being vented. If it burns with a blue and yellow flame, you can be sure that hydrogen is in the system and will have been produced by the chemical reaction of the two metals.

Once you've confirmed that corrosion is present within the system, you'll have to flush it through and introduce a reliable corrosion preventative chemical into the feed and expansion tank. By doing this, you should be able to prevent further corrosion and so save your system.

Removing the old radiator

One of the great deterrents to anyone wanting to remove a radiator is the prospect of having to drain the whole system. However, this won't be necessary provided the radiator to be replaced has a valve at both the hot water inlet and the outlet. Once these are closed, you'll be able to keep virtually all the system's water isolated in other parts.

At the inlet end you're likely to find the hand-valve which is the control by which you open and close the radiator. At the outlet end you'll find what is termed the lock-shield valve. When you come to inspect your radiator, don't worry if their positions are reversed – they will still be equally effective.

The first thing to do when removing a radiator is to close these valves. The hand-valve is straightforward, but you'll have to remove the cover to get at the lock-shield valve. You'll be able to close this valve using a spanner or an adjustable wrench with which to grip its spindle.

As you turn it, it's a good idea to note carefully how many turns it takes to close. And you'll find this task slightly easier if you mark the turning nut with a piece of chalk before you begin. The reason for all this is to maintain the balance of the system. After it was first installed, your system would have been balanced. The lock-shield valves of all the radiators were adjusted to give an equal level of water through-flow so that they were all heating up equally. So, by noting the number of turns taken to close the lock-shield, when you come to fit the new radiator you can simply open it up by the same amount – so avoiding the somewhat tedious task of re-balancing the whole system.

Once you've closed both valves, you can unscrew the nuts which connect the valves to the radiator inlet and outlet. Do these one at a time after having placed a low dish under each end to collect the water and protect the floor. Use an adjustable wrench to undo the coupling nuts. It's wise to hold the circulating pipe securely in place with another wrench. Otherwise, if you apply too much pressure to the coupling nut you risk fracturing the flowpipe, and this would cause

FITTING THE NEW RADIATOR

1 To ensure watertight connections to the new radiator, wrap PTFE tape round all threaded fittings and then smear on some jointing compound.

2 Screw in the valve couplings with a hexagonal radiator spanner. Use extension pieces if the new radiator is slightly narrower than the old one.

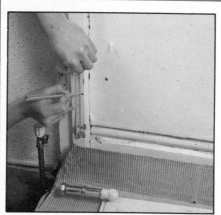

5 Mark the height taken in **4** on the wall above each valve, and join up the marks at each end with a pencil line. This marks the level of the new brackets.

6 Transfer the measurements taken in **3** to the wall to indicate the vertical position of each bracket. Accuracy is not so vital here as in **5**.

9 Lift the radiator into place on its brackets. You can move it slightly from side to side to align the valve couplings with the inlet and outlet valves.

10 Wrap the coupling threads in PTFE tape and jointing compound, and do up the couplings. Again, use a wrench to support the valve body and prevent strain.

3 Lay the radiator down in line with the two valves, and measure the distance from each valve coupling to the centre of the nearest bracket mounting.

4 Next, measure the height of the base of the radiator brackets from a line joining the centres of the inlet and outlet valves.

7 Hold the bracket against the wall in line with the vertical and horizontal marks you've made, and draw in the positions for the fixing screws.

8 Drill and plug the four holes – two to each bracket – and fix the brackets in position. Make sure the wallplug is well below the plaster to avoid cracking.

11 After connecting up the couplings, use a bleed key to open the air-bleed valve slightly so that air can escape as the radiator fills with water.

12 Open the inlet valve, allow the radiator to fill and then close the air-bleed valve. Finally open the lock-shield valve by as many turns as you took to close it.

you a lot of extra work and expense to mend – as well as causing quite a mess. As you unscrew each nut, the water from the radiator will flow out. If the system has been previously treated with corrosion proofer, it's well worth saving the water. That way you can pour it back into the feed-and-expansion tank when the job is complete.

Once the water has drained out, remove the tail pieces and coupling nuts from each end. Then block up each hole with a rag and lift the radiator from the brackets that hold it to the wall. It's a good idea to get the radiator out of your home as soon as possible – just in case it leaks any remaining dirty water on to your carpet.

Fitting a new radiator

Your new radiator will probably have four holes or tappings – one at each corner – and each one will have a female screwed thread. How you connect the radiator up to your system depends on the way in which the old one was fitted. Nowadays it is usual for the flow and return connections to be made to the bottom two holes but, of course, if your system had the flow pipe at a higher level then you'll have to reconnect it in the same way.

Fit an air-valve into one of the top tappings. First wrap PTFE thread sealing tape anti-clockwise round the male thread of the valve and then use a radiator key that grips inside the body of the valve to screw it home. Unless your radiator has a top inlet the other top tapping must be plugged with a blanking off plate. This should also be wrapped with PTFE tape and screwed home in the same way as the air vent.

You'll then have to fit tail pieces and coupling screws (either new ones, or the ones from the original radiator if you can remove them) on to the new one. Again wrap each thread with PTFE tape before fitting them. It's a good idea to buy new wall brackets for your replacement radiator. After all, you can't be sure the old ones will be suitable. You should drill and plug the wall and then fix the brackets in place. Fit the radiator so that the inlet end is a few millimetres higher than the outlet valve. This will make venting easier. You can now fix the radiator in place and connect the coupling nuts to the hand-valve and lock-shield valve and screw them up tightly.

You'll have to open the air-valve at the top of the radiator so that the air in it can be displaced as it fills with water. All you do is slowly open the hand-valve and allow the radiator to fill. When water starts to flow from the air-valve you'll know all the air has been displaced and you should immediately close the valve. Finally, open the lock-shield valve by the same number of turns and part turns it took originally to close it.

ELECTRICAL TECHNIQUES

Understanding ELECTRICS

In theory, you could do electrical jobs knowing nothing about electricity, given accurate step-by-step instructions. But you can't deal with any part of an electrical installation in isolation — everything is linked. And unless you understand how each part of the system works you have no way of knowing if you are making a mistake. With electricity, ignorance is dangerous.

We're all familiar with lights and power sockets, but how does the electricity reach them so we can use it? In fact, electricity enters your home along one thick cable (the service cable), passes through a large 'service fuse' and into a meter which records the amount you use. Everything up to and including that meter belongs to the electricity board, and is their responsibility. Everything beyond is the householder's property, which is perhaps why installations vary so much.

In a modern installation — one wired in the last 30 years — there are two wires carrying electric current that lead from the meter to what is called the consumer unit. These wires are known as the meter tails — one is termed live, the other neutral.

On the inlet side of the consumer unit there's a switch with which you can turn off the power altogether, but the unit's principal job is to divide up the power and send it round your home through a network of cables.

These cables are organized into circuits. There are circuits for lights, power sockets and so on, each with its own fuse in the consumer unit. The cables themselves run under the floor, above the ceiling and may even be visible on wall surfaces, although more often they are buried within them.

In older installations, instead of a consumer unit there may be individual fuse boxes protecting separate circuits. And each of these fuse boxes will have an isolating switch to cut off power to the circuit it controls. These fuse boxes are connected direct to the meter by

live and neutral meter tails. Alternatively the fuse boxes may be supplied from a distribution board which in turn is connected to the meter.

Sometimes, even with a consumer unit you may find separate fuse boxes. This is normally the result of the system having been extended.

What are circuits?

If you take a battery, and connect a wire to the positive (+) terminal, and another to the negative (−), then bring the free ends of the wires together, electricity will flow from positive to negative along them. That's a circuit. You can build a torch bulb and holder into it to prove it works. Break the circuit by cutting one wire, and the light goes out (the flow of current has stopped), and it will stay out until the cut ends are rejoined. That's a simple switch.

Of course, the circuits in your home are a good deal more complex than that, and their design varies according to whether they supply lights, power sockets or whatever. Even the electricity is different. Instead of flowing in one direction, it goes back and forth 50 times a second — hence its name *alternating current*, or AC for short.

But the principle is the same. Think of 'live' as positive, 'neutral' as negative, and you will see that for any appliance such as an electric fire to work it must have wires connecting it to the live and neutral terminals in the consumer unit. Those wires may be contained in a single cable, but the link must always be there, with switches *en route* to make or break it, and for safety reasons, switches are on the live wire.

What are fuses?

The main service cable has its fuse; the various circuits have theirs in the consumer

unit or fuse box and if you remove the back of a flat-pin plug you'll find a fuse in there.

Think of an electric light bulb. It gives out light because electricity passing through the filament (the fine wire just visible inside the bulb) makes it very hot. If you pass enough electricity through any wire, it will also heat up. If that wire happens to be a circuit cable, an appliance flex, or the service cable to the meter, then the consequences would be serious. So, to protect them, a weak link called a fuse is built into the circuit.

Most fuses are just thin pieces of wire. They can be fitted to rewirable fuse carriers, in which case you can replace them, or they may be in ceramic cartridges, in which case you throw them away and fit another. In any event, the fuse's thickness is described in terms of how much electricity — expressed in amps — is theoretically needed to melt it.

The word 'theoretically' is important because, in fact, fuses aren't particularly accurate or reliable. For this reason, a more sensitive device called a miniature circuit breaker (MCB) may be used instead. It's just a switch that turns off automatically when danger threatens. Once the fault responsible for the overload is put right, you switch on again.

Why cables?

It would be far too complicated to wire a house like a battery and bulb circuit using individual wires. Instead, the copper wires carrying the electricity are encased in PVC insulation to stop them touching and making their circuit in the wrong place — what's called a short circuit — and then bound together in PVC sheathing to form a cable. In this way, the live, neutral and earth wires can be run as one, even though each one is still connected up separately.

Different kinds of cable are used for different jobs. Follow the instructions in this section carefully to select the right one for each job.

Earthing

The purpose of the earth wire within the cable is to make up the earth continuity conductor (ECC). This is an essential safety feature of any electrical installation. Its role is to act as a 'safety valve' in the event of a fault, causing a fuse to blow or an MCB to trip to isolate a faulty circuit or faulty appliance from the mains supply. In doing so it could prevent the risk of fire or someone being electrocuted.

Earth wires are connected to the metal parts of switches, socket outlets, fittings and appliances (and even plumbing) in a really up-to-date system. Electricity will flow along the line of least resistance, so that if by some mishap any of these parts became live (by coming into contact with a live conductor) the earth wire would offer a line of 'less' resistance. In effect the faulty current would travel along the earth wire rather than through a person touching the live metal part. And the extra current passing through one circuit would

be sufficient to blow the fuse or activate the MCB.

Unfortunately this doesn't always happen – so, for added safety, a special device called a residual current device (RCD for short) can be fitted to detect the slightest leakage of current to earth. It shuts off the power within milliseconds – quickly enough to save a life – at the first sign of a fault.

RCD's can be added to an existing system, or included within the consumer unit in a new installation. They usually protect all the circuits in the house and also act as a mains on/off switch.

Ring circuits

For getting electricity to the power points, the most common system of wiring is what's called a 'ring' circuit. Wired in 2.5mm² two-core and earth cable, most homes have one such circuit for each floor of the house.

The two-cores and the earth wire are connected to their terminals in the consumer unit (or fuse box) and then pass through each power socket in turn before returning to their respective terminals in the consumer unit (fuse box). The circuit is protected by a 30A

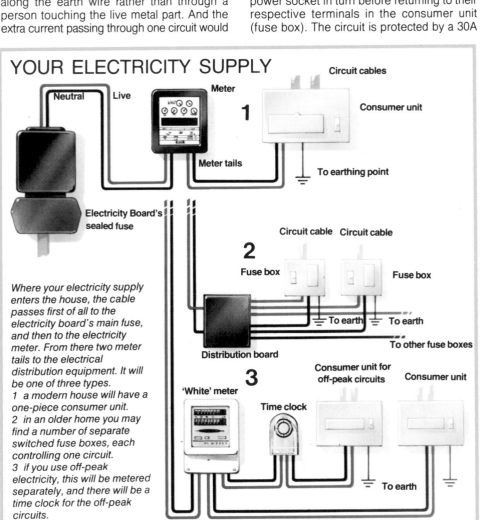

YOUR ELECTRICITY SUPPLY

Neutral / Live / Meter / Circuit cables / Consumer unit / 1 / Meter tails / To earthing point

Electricity Board's sealed fuse

Circuit cable / Circuit cable / 2 / Fuse box / Fuse box / To earth / To earth / To other fuse boxes / Distribution board

Consumer unit for off-peak circuits / Consumer unit / 3 / 'White' meter / Time clock / To earth / To earth

Where your electricity supply enters the house, the cable passes first of all to the electricity board's main fuse, and then to the electricity meter. From there two meter tails to the electrical distribution equipment. It will be one of three types.
1 a modern house will have a one-piece consumer unit.
2 in an older home you may find a number of separate switched fuse boxes, each controlling one circuit.
3 if you use off-peak electricity, this will be metered separately, and there will be a time clock for the off-peak circuits.

Trevor Lawrence

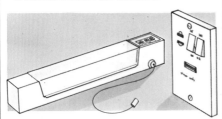

fuse. The advantage of this system is it allows the cable to cope with more sockets than if it made a one-way trip (as with radial circuits). In fact, you are allowed as many sockets as you like on the ring, so long as the floor area served by the circuit doesn't exceed 100 sq metres (1,080 sq ft). What's more, you can increase the number of sockets by adding 'branch lines' off the ring. These are called 'spurs' and break into the ring via a junction box, a spur connection unit, or an existing socket. You are allo-

wed as many spurs as can feed one single socket, one double socket, or one fixed appliance via a fused connection unit. Until a recent change in the IEE wiring regulations, a spur could feed two single sockets, and you may find such spurs on your existing circuits.

Of course, with all those sockets, there is a risk of overloading the circuit, but in the average family home it's unlikely that you'll have enough sockets in use at any one time. The circuit may carry up to 30 amps of current

which is equivalent to having appliances and portable lamps using 7,200 watts of power all switched on together. It's doubtful that you would want all this on at the same time, but it's wise not to go above this level of power use. If the circuit does overload, the fuse will blow, or the MCB will switch off.

Radial circuits

Unlike ring circuits, radial circuits consist of a single cable that leaves the fuse box and runs to one or more sockets. In older homes in the UK, before ring circuits were introduced, all power circuits were wired as radials. Since homes had (and needed) only a few sockets, individual circuits were usually run to each one from the fuse box. The sockets themselves were rated at 2A, 5A or 15A, and had round holes to accept round-pin plugs. Such circuits will probably have been wired in rubber- or lead-sheathed cables, which deteriorate with age (see pages 205–8), and are not able to satisfy the far greater electrical demands of a modern household. It's wise to have such circuits examined by a qualified electrician, and best of all to have them replaced.

Radial circuits are, however, also used in modern wiring systems where a ring circuit could be inappropriate for some reason. There are two types, with different current-carrying capacity.

A 20A radial circuit uses 2.5mm² cable and

A ring circuit originates from a 30A fuseway in the consumer unit. Protection may be by an MCB rather than a rewirable or cartridge fuse.

Spurs are sometimes added when the ring circuit is installed to save on the wiring runs. They are usually connected at a three-terminal junction box.

Socket outlets on a ring circuit take the fused 13A flat-pin plug. They can be one- or two-gang (ie, take one or two plugs); the best have switches.

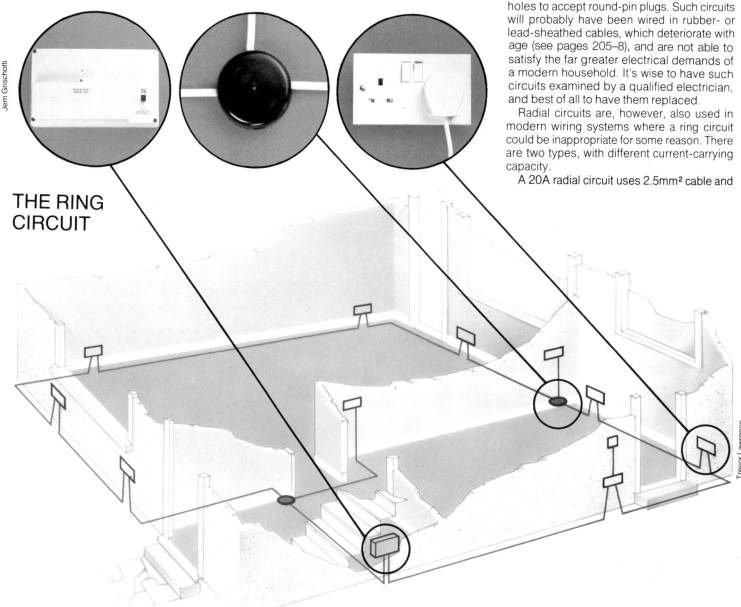

THE RING CIRCUIT

is protected by a 20A fuse (rewirable or cartridge) or an MCB in the consumer unit (or fuse box). It can supply an unlimited number of 13A socket outlets and fixed appliances using 3kW of power or less, providing they are within a floor area not exceeding 20 sq metres (about 215 sq ft).

The other type of circuit is the 30A radial which is wired in 4mm² cable and can feed a floor area of up to 50 sq metres (540 sq ft). It can be protected by a 30A cartridge fuse or MCB, but *not* by a rewirable fuse.

These restrictions on floor area mean that several radial circuits would have to be installed to cover the same area as a ring circuit. This is one of the reasons why the 'ring' is now the most common method of wiring in the UK, but radial circuits can supplement an overworked ring circuit.

Special purpose circuits

In addition to rings and radials, your home may have special circuits which supply only one outlet or appliance. Cookers, immersion heaters, instantaneous showers and the like are wired in this way and each has its own individual fuse. In effect, these circuits are just radials that have had both the cable and fuse sizes 'beefed up' to cope with the often heavy demands of the appliances they supply — for example, a large family-size cooker might need a 45A fuse, and 6mm² or even 10mm² cable.

Because electric night storage heaters all come on together they could overload a ring circuit; consequently each one is supplied by

The various radial power circuits originate from fuseways in a consumer unit or from individual fuse boxes. They are protected by rewirable fuses.

Modern radial circuits have sockets that take 13A flat-pin plugs. Older radials with lead or rubber-sheathed cable take round pin plugs.

Even if you have ring circuit wiring, radial circuits are used for special purposes, such as supplying a cooker. It may also contain a 13A socket outlet.

A fused connection unit sometimes supplies a fixed appliance on a radial circuit. This could be a wall mounted heater or an immersion heater.

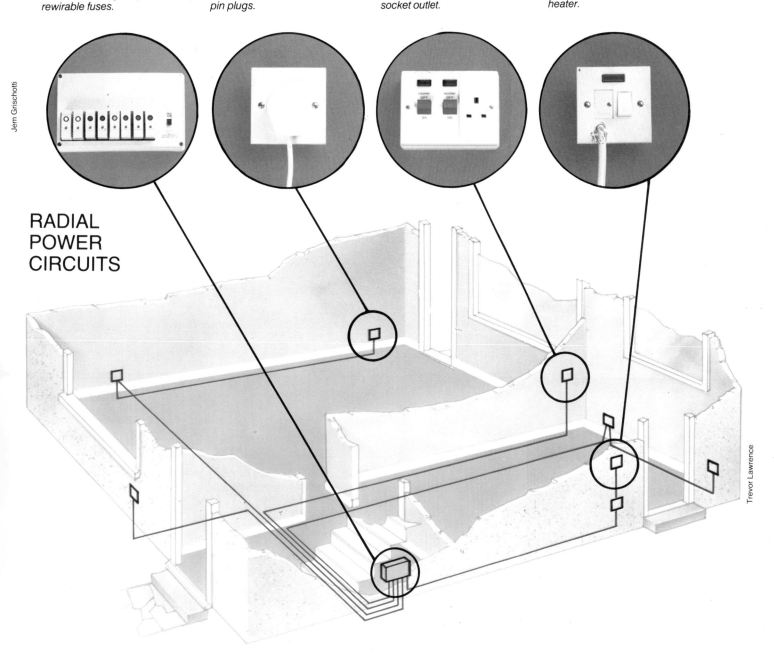

RADIAL POWER CIRCUITS

Jem Grischotti

Trevor Lawrence

LIGHTING CIRCUITS

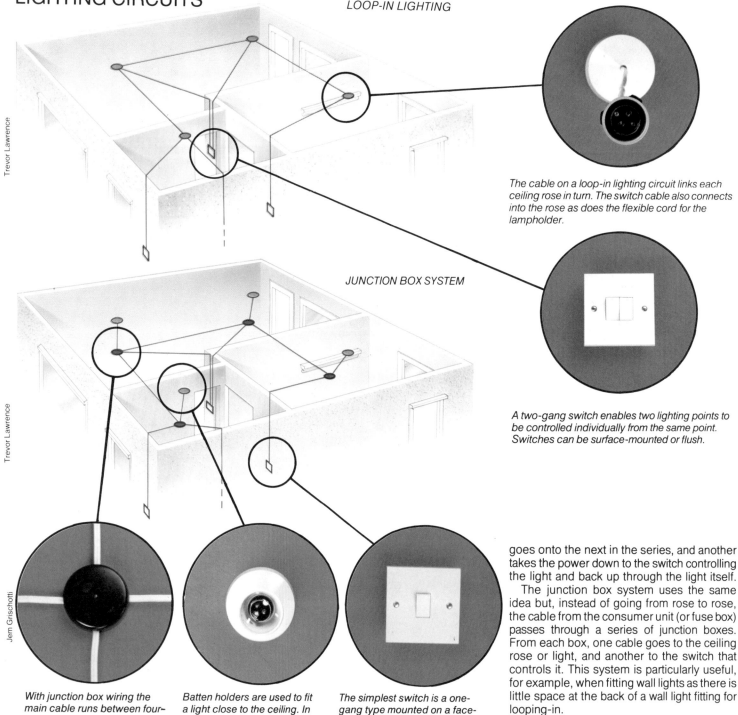

LOOP-IN LIGHTING

The cable on a loop-in lighting circuit links each ceiling rose in turn. The switch cable also connects into the rose as does the flexible cord for the lampholder.

JUNCTION BOX SYSTEM

A two-gang switch enables two lighting points to be controlled individually from the same point. Switches can be surface-mounted or flush.

Trevor Lawrence

Trevor Lawrence

Jem Grischotti

With junction box wiring the main cable runs between four-terminal junction boxes. The other cables go to the lighting point and the switch.

Batten holders are used to fit a light close to the ceiling. In bathrooms, they must have a 'skirt' to prevent contact with metal on the fitting or bulb.

The simplest switch is a one-gang type mounted on a face-plate. They can be either surface mounted or recessed to be flush with the wall.

a separate radial circuit protected by a 20A fuse. The fuses are housed in a separate consumer unit which is linked to a sealed time clock and uses off-peak electricity.

Lighting circuits
Two systems of wiring lighting circuits are in common use, and it is not unusual for an installation to contain a little bit of each. One is called the loop-in system; the other the junction (or joint) box system.

With the loop-in system, a cable (normally 1.0mm² but sometimes 1.5mm²) leaves a 5A fuse in the consumer unit (or fuse box) and is connected to the first in a series of special loop-in ceiling roses. From this rose, one cable goes onto the next in the series, and another takes the power down to the switch controlling the light and back up through the light itself.

The junction box system uses the same idea but, instead of going from rose to rose, the cable from the consumer unit (or fuse box) passes through a series of junction boxes. From each box, one cable goes to the ceiling rose or light, and another to the switch that controls it. This system is particularly useful, for example, when fitting wall lights as there is little space at the back of a wall light fitting for looping-in.

Lighting circuits are rated at 5 amps, which means they can take a load of up to 1,200 watts. In effect, they could supply 12 lampholders containing bulbs of 100w each or smaller. But as you may want to fit bulbs with higher wattages, it is usual for a lighting circuit to supply up to eight outlet points, so separate circuits are required for each floor.

Strictly speaking it's better to arrange the circuits so that there is more than one on each floor — this means that you won't be in total darkness if a fuse in the consumer unit blows.

TRACING ELECTRICAL FAULTS

When the lights go out or an electrical appliance won't work, the reason is often obvious. But when it isn't, it helps to know how to locate the fault and put it right.

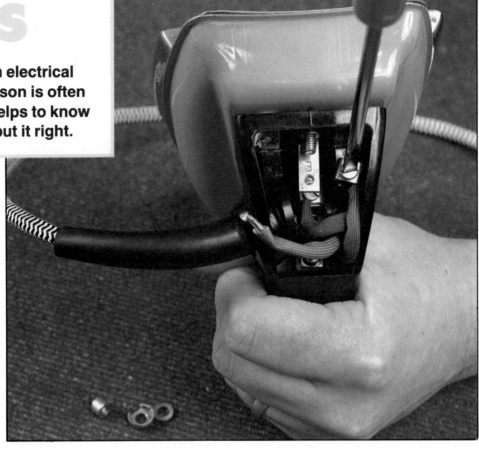

M ost people's immediate reaction to something going wrong with their electricity supply is to head for the meter cupboard, muttering darkly about another blown fuse. Fuses do blow occasionally for no immediately obvious reason, but usually there is a problem that needs to be pin-pointed and put right before the power can be restored. It's no use mending a blown fuse, only to find that when the power is restored the fuse blows again because the fault is still present.

Tracing everyday electrical faults is not particularly difficult. You simply have to be methodical in checking the various possible causes, and eliminating options until you find the culprit. More serious faults on the house's fixed wiring system can be more difficult to track down, but again some careful investigation can often locate the source of the trouble, even if professional help has to be called in to put it right.

Safety first

Before you start investigating any electrical faults, remember the cardinal rule and switch off the power at the main switch. When fuses blow, it is all too easy to forget that other parts of the system may still be live and therefore dangerous, and even if you know precisely how your house has been wired up it is foolish to take risks. If the fault appears to be on an electrical appliance, the same rules apply: always switch off the appliance *and* pull out the plug before attempting to investigate. Don't rely on the switch to isolate it; the fault may be in the switch itself.

It's also important to be prepared for things to go wrong with your electrics; even new systems can develop faults, and in fact a modern installation using circuit breakers will detect faults more readily than one with rewireable or cartridge fuses, so giving more regular cause for investigation. Make sure that you keep a small emergency electrical tool kit in an accessible place where it won't get raided for other jobs. It should include two or three screwdrivers, a pair of electricians' pliers, a handyman's knife, spare fuses and fuse wire, PVC insulating tape and a couple of spare light bulbs. Don't forget also a *working* torch.

Check the obvious

When something electrical fails to operate, always check the obvious first – replace the bulb when a light doesn't work, or glance outside to see if everyone in the street has been blacked out by a power cut before panicking that all your fuses have blown. Having satisfied yourself that you may have a genuine fault, start a methodical check of all the possibilities.

A fault can occur in a number of places. It may be on an appliance, within the flex or plug linking it to the mains, on the main circuitry itself or at the fuseboard. Let's start at the appliance end of things. If something went bang as you switched the appliance on, unplug it immediately; the fault is probably on the appliance itself. If it simply stopped working, try plugging it in at another socket; if it goes, there's a fault on the circuit feeding the original socket. If it doesn't go, either the second socket is on the same faulty circuit as the first one (which we'll come to later) or there may be a fault in the link between the appliance and the socket – loose connections where the cores are connected to either the plug or the appliance itself, damaged flex (both these problems are caused by abuse of the flex in use), or a blown fuse in the plug if one is fitted.

Plug and flex connections

The next step is to check the flex connections within the plug and the appliance. The connections at plug terminals are particularly prone to damage if the plug's cord grip or flex anchorage is not doing its job; a tug on the flex can then break the cores, cutting the power and possibly causing a short circuit. If the connections are weak or damaged, disconnect them, cut back the sheathing and insulation and remake the connections. Make sure that the flex is correctly anchored within the body of the plug before replacing the cover.

If the plug contains a fuse, test that it has not blown by using a continuity tester, or by holding it across the open end of a switched-on metal-cased torch – see *Ready Reference*. Replace a blown fuse with a new one of the correct current rating; 3A for appliances rated at 720W or below, 13A for higher-rated appliances (and all colour televisions).

Next, check the flex connections within the appliance itself. Always unplug an appliance before opening it up to gain access to the terminal block, and then remake any doubtful-looking connections by cutting off the end of the flex and stripping back the outer and inner insulation carefully to expose fresh conductor strands. If the flex itself is worn or

Ready Reference

COMMON FAULTS

Many electrical breakdowns in the home are caused by only a few common faults. These include:

● overloading of circuits, causing the circuit fuse to blow or the MCB to trip
● short circuits, where the current by-passes its proper route because of failed insulation or contact between cable or flex cores; the resulting high current flow creates heat and blows the plug fuse (if fitted) and circuit fuse
● earthing faults, where insulation breaks down and allows the metal body of an appliance to become live, causing a shock to the user if the appliance is not properly earthed and blowing a fuse or causing the RCD to trip otherwise.
● poor connections causing overheating that can lead to a fire and to short circuits and earthing faults.

TIP: TESTING FUSES

You can test suspect cartridge fuses (both circuit and plug types) by holding them across the open end of a switched-on metal-cased torch, with one end on the casing and the other on the battery. A sound fuse will light the torch.

CHOOSE THE RIGHT FLEX

When fitting new flex to an appliance, it's important to choose the correct type and current rating. The table below will help:

Size (mm²)	Rating amps	watts	Use
0.5	3	720	Light fittings
0.75	6	1440	Small appliances
1.0	10	2400	Larger appliances
1.5	15	3600	
2.5	20	4800	

If you are buying flex for pendant lights, remember that the maximum weight of fitting that each size of twin flex can support is
● 2kg (4½lb) for 0.5mm² flex
● 3kg (6½lb) for 0.75mm² flex
● 5kg (11lb) for larger sizes.

Select circular **three-core PVC-insulated flex** for most appliances, **unkinkable** or **braided flex** for irons, kettles and the like, **two-core flex** for non-metallic lamps and light fittings and for double-insulated appliances, and **heat-resisting flex** for powerful pendant lights and for heater connections.

REWIRING A PLUG

1 *Strip the outer sheathing carefully, cut each core 12mm (½in) longer than is necessary to reach its correct terminal and then remove 12mm of core sheathing.*

2 *Twist the strands of each core neatly and form a loop that will fit round the terminal screw. Connect the cores as shown here and screw down the studs.*

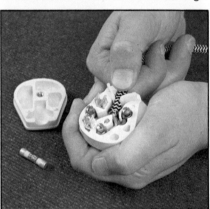

3 *Check that the core insulation reaches right to each terminal, and that there are no loose strands visible. Then fit the flex securely in the cord grip.*

4 *Lastly, in a fused plug press in a cartridge fuse of the correct rating for the appliance concerned, and screw the plug top firmly on.*

damaged, take this opportunity to fit new flex of the correct type and current rating – see the *Ready Reference* panel (left) and the step-by-step photographs for more details. Make sure you re-use any grommets, heat-resistant sleeving, special captive washers and the like that were fitted to the appliance.

Lastly, check the flex continuity; it is possible that damage to the flex itself has broken one of the cores within the outer sheathing. Again use a continuity tester for this, holding the two probes against opposite ends of each core in turn, or use your metal-cased torch again, touching one core to the case and the other to the battery. Replace the flex if *any* core fails the test; the appliance may still work if the earth core is damaged, but the earthing will be lost and the appliance could become live and dangerous to anyone using it in the event of another fault developing in the future.

Lighting problems

Similar problems to these can also occur on lighting circuits, where the pendant flex linking ceiling roses to lampholders can become disconnected or faulty through accidental damage or old age. If replacing the bulb doesn't work, switch off the power at the mains and examine the condition of the flex carefully.

Look especially for bad or broken connections at the ceiling rose and within the lampholder. You must replace the flex if the core insulation has become brittle, and fit a new lampholder if the plastic is at all discoloured. Both of these problems are caused by heat from the light bulb.

Mending blown fuses

A circuit fuse will blow for two main reasons, overloading and short circuits – see *Ready Reference*. Too many appliances connected to a circuit will demand too much current, and this will melt the fuse. Similarly, a short circuit – where, for example, bare live and neutral flex cores touch – causes a current surge that blows the fuse.

If overloading caused the fuse to blow, the remedy is simple: disconnect all the equipment on the circuit, mend the fuse and avoid using too many high-wattage appliances at the same time in future. If a short circuit was to blame, you will have to hunt for the cause and rectify it before mending the fuse – see photographs on the next page.

When a circuit fuse blows, turn off the main switch and remove fuseholders until you find the one that has blown. Then clean out the remains of the old fuse wire, and fit a new piece of the correct rating for the circuit – 5A for lighting circuits, 15A for circuits to immersion heaters and the like, and 30A for ring circuits. Cut the wire over-long, thread it loosely across or through the ceramic holder and connect it carefully to the terminals. Trim the ends off neatly, replace the fuseholder in the consumer unit and turn on the power again. If the fuse blows again, and you have already checked for possible causes on appliances, flexes and lighting pendants, suspect a circuit fault – see below.

If you have cartridge fuses, all you have to do is find which cartridge has blown by removing the fuseholder and·testing the cartridge with a continuity tester or metal-cased torch. A blown cartridge fuse should be replaced by a new one of the same current rating. Again, if the new fuse blows immediately, suspect a circuit fault.

If you have miniature circuit breakers (MCBs) you will not be able to switch the MCB on again if the fault that tripped it off is still present. Otherwise, simply reset it by switching it to ON or pressing in the centre button.

Residual current devices (RCDs)
If you installation has an RCD, it will trip off if an earthing fault occurs – for example, if a live wire or connection comes into contact with earthed metal. Like an MCB, it cannot be switched on again until the fault is rectified – a useful safety point. However, it will not trip off in the event of a short circuit between live and neutral, or when overloading occurs.

The modern high-sensitivity type of RCD, in addition to detecting earth faults, also protects against the danger of electric shocks by tripping off if it detects current flowing to earth through the human body. It can do this quickly enough to prevent the shock from causing death.

Tracing circuit faults
If you have checked appliances, flexes, plug connections and pendant lights, and a fault is still present, it is likely to be in the fixed

REPLACING FLEX

1 *To replace damaged flex, remove the appropriate cover plate or panel from the appliance. Make a note of which core goes where before undoing it.*

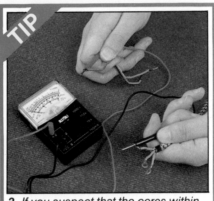

3 *If you suspect that the cores within apparently undamaged flex are broken, test each core in turn with a continuity tester.*

2 *Loosen the cord grip within the appliance and withdraw the old flex. Here heat-resisting sleeving has been fitted; save this for re-use.*

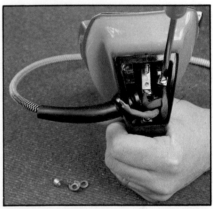

4 *Connect in the new flex by reversing the disconnection sequence, re-using grommets, sleeving and washers. Make sure each connection is secure.*

wiring. Here, it is possible to track down one or two faults, but you may in the end have to call in a professional electrician.

The likeliest causes of circuit faults are damage to cables (perhaps caused by drilling holes in walls or by nailing down floorboards where cables run), ageing of cables (leading to insulation breakdown, and overheating) and faults at wiring accessories (light switches, socket outlets and so on). Let's look at the last one first, simply because such items are at least easily accessible.

If the cable cores are not properly stripped and connected within the accessory, short circuits or earth faults can develop. To check a suspect accessory such as a socket outlet, isolate the circuit, unscrew the faceplate and examine the terminal connections and the insulation. Ensure that each core is firmly held in its correct terminal, and that each core has insulation right up to the terminal,

so that it cannot touch another core or any bare metal. There is usually enough slack on the mains cable to allow you to trim over-long cores back slightly. Check that the earth core is sleeved in green/yellow PVC, and try not to double over the cable as you ease the faceplate back into position; over-full boxes can lead to short circuits and damage to cable and core insulation ... and more trouble. You can carry out similar checks at light switches and ceiling roses. Any damaged accessories you find should be replaced immediately with new ones.

Damage to cables is relatively easy to cure provided that you can find where the damage is. If you drilled or nailed through a cable, you will of course be able to pin-point it immediately. Cable beneath floorboards can be repaired simply by isolating the circuit, cutting the cable completely at the point of damage and using a three-terminal junction

CHECKLIST FOR ACTION

When something goes wrong with your electrics, use this checklist to identify or eliminate the commonest potential causes of trouble.

Fault 1
Pendant light doesn't work
Action
● replace bulb
● check lighting circuit fuse/MCB
● check flex connections at lampholder and ceiling rose
● check flex continuity.

Fault 2
Electrical appliance doesn't work
Action
● try appliance at another socket
● check plug fuse (if fitted)
● check plug connections
● check connections at appliance's own terminal block
● check flex continuity
● check power circuit fuse/MCB
● isolate appliance if fuses blow again.

Fault 3
Whole circuit is dead
Action
● switch off all lights/disconnect all appliances on circuit
● replace circuit fuse or reset MCB
● switch on lights/plug in appliances one by one and note which blows fuse again
● isolate offending light/appliance, and see Faults 1 and 2 (above)
● check wiring accessories on circuit for causes of short circuits
● replace damaged cable if pierced by nail or drill
● call qualified electrician for help.

Fault 4
Whole system is dead
Action
● check for local power cut
● reset RCD if fitted to system (and see Faults 1, 2 and 3 if RCD cannot be reset)
● call electricity board (main service fuse may have blown).

Fault 5
Electric shock received
Action
● turn off the power supply *or*
● pull person clear immediately but DON'T TOUCH his/her body – grab the clothes or use a wooden stick, length of rubber or leather *(no metal; no moisture)*
● if victim is conscious, call a doctor; don't give brandy or food or wrap in blankets
● if breathing and/or heartbeat has stopped, give artificial respiration and/or heart massage, then CALL AN AMBULANCE

REPAIRING A CIRCUIT FUSE

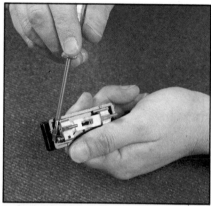

1 *Switch off the mains and locate the blown fuse. Then remove the remains of the old fuse wire and clean off any charring that has occurred.*

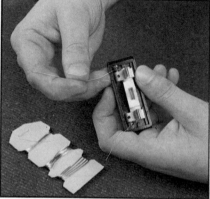

2 *Feed in a length of fuse wire of the correct rating and wind each end round the terminal before tightening up the screw. Don't pull the wire taut.*

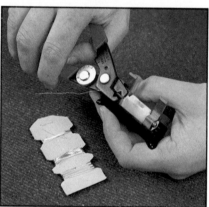

3 *Trim off the unwanted ends of fuse wire neatly with wire strippers, then replace the fuse carrier in the fuse box and restore the power.*

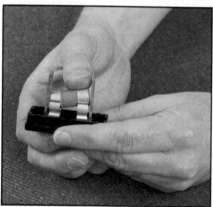

4 *Test a suspect cartridge fuse with a continuity tester or torch (see Ready Reference) and replace it by pressing in a new fuse of the correct rating.*

box to link the cut ends. Cable buried in plaster must be cut out and a new length of cable inserted between adjacent accessories to replace the damaged length. Where this would involve a long length of cable (on a run to a remote socket, for example) it is acceptable to use junction boxes in nearby floor or ceiling voids to connect in the new length of cable. You will then have to make good the cutting-out.

Tracking down a break in the cable elsewhere in the installation is a difficult job best left to a qualified electrician. If, however, you find that your house is wired in rubber-sheathed cable and faults are beginning to occur, don't waste time and effort trying to track them down. It is very likely that your house needs rewiring. This will save you time and prevent problems in the long run.

If you are unable to trace an electrical fault after checking all the points already de-scribed, call in a professional electrician who will be able to use specialist test equipment to locate the fault. Do *not* attempt to bypass a fault with a makeshift wiring arrangement, and NEVER use any conducting foreign body such as a nail to restore power to a circuit whose fuse keeps blowing. Such tricks can kill.

Regular maintenance
You will find that a little common-sense maintenance work will help to prevent a lot of minor electrical faults from occurring at all. For example, it's well worth spending a couple of hours every so often checking the condition of the flex on portable appliances (especially those heavily used, such as kettles, irons, hair driers and the like) and the connections within plugs. Also, make a point of replacing immediately any electrical accessory that is in any way damaged.

CEILING LIGHTS AND SWITCHES

Most ceiling lights are positioned centrally in a room to give general lighting. But by adding another light, or changing the position of an existing fitting, you can highlight particular areas and enhance the decoration.

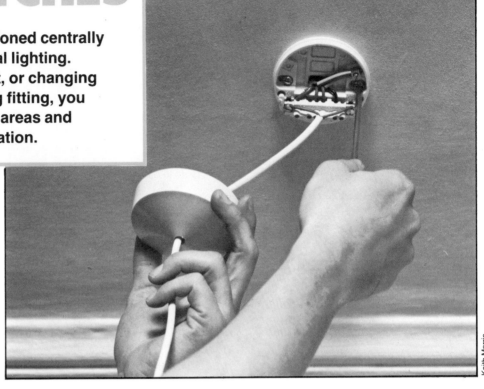

Keith Morris

Putting in a new pendant ceiling light and switch, or changing the position of an existing one, usually presents few problems – even if you have little or no experience of electrical work.

A pendant is the most common ceiling light and consists of a lampholder wired to a length of flexible cord which hangs from a ceiling rose. Another type can be plugged into the ceiling rose – in this case the flexible cord has to have a special fitting which slots into a batten holder.

Know your system

Installing a new ceiling light requires making a simple connection into a nearby lighting circuit either by inserting a junction box or at an existing loop-in rose and then running a cable to a switch. In order to connect into the circuit you'll first need to know how the lights in your house are wired and which lights belong to which circuit. Then you'll be able to work out whether you can actually add another light to the circuit that is nearest to the new light's position.

There are two principal methods of wiring a lighting circuit. In the loop-in method the cable runs from ceiling rose to ceiling rose, stopping at the last one on the circuit, and the switches are wired into the roses. With the junction box system the cable runs to a number of junction boxes each serving a switch and a light. You may well find that both methods have been used in the same circuit to simplify and reduce the cable runs.

It's possible to connect into a nearby rose provided it's a loop-in type. You can check this simply by turning off the power and unscrewing the rose cover. A loop-in rose will have more than one red insulated wire going into the central terminal bank of the three in-line terminal banks. However, it can be quite fiddly to fit another cable, given that the terminal banks are very small, so you might find it easier to insert a junction box in the main circuit. And if there isn't a loop-in rose you'll have to use this method anyway.

Earthing for lighting circuits

Modern lighting circuits are protected by an earth. But if you've got a fairly old system (it's

likely to be based on junction boxes), you might find that it doesn't have one. So when you're extending such a circuit, you're now required to protect the new wiring, light fitting and switch by installing an earth. Consequently, you have to use two-core and earth cable for the extension, which will most probably connect into the existing circuit at a junction box. You then have to run a 1.5mm^2 earth cable from this point to the main earthing point.

Circuit additions

Usually there's a lighting circuit for each floor of a house and in a single storey dwelling there are likely to be two or more. But it's easy to identify the individual circuits simply by switching on all the lights, turning off the power and taking out a 5A fuse from the consumer unit or switching off an MCB. When you restore the power you'll know that the lights that remain off all belong to the same circuit.

Generally speaking, a lighting circuit serves six to eight fixed lighting points. In fact it can serve up to 12 lampholders provided the total wattage of the bulbs on the circuit doesn't exceed 1,200 watts. This means that unless other lights have previously been added – wall lights for example – there shouldn't be a problem of connecting in another light.

Remember, when adding up the bulb wattages, a bulb of less than 100 watts counts as 100 watts and not its face value.

The place for lights

Apart from bathrooms, where special regulations apply, you can position lights and switches in any place you like inside the house. But bear in mind they are there to fulfil a function, so switches, for example, should be conveniently located – by a door is often the most satisfactory position. Usually they are set on the wall 1.4 metres (4ft 6in) above floor level. But they can be higher or lower to suit your needs.

You mustn't install pendant lights, especially plain pendants with exposed flexible cords, in a bathroom. This is for your safety. Flexes can become frayed, and if, say, you tried to change a bulb while standing in the bath and touched an exposed conductor you could electrocute yourself. Consequently, all light fittings here must be of the close-mounted type and preferably totally enclosed to keep off condensation. If instead you use an open batten lampholder it must be fitted with a protective shield or skirt which makes it impossible for anyone changing the bulb to touch the metal clamp.

A wall-mounted switch must also be out of reach of a person using the bath or shower. In modern small bathrooms, however, this is often impossible. The alternative is to place the switch just outside the room by the door, or to fit a special ceiling switch operated by an insulating cord which doesn't have to be out of reach of the bath or the shower.

Ready Reference

LIGHTING BASICS

● Extensions to lighting circuits are usually wired in 1.00mm² two-core and earth PVC-sheathed and insulated cable.
● You can extend from an existing rose only if it is of the loop-in variety with three banks of terminals; such roses can accommodate up to four cables. If you have older roses, extensions must be made via a junction box.

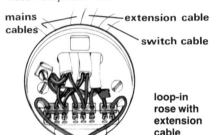

mains cables

extension cable

switch cable

loop-in rose with extension cable added

TOOLS FOR THE JOB

Electrician's pliers have cutting edges on the jaws and insulated handles.
Wire strippers can be adjusted to the diameter of the insulation to be stripped.
Handyman's knife – ideal for cutting back the sheathing of the cable.
Screwdrivers – a small one is best for the terminal fixing screws and a medium sized one for the fixing screws on the rose and switch.

HOW TO STRIP CABLE

● Use handyman's knife to cut sheathing between neutral and earth cores.
● Use wire strippers to remove core insulation.

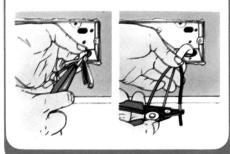

Mounting box: MK

PREPARING THE CABLE RUN

1 Raise the floorboard above the proposed location of the new light and any others necessary for laying the power supply and switch cables.

2 Mark the position of the new rose, then bore a 12mm (¹/₂in) hole. Where the cable crosses a joist, drill a 16mm (⁵/₈in) hole 50mm (2in) below the top.

3 If the new rose can't be screwed to a joist, drill a 12mm (¹/₂in) hole in a wooden batten to coincide with the hole in the ceiling and fix the batten in position.

4 If flush-fitting the switch and chasing in the cable, use a mounting box and a length of conduit to mark their positions on the wall.

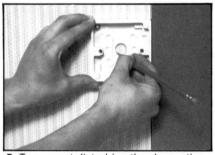

5 To prevent disturbing the decoration in one room, you can bring the switch cable down the other side of the wall and surface-mount the switch.

6 Use a small bolster chisel and club hammer to channel out a groove in the wall to take the switch cable and to chop out the recess for the switch.

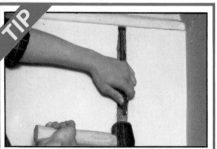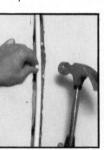

TIP

7 With cornices, make the channel in the wall first, then drive a long cold chisel gently up the back.

8 Fix the conduit in place with old nails, although you can also use clout nails. Drill and plug the fixing holes for the box and screw it into place.

Keith Morris

LAYING THE CABLE

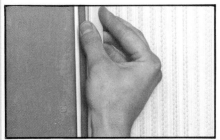

1 *Run the cable from where it joins the existing circuit to the new rose and lay in the switch cable. Allow 200mm (8in) for connections.*

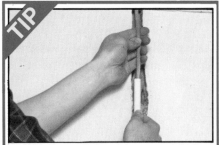

2 *With the switch cable, you might find it easier to pull down the required length and then slide on the conduit before fixing it in place.*

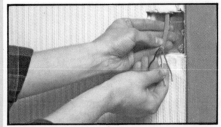

3 *It's not a good idea to leave cable exposed on a wall. When surface-mounting, the cable should be laid in PVC trunking with a clip-on cover.*

4 *If the cable is brought down on the other side of the wall to the switch, you'll need to drill a hole through so the cable enters the back of the box.*

FIXING THE SWITCH

1 *After making good, strip back about 100mm (4in) of sheathing; take off 15mm (⁵⁄₈in) of insulation and bend over the exposed wire; sleeve the earth wire.*

2 *Because the switch is wired into the 'live' of the circuit, the black wire is live and not neutral; mark it as such with red PVC tape.*

3 *Connect the earth wire to the earth terminal of the metal box and the two conductors to the terminals on the back of the faceplate.*

4 *Make sure a surface-mounted box is square before connecting the switch. With a flush fitting squareness can be adjusted when attaching the faceplate.*

Keith Morris

Switch: MK

Putting in switches

There is a great variety of switches available, but all perform the same function of breaking or completing an electrical circuit so you can turn the light off or on. Modern switches are of the rocker type; a one-gang switch has a single switch on the faceplate; a two-gang switch has two switches on the same faceplate, and so on. Dimmer switches are slightly different in that you can vary the power flowing to the bulb (so reducing or increasing its brightness) by rotating a control knob.

With a new light, you can either connect it into an existing switch position (fitting a two-gang switch in place of a one-gang one, for example) or a new switch. Depending on how you connect into the existing circuit, you'll have to run the switch cable above the ceiling from a rose or a junction box down the wall to where you are going to locate it. If you want to conceal the cable on the down drop you'll have to cut a shallow channel – which will damage the existing decoration. Or, you can surface-mount it in trunking.

Making the connection

Once you've decided where you want to put the light fitting and switch, you then have to decide where it's best to make the connection into the existing circuit.

Wiring runs may require some detective work to find out what each cable is doing – you don't want to connect into a switch cable by mistake. This may mean climbing into the roof space or raising a few floorboards. You'll need to do this anyway to run in the new cables to the required positions. As cable is expensive, it's best to plan your runs to use as little as possible. But when you measure along the proposed route, don't forget to allow about 200mm extra at the switch, rose and junction box for stripping back the conductors and joining in.

Changing the position of a ceiling light is even easier than adding a new one. If after you've turned off the power you undo the existing rose you'll see immediately the type of lighting circuit you are dealing with.

If there is only a black, a red and an earth wire going into it on the fixed wiring side then you have a junction box system. All you have to do is to disconnect the wires from the rose and reconnect them to the respective terminals of a new three-terminal junction box that you'll have to put in directly above the old fitting. You can then lead off another cable from this junction box to the re-positioned ceiling rose. The switch remains unaffected.

If the rose is a loop-in type, you have to carry out a similar modification, but this time the switch wires have to be incorporated in the new junction box, which must be a four-terminal type.

FITTING THE NEW ROSE AND LAMPHOLDER

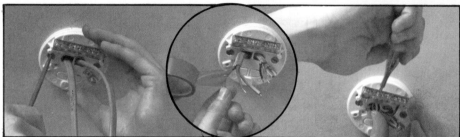

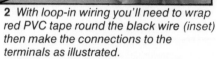

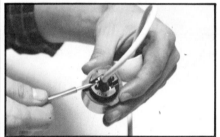

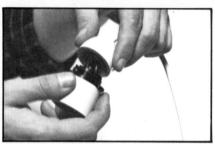

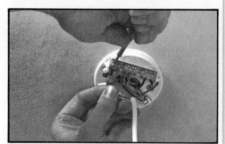

1 *Fix the new rose to the ceiling.Strip back 75mm (3in) of sheathing and 8mm (1/3in) of insulation from the conductors, and sleeve the earth wires.*

2 *With loop-in wiring you'll need to wrap red PVC tape round the black wire (inset) then make the connections to the terminals as illustrated.*

3 *With junction box wiring, the earth is connected to the earth terminal, the black conductor goes to the neutral bank and the red to the SW terminal.*

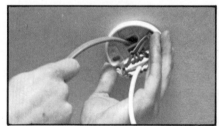

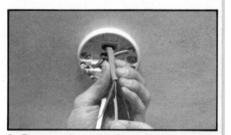

4 *Strip back the sheathing and insulation of one end of the flex and connect the blue and brown conductors to the two terminals of the lampholder.*

5 *Screw on the cap and then slip the rose cover over the flex. Cut the flex to length and prepare the free end for connecting to the rose.*

6 *At the rose, connect the blue conductor to the terminal on the neutral side and the red to the SW side. Hook the wires over the cord grips.*

CONNECTING INTO THE CIRCUIT

1 *When connecting into a loop-in rose, undo the fixing screws and pull the fitting a little way from the ceiling. But keep all the wires in place.*

2 *Tap out a knockout, then draw down through it about 200mm (8in) of the cable that leads to the new ceiling rose, or else feed the cable up from below.*

3 *Prepare the cable by stripping back about 75mm (3in) of sheathing and 10mm (3/8in) of insulation from the conductors. Sleeve the earth wire.*

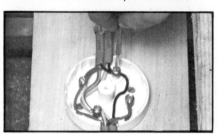

4 *Connect the earth to the earth terminal, the black to the neutral terminals and the red to the central in-line terminals.*

5 *When connecting in at a junction box, use a four-terminal type mounted on a batten. Connect the wires to the terminals as shown.*

6 *When taking out an old loop-in rose, disconnect the switch and feed cables and connect up the two feed cables as shown in a three-terminal junction box.*

TWO-WAY SWITCHING

In a room lit by a single pendant light, controlling that light from a single switch is no great hardship. But if the room contains wall lights it's useful to be able to control them from different parts of the room and that's exactly what two-way switching lets you do.

In most rooms, lights or groups of lights are controlled by just one switch. It's the standard set-up, and electricians call it one-way switching. However, there are situations where a one light, one switch arrangement isn't very convenient.

Take the light over a flight of stairs as an example. Having the light switch at the bottom of the flight is fine if you want to go upstairs. You can turn on the light before you go up without difficulty. But what happens when you reach the top? You can't turn the light off again. And suppose you want to come downstairs and the light is turned off? You can't switch it on without negotiating the stairs in the dark, which rather defeats the object of having a light there at all.

Obviously, what's needed is another switch at the top of the stairs and a system of wiring that allows either switch to turn the light on and off independently of the other. This system is called two-way switching.

Where it can be used

The example of the light above the stairs is such a common one that providing two-way switching for stair lights is now more or less standard procedure. There are, however, many other situations where two-way switching may be useful.

Think of the advantages of having a switch at both ends of a long hallway. And what about rooms with more than one entrance? It makes sense to have a switch beside each of the doors. The same applies to a garage with a side door in addition to the main one.

There are also situations where two-way switching is not vital but still worth considering. For example, where you have installed wall-mounted bedside reading lamps: it is a great advantage when you can control these from the door, as well as from a switch by the bed. You might also want to install a two-way switch for the main bedroom light so you can turn it on and off without getting out of bed.

And don't forget the hall light: in many homes this is one-way switched despite the fact that it often serves as a stair light by illuminating the bottom steps of the staircase. It's all too easy to go upstairs having forgotten to switch it off.

How it works

The key to two-way switching lies in using a special switch at both switching positions.

An ordinary one-way switch has two terminals and when you operate it you either make or break the electrical connection between them. For the current to reach the lightbulb and make it work, it must pass down one of the cores in the switch-drop cable, and back up the other. Making or breaking the link between terminals also makes or breaks the link between the two cores and therefore switches the light on or off.

A two-way switch works in a completely different way. It has three terminals, marked 'Common', L1, and L2, and when you operate it, flicking the switch one way provides a link between L1 and Common; flicking it the other way provides a link between Common and L2. If you link the terminals of two two-way switches in a certain way, then one switch can complete the circuit (and turn the light on) while the other can over-ride it and turn the light off again. The reverse also applies.

So, what is this remarkable wiring arrangement? Well, in its traditional form – the one normally illustrated in text-book wiring diagrams – the switches are linked with a pair of single-core cables called straps. Each joins the L1 terminal in one switch to the L2 terminal in the other. The switch drop from the light is

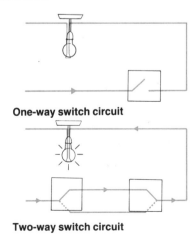

THE THEORY OF TWO-WAY SWITCHING

How a two-way switching circuit works can be seen in the way in which the switches are linked and how the power flows between them.

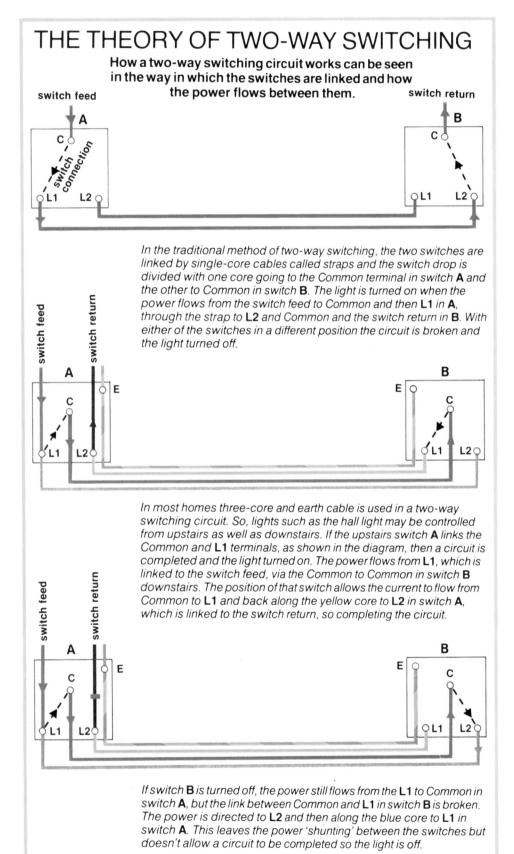

In the traditional method of two-way switching, the two switches are linked by single-core cables called straps and the switch drop is divided with one core going to the Common terminal in switch A and the other to Common in switch B. The light is turned on when the power flows from the switch feed to Common and then L1 in A, through the strap to L2 and Common and the switch return in B. With either of the switches in a different position the circuit is broken and the light turned off.

In most homes three-core and earth cable is used in a two-way switching circuit. So, lights such as the hall light may be controlled from upstairs as well as downstairs. If the upstairs switch A links the Common and L1 terminals, as shown in the diagram, then a circuit is completed and the light turned on. The power flows from L1, which is linked to the switch feed, via the Common to Common in switch B downstairs. The position of that switch allows the current to flow from Common to L1 and back along the yellow core to L2 in switch A, which is linked to the switch return, so completing the circuit.

If switch B is turned off, the power still flows from the L1 to Common in switch A, but the link between Common and L1 in switch B is broken. The power is directed to L2 and then along the blue core to L1 in switch A. This leaves the power 'shunting' between the switches but doesn't allow a circuit to be completed so the light is off.

then divided in two: the first core goes to the Common terminal in one switch, the second to the Common terminal in the other. It's all run in single-core cable, and is designed for use where your home's wiring is run entirely in conduit – as it may well be if you live in a flat.

In most homes, though, the wiring takes the form of multi-cored PVC-sheathed cables, and in this case, a different two-way switching circuit is generally more convenient. What happens is that the switch drop, run in two-core and earth cable, is connected to only one of the two-way switches: one core to L1, the other to L2. This switch is then linked to its partner with three-core and earth cable, a cable which has rather oddly colour-coded wires – one red, one yellow, and one blue. However, this doesn't make the wiring up any more complicated. The yellow and blue cores are connected in the same way as the straps in the traditional system, and the red core is used to link the two Common terminals.

Converting an existing switch

That's the theory, but how does it work in practice? How do you convert an existing one-way switching circuit to two-way switching? You may be surprised at just how simple it is. Using a club hammer and cold chisel, make a hole in the wall to take a one-gang, plaster-depth mounting box at the spot where you want the new switch to go. This should be secured to the wall with a couple of screws and wallplugs.

Then, before running a length of 1.0 or 1.5mm² three-core and earth PVC-sheathed cable to the original switch position, connect up the new switch in order to minimise the time the power has to be switched off at the mains. The red core should go to the Common terminal with the yellow and blue cores acting as strap wires. The running of the cable shouldn't pose any difficulty. The cable is taken up the wall, above the ceiling and back down the wall to the old switch.

Chop a channel in the plaster at the wall sections of the run, insert a length of PVC conduit and pass the cable through that. Above the ceiling, if the cable runs at right angles to the joists, feed it through holes drilled at least 50mm below their top edge.

If the cable runs parallel to the joists, simply rest it on top of the ceiling, unless it is likely to be disturbed – as in a loft, for example. In that case it must be secured to the sides of the joists with cable clips. Turn off the power at the mains before removing the fixing screws. Then, ease the original switch from the wall so you can pass the cable into the mounting box.

With the cable in position, all that remains to be done is connect it up to the new two-way switch at the original switch position. Finally, connect the two cores of the switch drop to terminals L1 and L2, screw the switch securely to its mounting box and restore the power.

New circuits

The same system can also be employed in new work where you require two-way switching. For example, if you are installing a new wall light and want to be able to control it from a switch at the door of the room, as well as from a switch near the light itself, all you need to do is to install a new two-way switch in the normal way (see pages 213–214) and then run a length of three-core and earth cable from this switch to the switch by the door (the one controlling the room's main light). Here, you replace the old one-gang, one-way switch with a two-gang, two-way switch and connect the three-core and earth cable to one gang for two-way switch-

ing. Then connect the switch drop belonging to the room's main light to the other gang, this time connecting it up for one-way switching with one of the cores going to the L2 terminal and the other to the Common.

This method is quite straightforward, but it is not necessarily the most convenient way of setting about the job. Suppose you were installing not one new wall light, but two or more. If they are all to have two-way switches then you'll be involved in a great deal of cable running and, therefore, a great deal of work. After all, for each light you have to run a cable down to the new switch, back up above the ceiling, then back down the wall again to the second switch position.

This extra work can be avoided by using a junction box and a variation on the traditional two-way switching circuit. You run the circuit using three-core and earth PVC-sheathed and insulated cable. Doing this you are using the cable's red core as one half of the switch drop and the yellow and blue cores as straps. Then connect them up, together with the cables to the wall lights and the cable supplying the new circuit with power (taken from a loop-in ceiling rose, or from a junction box inserted into one of your home's main lighting circuits) in a large multi-terminal joint box called an RB4. The step-by-step photographs will explain what is happening but note that only one cable need be run to each wall-light.

INSTALLING A NEW TWO-WAY CIRCUIT

Using an RB4 multi-terminal junction box can save you running extra cable when you install a new two-way circuit with more than one light. Here it has been used to install a bedside lighting circuit, shown diagramatically. Overleaf we show you how the circuit is wired up, step by step.

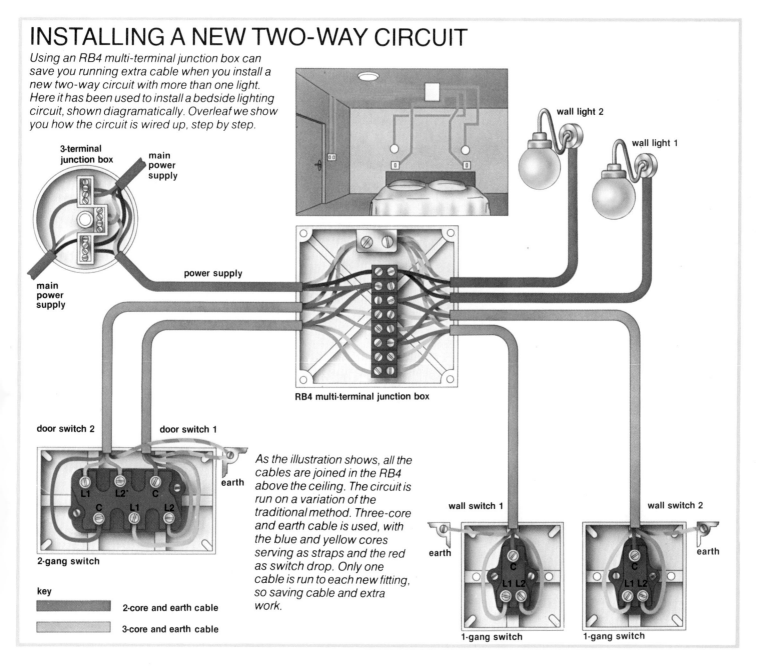

3-terminal junction box

main power supply

main power supply

power supply

RB4 multi-terminal junction box

wall light 2

wall light 1

door switch 2

door switch 1

earth

2-gang switch

As the illustration shows, all the cables are joined in the RB4 above the ceiling. The circuit is run on a variation of the traditional method. Three-core and earth cable is used, with the blue and yellow cores serving as straps and the red as switch drop. Only one cable is run to each new fitting, so saving cable and extra work.

wall switch 1

earth

1-gang switch

wall switch 2

earth

1-gang switch

key

2-core and earth cable

3-core and earth cable

CHANGING THE DOOR SWITCH

1 *Turn off the power at the mains and remove the screws in the old switch's faceplate. Ease the switch from the wall until you can disconnect it.*

2 *Run one three-core and earth cable per light from the RB4 box to the switch mounting box, using an existing conduit to carry it down the wall.*

3 *For two wall lights, install a three-gang, two-way switch. Use two gangs to connect the three-core cables – yellow to L1, blue to L2 and red to Common.*

FITTING THE BEDSIDE SWITCHES

1 *Using a club hammer and bolster chisel, chop a channel in the wall from the ceiling down to the new switch position ready for the cable.*

2 *Mark the exact position of the switch on the wall, then chop out a recess, taking care to ensure that it is deep enough to take the metal mounting box.*

3 *Before running the cable, insert a length of PVC conduit into the channel; where possible poke it through into the void above the ceiling.*

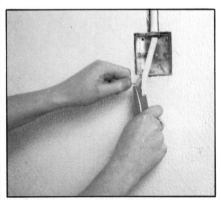

5 *Strip the ends of the three-core and earth cable from the RB4 ready for connection, remembering to fit the earth wires with green and yellow sleeving.*

6 *Next connect the cable to a one-gang, two-way switch, linking the yellow core to the L1 terminal, the blue core to L2 and the red core to Common.*

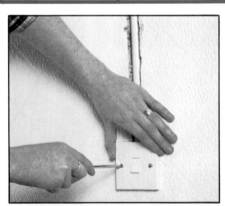

7 *Having connected the earth core to the terminal on the mounting box, screw the new switch securely into place and check that it is level.*

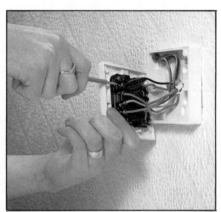

4 *Connect the switch drop from the room's main light to the third gang to give one-way switching. One core goes to L2, the other to Common.*

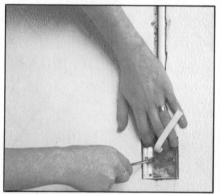

4 *At the second switch position of each light, use screws and wallplugs to fix a one-gang, plaster-depth mounting box in a hole cut into the wall.*

8 *Finally, join up all the cables in the RB4 junction box. It's much easier than it looks.*

Intermediate switching

There is one other kind of two-way switching that could be useful in your home. It's called an intermediate switching circuit and it means that a light or group of lights can be controlled by three or more separate switches. It's easy to install because all you do is introduce one or more additional switches into the circuit between the two two-way switches. This can, of course, be very convenient because you can then control a light from as many positions as you like. For example, you could control a hall light from a switch near the front door, from one near the living room door and from another switch on the landing upstairs.

There are two ways of carrying out the wiring but with both methods a special switch called an intermediate switch is needed. This has four terminals: two marked L1 and two marked L2. To install an intermediate switch in a two-way switching circuit all you do is use the switch to interrupt the three-core and earth cable – or the strap wires in a traditional circuit that has been installed in a flat or where the cables are all run in conduit.

The cores from the L1 terminals and L2 terminals in one two-way switch go to the L1 terminals on one side of the intermediate switch and the L1 and L2 cores from the second two-way switch go to the L2 terminals on the other side. However, with a three-core and earth circuit this leaves a break in the core linking the two-way switches' Common terminals. One way of solving this problem is to join the ends of the two cores with a cable connector. Once the two red cores have been joined the connector unit is then placed in the space behind the intermediate switch. However, it's better to interrupt the three-core and earth cable with a multi-terminal junction box above the ceiling near the intermediate switch position. You need six terminals in the junction box: one for the earth cores, one for both the red cores from the Common terminals and one each for the remaining cores.

At this stage you should introduce two lengths of two-core and earth cable which, by connecting up to the appropriate terminals, are used to extend the yellow and blue cores from each two-way switch. When that's done, run the two two-core and earth cables down to the intermediate switch and connect them up just as if they were the two pairs of yellow and blue cores in the three-core and earth cable. It is worth remembering that if one of the switches in an intermediate circuit is to be cord-operated then it should be one of the end switches. This is because there are no cord-operated intermediate switches available.

Ready Reference

TWO-WAY SWITCHING

Two-way switching lets you control a light from two separate switches. The illustration shows the back of a two-way switch with its

three terminals labelled Common, L1 and L2. In any two-way switching circuit, both switches are exactly the same and have equivalent terminals. But wiring up the switches is completely different from connecting up one-way switches.

This is because each two-way switch must be able to control the light independently of the other.

The traditional way of wiring two-way switches as used in flats or all-conduit installations is to use single core to make the connections:

● the L1 and L2 terminals of each switch are linked by single-core cables that are known as straps

● the switch drop cable that provides the power to the circuit is divided with the feed going to one Common terminal and the return going to the other.

More often PVC-sheathed three-core and earth cable, colour coded red, yellow and blue, is used:

● the Common terminals are linked by the red cores, with the yellow and blue cores acting as straps

● the switch drop is then connected to the L1 and L2 terminals of just one of the switches.

CONVERTING A CIRCUIT

To convert an existing one-way switching circuit to two-way switching:
● replace the existing switch with a two-way switch
● run 1.0 or 1.5mm² PVC-sheathed and insulated three-core and earth cable to the new switch position
● connect it to another two-way switch.
This method can also be used to create new two-way switching circuits.

INSTALLING WALL LIGHTS

Ceiling lights are simple and effective, but if you want a lighting scheme that is a little more exciting, more decorative and more versatile, they are not enough. One solution is to fit wall lights. Here's how.

There are two keys to a really successful lighting scheme: variety and versatility. Variety, because having a uniform level of light throughout a room is just plain boring. And versatility because your lighting needs change from one part of the room to another. In a living room, for example, you may prefer the overall lighting level to be fairly low and restful, but you will still need pools of intense light for reading, or perhaps simply to show off decorative feature like pictures, plants or ornaments. That's where wall lights come in. They are very good at creating interesting pools of light.

Choosing a light

With so many wall lights to choose from where do you start? It really depends on what you want the light to do. Few provide a light you can put to practical use. Most are purely decorative.

The traditional wall light is a good example. It normally has a low wattage, candle-shaped lamp, mounted on a wooden base, and concealed behind a pretty parchment shade, so that it spreads a fan of soft light across the wall.

More recent versions take the imitation candelabra and gaslight theme still further, having ornate brass, copper, and aluminium stems, and, instead of shades, translucent bowls in plain, coloured, frosted, smoked, and sculpted glass or plastic. They tend to use more powerful bulbs, and can be made to light the top or bottom of the wall, but the net result is the same. They are for looking at, rather than seeing by.

This is also true of many modern wall light designs. There are, for example, cylindrical fittings open at top and bottom to spread a shaft of light in two directions, either vertically or horizontally.

Still attractive, but producing a more useful light, there are the fully enclosed fittings. 'Opals', for example, create a beautifully soft, even light, and look rather like round, square or rectangular blocks of milky glass or plastic. For those who prefer more ornate lights, sculpted glass versions (they look like cut crystal) are also available. Enclosed fittings are particularly handy

CABLE RUNS

1 From a loop-in rose

To install a new wall light you need to run a supply cable from an existing loop-in ceiling rose to a new four-terminal junction box and then run cables to the switch and fitting.

2 From a nearby circuit

You can also get the power for the wall light by connecting a three-terminal junction box to an existing circuit cable and run cable from this to the new four-terminal junction box.

——— existing cable runs
- - - - new cable runs

where space is limited – in a hallway, perhaps – and since many are weatherproof, they are an excellent choice for the humid atmosphere of a bathroom or an outside porch.

More useful still are the spotlights. Usually mounted on adjustable arms away from the wall, they can be used to send a strong beam of light almost anywhere – back onto the wall, say, to light a picture, or out into the room to illuminate a desk or sitting area. Their only real snag is that they need careful shading, if they are not to dazzle you. Mounting them on the ceiling may overcome this problem.

And finally, don't forget fluorescent lights. Slimline fluorescent tubes, though inhospitable looking, give off little heat and are easily concealed. Use them to spread a sheet of light over a wall. The light assembly can be mounted on a wooden batten and

shaded by a pelmet or baffle. If you wish, the pelmet can be painted or papered to match the wall. Miniature fluorescents are also handy for lighting pictures and shelves, but whatever the size, be sure to use a 'de luxe' warm white' tube, or the light will look cold and harsh.

Positioning the fitting

Choosing a light is only half the battle. To give of its best it must be carefully positioned. With the exception of enclosed fittings, which stand very well on their own, most need to be arranged at least in pairs, and sometimes even in a group. Traditional wall lights and mock candelabra, for example, tend to look best when arranged symmetrically in pairs – say, on each side of a chimney breast. Spotlights, on the other hand, are often most effective in a cluster.

Of course, there are no hard and fast

INSTALLING THE FITTING

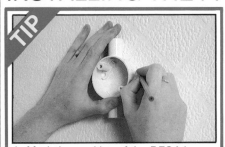

1 Mark the position of the BESA box on the wall where the light is to go. Use a through box if the light's switch is to be immediately below the BESA box.

2 With a club hammer and bolster chisel, chop out the hole to take the box, and channels to take cables up to the ceiling and down or across to the switch.

3 Fix the box in place with screws and wall plugs, then run in the cables for the light and switch. Note that the switch cable passes straight through the box.

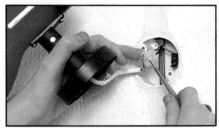

4 Connect the light cable to the light with insulated cable connectors Tuck the earth wire out of the way if it is not needed.

INSTALLING A SWITCH

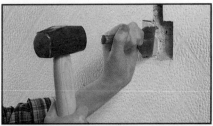

1 To install a new switch, mark out the position of the switch mounting box (a plaster-depth box) and chop out the hole to receive it.

2 Drill and plug the wall, then screw the mounting box in place, checking it is level. Next, feed in the cable coming from the new circuit's junction box.

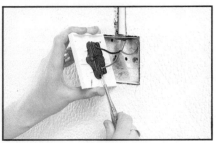

3 Connect the cable to a one-gang one-way switch. Ensure the terminal marked 'TOP' is at the top. Connect the earth wire to the box terminal.

4 If using an existing switch position, insert a new two-gang plate switch. Connect existing cable to one set of terminals, new cable to the other.

Ready Reference

POSITIONING WALL LIGHTS
● fix ordinary wall lights about 1.5m (5ft) above floor level
● bedside lights are best set about 1.2m (4ft) above floor level.

WHAT SWITCH TO USE
Use a one-way plate switch for the wall light. Set it on a metal mounting box sunk into the wall or on a plastic box mounted on the surface.
● a separate switch is needed to isolate a wall light from the main circuit even if it has a built-in switch of its own

● alternatively you can use an existing switch position to control an extra wall light by replacing a one-gang switch unit with a two-gang unit.

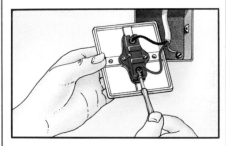

FITTING THE WALL LIGHT
The wires of the fitting are linked to the circuit cable using insulated cable connectors. These are housed in a BESA box or an architrave box which is sunk into the wall and hidden by the light fitting.

ALTERNATIVES

1 *If the light switch is not to be vertically below the light position, use a single entry BESA box instead of a through one, fitting it in the same way.*

2 *If the light cannot be mounted on a BESA box, connect the wires in an architrave mounting box. Knockouts let this act as a single entry or through box.*

LIGHTING CIRCUIT CONNECTIONS

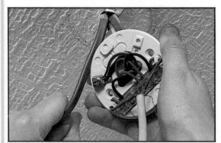

1 *Turn off the power at the mains, unscrew the rose and ease it away from the ceiling so you can pull through new 1.0 or 1.5mm^2 cable.*

3 *Run the cable to a junction box between the switch and light. Then run one cable to the light, another to the switch position.*

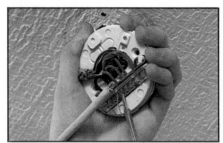

2 *Connect the cable to the rose's loop-in terminals; the red wire to the centre terminal block, the black to the neutral block, and the earth to the earth block.*

4 *If you can't connect to the rose, insert a junction box at some point along one of the rose's feed cables. Run cables down to the light and switch as before.*

CONNECTING TO A RING CIRCUIT

1 *The easiest way to link a lighting spur to the ring circuit is to connect a 2.5mm^2 cable to the back of a socket. Ensure the socket isn't already on a spur.*

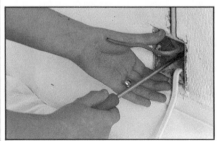

4 *Fix the mounting box for the connection unit into the whole, and then run the cable into it from the power socket or three-terminal junction box.*

2 *Alternatively, cut the ring circuit cables and connect them to a three-terminal junction beneath the floor; then run the spur cable into that.*

5 *Having run the cable to the light position (or four-terminal junction box), fit the connection unit with a 5A fuse and connect it up.*

3 *Mark the position of the fused connection unit. Cut through the wallpaper with a sharp knife before you chisel out the hole for the mounting box.*

6 *Finally, fit an architrave box or a stopped BESA box at the light position and install the light as before. Note the cable will now enter from below.*

rules. In the end, it's all down to what looks and works best in your particular situation. Try to imagine how the lights will affect the room – not only the lights themselves and their position, but also the direction of the light they will give out.

You ought to pay particular attention to the light's height above the floor. The general rule is to place the light at just below eye level – about 1,500mm (5ft) – but you can vary this as necessary to stop the light getting in your eyes or to help direct it where it's needed. Wall lights used as bedside lamps, for example, should be about 1,220mm (4ft) above the floor and positioned so they can't get knocked as someone walks past them.

Installing the light
If you've read pages 209–212 and 213–217, then you shouldn't experience too much difficulty in fitting the light. But remember electricity can be dangerous if abused, so follow the instructions to the letter. If they don't tie in with your home's existing wiring, or you're unsure about what you're doing, don't take chances – seek expert advice before attempting anything yourself.

The first step is to find a power source, though it is best to leave the connections into the existing circuit until last. That way, you can do almost all the work with your home's electrics working normally; you'll have to turn off the power at the mains only for the few minutes needed to make the final connection.

In most cases, taking a spur off the existing lighting circuit is your best bet. Do check, though, that the wall light will not overload it. Isolate the circuit in question by removing the fuse carrier from the consumer unit, or by turning off its MCB, and add up the total wattage of the bulbs it feeds – those that are now dead, in other words. Bulbs rated at 100W or more count at face value; less powerful bulbs count as 100W. When you've done that, add on the wattage of the new light and make sure the grand total is less than 1,200 watts.

Assuming this is so, there are two ways to break into the circuit. In theory, the simplest is to connect a 1.0 or 1.5mm² two-core and earth cable to a loop-in ceiling rose, and run it to a four-terminal junction box above the ceiling. In practice, it's often hard to fit the extra wires in, so, as an alternative, trace a mains feed cable out of the rose, and connect the junction box into this cable.

Once you've got power to the junction box, wire up the wall light and its switch on the conventional junction box system (see pages 209–212 and 213–217) with one cable going to the light, and another to the switch. The switch can be anywhere convenient, either close to the light or away from it. You can use the switch position by the room's door if

you wish. It's a simple matter to convert the existing one-gang switch there (for ceiling light) to a two-gang switch (for ceiling light and wall light).

Many wall lights have a built-in switch, so you may wonder why a switch is necessary. Although these are fine for everyday use, you ought to be able to isolate the wall light completely so an additional ordinary plate switch is required.

Though fitting a wall light is not complicated there are two problems you may meet. The first is in fixing the light to the wall. Many can be screwed to the holes provided in the BESA box housing connections between light and cable. Failing that, you can fix the light to the wall using screws and wall plugs, and house the connections in a metal architrave mounting box sunk into the wall behind it.

The second problem is earthing. Even if the wall light doesn't need to be earthed, the earth wire in the new cables must be linked to your home's main earthing point at the fuse box or consumer unit. (Never connect earth wires to water or gas pipes.) You can, of course, do this by connecting it to the earth wire in the existing wiring, but, if the existing wiring is old, it may not have an earth wire. In this case, you should run a single sheathed earth core from the new junction box back to the earthing point.

Connecting to a ring circuit
You might find that it's inconvenient or impossible to take power from the lighting circuit – if this is the case you can connect the wall light to a ring circuit. Essentially, what you do is run a spur to the wall light's junction box. You break into the ring either by connecting a 2.5mm² two-core and earth cable to the back of a power socket, or by joining it to a three-terminal junction box and connecting this to the ring circuit cable beneath the floor.

However, there is a snag. The ring circuit fuse has too high a rating for a lighting circuit (remember, these need a 5A fuse). To get round this, you have to run the 2.5mm² cable into a fused connection unit fitted with a 5A fuse, and continue the circuit to a four-terminal junction box and then on to the light and switch junction box with 1.0 or 1.5mm² cable.

Obviously, this involves considerable extra work and expense, but there is a short cut. You can do away with the junction box and separate switch, and instead use a switched fused connection unit to control the wall light. It sounds appealing, but it too has its drawbacks. The connection unit will not match the other light switches in the room, and it needs to be as close as possible to the light – an unnecessarily complex cable run would be needed to control the light from the far side of the room.

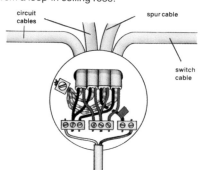

Ready Reference

WIRING THE CIRCUIT
The easiest way to provide wall lights with power is to run a 1.0mm² two-core and earth, PVC-sheathed and insulated cable from a loop-in ceiling rose.

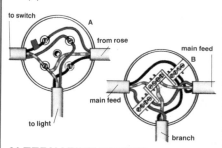

● run a cable from the rose to a junction box. Two cables then run from the box – one to the light and one to its switch (A)
● rather than connecting into the main lighting circuit at a rose, you can break into the main feed cable and install a junction box (B).

ALTERNATIVE WIRING
Wall lights can also take their power from a ring circuit.
● install a three-terminal junction box (A). Then run a 2.5mm² cable to a fused connection unit fitted with a 5A fuse (B). Continue the wiring to the light (C) and a switch (D) as if the power had been taken from the lighting circuit (ie, use 1.0mm² cable)

● alternatively use a switched fused connection unit (A), and run the 1.5mm² cable straight to the wall light. The unit then acts as an isolating light switch.

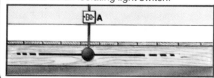

ADDING A POWER POINT

Electrical equipment is now used more and more in the home, so an extra power socket is always useful. Here's how to fit one.

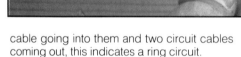

Keith Morris

There's nothing really difficult about installing a new power point. It's easier than putting in a new light as you don't have to worry about a switch cable.

Ever since the early 1950s, the power supply to the sockets has almost always been wired as a ring circuit (see pages 200–204), and it is almost certain that any house rewired since then will have had this system installed. This means that once you've decided where you want the new outlet point – by a shelf in the living room for a hi-fi system, or over a work-top in the kitchen, for example – all you have to do is to run a 'branch' or 'spur' to it from a convenient point on a nearby ring circuit.

The connection could be made at any socket on the ring (unless it already has a spur coming from it), or by using a three-terminal junction box inserted into the cable run. Each spur can have either one single or one double socket connected to it, or else one fused connection unit. Until a recent change in the Wiring Regulations, you were allowed two single sockets on a spur, but this is no longer permitted.

Checking your circuits

Although it's very likely that your house has ring circuits for the power supply, it's important to make sure. A ring circuit serves a number of 13A power outlets, and the sockets themselves take the familiar three-pin plugs with flat pins. But having this type of socket doesn't necessarily mean you've got a ring circuit – a new radial circuit may have been installed with these fittings, or an old radial circuit may simply have been modernised with new socket outlets. Pages 200–204 explain the distinction.

First you've got to check whether you've got a modern consumer unit or separate fuse boxes for each of the circuits. Having a consumer unit is a fair indication that you've got ring circuit wiring, and if two cables are connected to each individual 30A fuseway in the unit this will confirm it. Normally each floor of the house will have a separate ring circuit, protected by a 30A fuse or MCB.

If you have separate fuse boxes, look for the ones with 30A fuses. If they have one supply

cable going into them and two circuit cables coming out, this indicates a ring circuit.

It's easy to identify the sockets on any particular circuit simply by plugging in electrical appliances, such as table lamps, turning off the power and then removing a 30A fuse from the fuse box or consumer unit, or switching off a 30A MCB. When you restore the supply, the equipment that remains off will indicate which sockets are on the circuit.

Dealing with radial circuits

Where a house hasn't got ring circuits, then the power sockets will be supplied by some form of radial circuit. Because there are different types of radial circuit, each governed by separate regulations controlling the number and location of sockets on the circuit, size of cable to be used and the size and type of circuit fuse protecting it, you should only add a spur to an existing radial circuit if you can trace its run to the fuse box and identify its type, and if it has been wired up in modern PVC-sheathed cable throughout.

If you've still got unfused 15A, 5A and 2A round-pin plugs, then this is a sure sign of very old radial circuits, which were installed more than 30 years ago. Rather than extending the system you should seriously consider taking these circuits out and replacing them with ring circuits, as the wiring will almost certainly be nearing the end of its life. You'll then be able to position the new sockets exactly where 'you want them. If you're in any doubt about the

circuitry in your house you should contact your local electricity authority or a qualified electrician before carrying out any work.

Adding a spur to a ring

Once you've established you're dealing with a ring circuit and what sockets are on it, you'll need to find out if any spurs have already been added. You can't have more spurs than there are socket outlets on the ring itself. But unless the circuit has been heavily modified, it's unlikely that this situation will arise. You'll also need to know where any spurs are located – you don't want to overload an existing branch by mistake.

You can distinguish the sockets on the ring from those on a spur by a combination of inspecting the back of the sockets and tracing some cable runs (see *Ready Reference*). But remember to turn off the power first.

When you've got this information, you can work out whether it's feasible to add to the ring circuit. And you'll have a good idea where the cable runs.

Installing the socket

It's best to install the socket and lay in the cable before making the final join into the ring, since by doing this you reduce the amount of time that the power to the circuit is off.

You can either set the socket flush with the wall or mount it on the surface. The latter is the less messy method, but the fitting stands proud of the wall and so is more conspicuous.

FLUSH FITTING IN A BRICK WALL

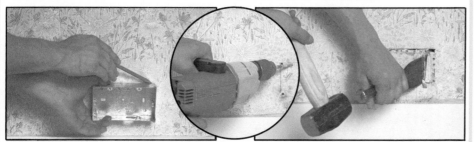
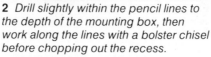

1 *Decide where you want to position the socket, then pencil round the mounting box as a guide for where to chop out the wall.*

2 *Drill slightly within the pencil lines to the depth of the mounting box, then work along the lines with a bolster chisel before chopping out the recess.*

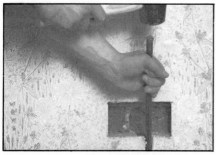
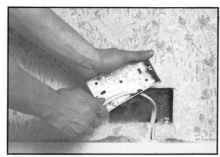

3 *Channel a cable run down the back of the skirting using a long, thin cold chisel. Alternatively, use a long masonry bit and an electric drill.*

4 *Thread the cable up from under the floor, through some PVC conduiting behind the skirting and into the mounting box.*

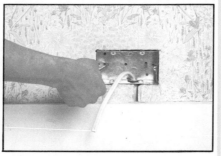

5 *Push the box into position, then use a bradawl to mark where the fixing holes are to go in the recess. Remove the box and drill and plug the holes.*

6 *Set the box back into place and screw it tightly into the recess. Check that it is level, and then make good if necessary with plaster or filler.*

Keith Morris

Flush-fixing a socket on a plasterboard wall is a little more involved.

If you choose to surface-mount the socket, all you have to do is to fix a PVC or metal box directly to the wall after you've removed the knockout (and, if metal, use a grommet) where you want the cable to enter. The socket can then be screwed directly to this.

Laying in the cable

Because cable is expensive, it's best to plan the spur so that it uses as little cable as possible. When you channel cable into a wall you'll need to chase out a shallow run, fix the cable in position with clips, then plaster over it. But the best method of all is to run the cable in oval PVC conduiting. It won't give any more protection against an electric drill, but it'll prevent any possible reaction between the plaster making good and the cable sheathing. Always channel horizontally or vertically, and never diagonally, so it's easier to trace the wiring run when you've completed decorating. You can then avoid the cable when fixing something to the wall.

Normally the cable will drop down to below floor level to connect into the circuit. Rather than remove the skirting to get the cable down

WARNING
The power supply to the sockets will probably be wired as a ring circuit. You can add a spur to this provided the number of spurs doesn't exceed the number of sockets on the ring.

CABLE SIZE
New spurs should be in 2.5mm^2 cable

CHECKING OUT A RING CIRCUIT
These instructions assume that your installation conforms to the Wiring Regulations. If it seems to have been modified in an unauthorised way, get a qualified electrician to check it.

TURN OFF THE POWER SUPPLY. Start by undoing a socket near where you want to install the new socket.

AT A SINGLE SOCKET
One cable entering
Socket is on the end of a spur. There could be another single socket on the branch.
Action: trace cable. If it goes to another single socket and this socket has only two cables going to it, then you have found an intermediate socket on the spur. It it goes to a double socket where there are three cables, then the single socket is the only socket on the spur. It's the same if the cable goes to a junction box.

Two cables entering
Socket could be on the ring, or it could be the intermediate socket on a spur.
Action: You'll need to trace the cable runs. If the cable is the only one going to another single socket, then the socket is on a spur. If the cable makes up one of two cables in another socket then it's on the ring.

Three cables entering
Socket is on the ring with a spur leading from it.
Action: to check which cable is which you'll need to trace the cable runs.

AT A DOUBLE SOCKET
One cable entering
Socket is on a spur. You can't connect a new socket from this.
Two cables entering
Socket is on the ring. You can connect a spur into this.
Three cables entering
Socket is on the ring with a spur leading from it. Checking to see which cable is which is the same as for a single socket with three cables. You can't connect a spur from this socket.

FLUSH FITTING IN A PLASTERBOARD WALL

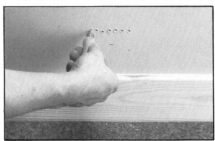

1 Knock along the cavity wall to locate a stud near where you want the socket. Pierce the wall with a bradawl to locate the centre of the upright.

2 Position the box centrally over the stud and pencil round it. Be as accurate as you can because eventually the box should fit neatly in the opening.

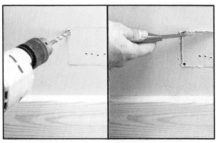

3 Drill the corners of the guidelines. Push a pad saw (or keyhole saw) into one of them and cut along the lines. The plasterboard will come out in one piece.

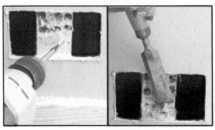

4 Once you've exposed the stud, you'll need to remove some of the wood so the box can be fully recessed. You can do this with a drill and chisel.

5 Use a long drill bit to drill down through the baseplate of the stud partition. Try and keep the drill as upright as possible.

6 Lay the cable from the point where it joins the main circuit and thread it up through the hole in the baseplate and into the box.

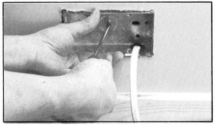

7 Set the box in the recess and fix it in place by screwing to the stud. The cable end can now be prepared and connected to the socket terminals.

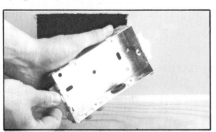

8 Where there is no stud to fix to, fit special lugs to the box sides. These press against the plasterboard's inner face when the faceplate is attached.

TIP

9 Before manoeuvring the box into the recess, thread some string through the front so you can hold it in position.

Jem Grischotti

CONNECTING THE NEW SOCKET

1 Strip back the sheathing of the cable by running a sharp knife down the side of the uninsulated earth. Avoid damaging the other cores.

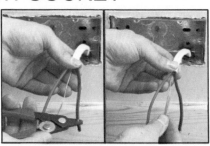

2 Set the wire strippers to the correct gauge and remove about 9mm (³/₈in) of insulation from the cores. Sleeve the earth core in green/yellow PVC.

3 Connect the three cores to the relevant terminals of the socket, making sure no exposed core is showing. Then screw the socket into position.

Keith Morris

the back you can use a long steel cold chisel to chip out a groove. You'll then have to drill down through the end of the floorboard with a wood bit. Alternatively, you can use a long masonry bit with an electric drill to complete the task.

But if the floor is solid, the ring is usually in the ceiling void above, in which case the branch will drop down from the ceiling. And this will involve a considerable amount of channelling out if you want to install the new socket near floor level.

Stud partition walls also present a few problems. If the socket is near the floor, you should be able to get a long drill bit through the hole you cut for the socket to drill through the baseplate and floorboard. You can then thread the cable through. But if the socket is to be placed higher up the wall, noggings and sound insulation material may prevent the cable being drawn through the cavity. In this case you will probably have to surface-mount the cable.

In fact, surface-mounting is the easiest method of running the cable. All you do is fix special plastic conduit to the wall and lay the cable inside before clipping on the lid. But many people regard this as an ugly solution.

When laying cable under ground floor floorboards you should clip it to the sides of the joists about 50mm (2in) below the surface so that it doesn't droop on the ground. Cable in the ceiling void can rest on the surface.

When you have to cross joists, you'll need to drill 16mm (5⁄8in) holes about 50mm (2in) below the level of the floorboards. The cable is threaded through them and so is well clear of any floorboard fixing nails.

Connecting into the circuit

If you use a junction box, you'll need one with three terminals inside. You have to connect the live conductors (those with red insulation) of the circuit cable and the spur to one terminal, the neutral conductors (black insulation) to another, and the earth wires to the third. Sleeve the earth wires in green/yellow PVC first.

You might decide that it's easier to connect into the back of an existing socket rather than use a junction box, although this will probably mean some extra channelling on the wall. Space is limited at the back of a socket so it may be difficult to fit the conductors to the relevant terminals. However, this method is ideal if the new socket that you're fitting on one wall is back-to-back with an existing fitting. By carefully drilling through the wall a length of cable can be linked from the old socket into the new.

CONNECTING INTO THE CIRCUIT

1 *Unscrew a nearby socket to check that it's on the ring – normally there'll be two red, two black and two earth wires. Sometimes the earths are in one sleeve.*

2 *Usually it's easier to push the new cable up into the mounting box from below the floor, although you might prefer to take it the other way.*

3 *Prepare the cores and sleeve the earth of the new cable, then connect them into the appropriate terminals on the back of the socket.*

4 *If installing a junction box use a three-terminal type. Connect the red conductors to one terminal, the blacks to another and the earths to a third.*

Keith Morris

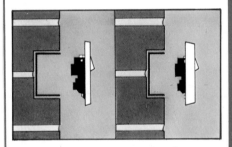
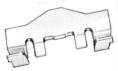

LAYING CABLE

The hardest part of the average electrical job is running the cables: it takes up a lot of time and a lot of effort. But there are certain techniques used by experts which can make it much easier.

Before you get involved in the details of how to install the wiring, there's one simple question you must answer. Does it matter if the cable runs show? This is because there are only two approaches to the job of running cable. Either you fix the cable to the surface of the wall, or you conceal it. The first option is far quicker and easier but doesn't look particularly attractive; it's good enough for use in, say, an understairs cupboard. For a neater finish, using this method, you can smarten up the cable runs by boxing them in with some trunking. Many people, however, prefer to conceal the wiring completely by taking it under the floor, over the ceiling, or in walls.

TYPICAL CABLE RUNS

More and more electrical equipment is now being used in the home. And the chances are that sooner or later you will want to install a new power point, wall or ceiling light, or another switch. In which case you will have to get power to your new accessory. To do that will involve running cable from an existing circuit or installing a completely new one. Running cable to a new appliance can be the hardest part of any job and, as the illustration on the right shows, you will be involved in trailing cable across the roof space or ceiling void, channelling it down walls and threading it behind partitions as well as taking it under floorboards. But it's much easier than it seems. There are a number of tricks of the trade that will make any electrical job simpler and less time consuming. For example, once you can 'fish' cable, the daunting task of running it under a floor is simple.

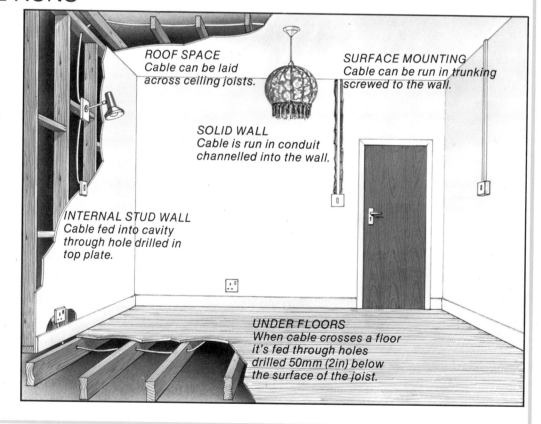

ROOF SPACE
Cable can be laid across ceiling joists.

SURFACE MOUNTING
Cable can be run in trunking screwed to the wall.

SOLID WALL
Cable is run in conduit channelled into the wall.

INTERNAL STUD WALL
Cable fed into cavity through hole drilled in top plate.

UNDER FLOORS
When cable crosses a floor it's fed through holes drilled 50mm (2in) below the surface of the joist.

SURFACE MOUNTING CABLE

1 *To run cable in trunking, cut the trunking to length and fix the channel half to the wall with screws and wall plugs at 450mm (18in) centres.*

2 *Run the cable and press it firmly into the channel as far as it will go, carefully smoothing it out to avoid kinks and twists.*

3 *Next, snap the trunking's capping piece over the channelling, tapping it firmly along its length with your hand to lock it into place.*

4 *If the cable is to be on show, merely secure it every 225mm (9in) with cable clips. Fit them over the cable and drive home the fixing pins.*

Planning the route

Having made your decision you must now work out a suitable route for the cable to follow.

If it is to be surface-mounted – with or without trunking – run the cable around window and door frames, just above skirting boards and picture rails, down the corners of the room, or along the angle between wall and ceiling. This not only helps conceal the cable's presence, but also protects it against accidental damage. This last point is most important, and is the reason why you must never run cable over a floor.

With concealed wiring, the position is more complicated. When running cable under a floor or above a ceiling, you must allow for the direction in which the joists run – normally at right angles to the floorboards – and use an indirect route, taking it parallel to

the joists and/or at right angles to them.

When running cable within a wall, the cable should *always* run vertically or horizontally from whatever it supplies, *never* diagonally.

Surface-mounting techniques

If you are leaving the cable on show, all you need do is cut it to length, and fix it to the surface with a cable clip about every 225mm (9in), making sure it is free from kinks and twists. With modern cable clips, simply fit the groove in the plastic block over the cable and drive home the small pin provided.

Surface mounting cable within trunking involves a bit more work. Having obtained the right size of PVC trunking, build up the run a section at a time, cutting the trunking to length with a hacksaw. Once each piece is cut, separate it into its two parts – the

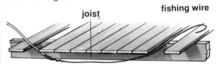

channelling and capping – and fix the channel to the wall with screws and wall plugs at roughly 450mm (18in) intervals (you may have to drill screw clearance holes in the channelling yourself).

Continue in this way until the run is complete. Turn corners by using proprietary fittings or by angling the ends of two pieces of trunking to form a neatly mitred joint, then run the cable. Press this firmly into the channel, and finish off by snapping the capping pieces firmly into place.

Concealing cables in walls

There are two ways to conceal cable in a wall. With a solid wall, chop a channel (called a 'chase') out of the plaster using a club hammer and bolster chisel, carefully continuing this behind any skirting boards, picture rails, and coverings. You could now run the cable in this chase and plaster over it. However, to give the cable some protection, it is better to fit a length of PVC conduit into the chase and run the cable through this before replastering.

To continue the run either above the ceiling or through the floor before you position the conduit, use a long drill bit so you can drill through the floor behind the skirting board. If a joist blocks the hole, angle the drill sufficiently to avoid it.

With a hollow internal partition wall, the job is rather easier, because you can run the cable within the cavity.

First drill a hole in the wall where the cable is to emerge, making sure you go right through into the cavity. Your next step is to gain access to the timber 'plate' at the very top of the wall, either by going up into the loft, or by lifting floorboards in the room above. Drill a 19mm (¾in) hole through the plate, at a point vertically above the first hole, or as near vertically above it as possible.

All that remains is to tie the cable you wish to run to a length of stout 'draw' wire – single-core earth cable is often used – and then to tie the free end of this wire to a length of string. To the free end of the string, tie a small weight, and drop the weight through the hole at the top of the wall. Then all you do is make a hook in a piece of stout wire, insert it in the cavity, catch hold of the string and pull it (and in turn the draw wire and cable) through the hole in the room below.

What are the snags? There are two. You may find that, at some point between the two holes, the cavity is blocked by a horizontal timber called a noggin. If this happens, try to reach the noggin from above with a long auger bit (you should be able to hire one) and drill through it. Failing that, chisel through the wall surface, cut a notch in the side of the noggin, pass the cable through the notch, and then make good.

The second snag is that you may not be

CHASING OUT SOLID WALLS

1 Mark out the cable run using a length of conduit, and chop a channel ('chase') in the wall to receive it, using a club hammer and a bolster chisel.

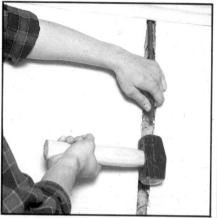

2 Continue the chase behind any coving, skirting board, or picture rail by chipping out the plaster there with a long, narrow cold chisel.

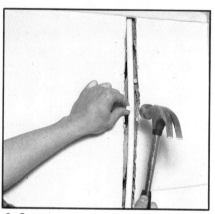

3 Cut a length of PVC conduit to fit, and lay it in the chase, securing it temporarily with clout nails driven into the wall's mortar joints.

4 Pull the cable through the conduit, then make good the wall by filling in over the conduit with plaster or cellulose filler.

able to reach the top plate to drill it. In which case, either give up the ideas of having concealed wiring, or try a variation on the second method used to run cable into the cavity from below the floor.

Here, it is sometimes possible to lift a couple of floorboards and drill up through the plate forming the bottom of the wall. Failing that you have to take a very long drill bit, drill through the wall into the cavity, then continue drilling through into the timber plate. You can now use the weighted string trick to feed the cable in through the hole in the wall, and out under the floor.

Running cable beneath a floor

The technique for running cable beneath a suspended timber floor depends on whether the floor is on an upper storey and so has a ceiling underneath, or is on a ground floor with empty space below. If it's a ground floor, it may be possible to crawl underneath and secure the cable to the sides of the joists with cable clips, or to pass it through 19mm (¾in) diameter holes drilled in the joists at least 50mm (2in) below their top edge. This prevents anyone nailing into the floor and hitting the cable.

If you cannot crawl underneath, then the cable can be left loose in the void. But how do you run it without lifting the entire floor? The answer is you use another trick, called 'fishing'.

For this, you need a piece of stiff but reasonably flexible galvanised wire, say 14 standard wire gauge (swg), rather longer than the intended cable run, and a piece of thicker, more rigid wire, about 1m in length. Each piece should have one end bent to form a hook.

Lift a floorboard at each end of the

COPING WITH STUD WALLS

1 Drill a hole in the wall where the cable is to emerge, then bore a second hole in the wooden plate forming the top of the wall.

2 Tie a weight to a length of string and lower this through the hole in the wall plate. Tie the free end of the string to a stout 'draw' wire.

3 If the weight gets blocked on its way to the hole in the wall, use a long auger bit to drill through the noggin obstructing it.

4 Fish out the weighted string through the hole in the wall, using a piece of wire bent to form a hook. Now, pull through the draw wire.

5 Tie the draw wire to the cable you wish to run, then return to the hole in the wall's top plate, and use the string to pull up the draw wire.

6 Then use the draw wire to pull the length of cable through. Remember, do this smoothly and don't use force if there's an obstruction.

proposed cable run and feed the longer piece of wire, hook end first, into the void through one of the resulting gaps in the floor. Hook it out through the second gap using the shorter piece of wire, and use it to pull through the cable in the same way as the draw wire used to pull cable through a hollow wall.

This technique is also used where there is a ceiling below the floor, and where you wish to run cable parallel to the joists, but in this case, check for any ribs and struts between the joists which might stop the fish wire getting through. Do this with the aid of a small mirror and a torch. If there is an obstruction, lift the floorboard above it, and drill a hole through which the cable can pass.

If the cable is to run at right angles to the joists, lift the floorboard above the line of the cable run, and feed the cable through holes drilled in the joists, 50mm (2in) below their top edge.

And what about solid floors? Obviously there is no way to run cable beneath these. Instead run the cable around the walls of the room, surface-mounting it just above the skirting board.

Running cable above a ceiling

Running cable above a ceiling is essentially the same as running it below a suspended timber floor. In fact, if there is a floor above the ceiling, it is generally easier to tackle the job from there, rather than from the room below.

If running the cable above the ceiling means taking it into the loft, then you can tackle it in much the same way as if you were running it below a suspended ground floor. If you cannot gain access to the loft, fish the cable through. If you can get into the loft, run the cable by hand, clipping it to the sides of the joists where it runs parallel to them.

You can run the cable at right angles to the joists by passing it through holes as already described, but this is frowned on by many electricians. Instead, they prefer to run it parallel to the joists as far as the 'binder' – the large timber cross-member linking the joists. They then clip the cable to the binder to traverse the ceiling, before running it to the desired position, again working parallel to the joists.

Unfortunately, there are situations in which running cable above a ceiling is almost impossible. The main ones are where the ceiling is solid concrete, as in many modern flats; where the ceiling is below a flat roof; and where, although there is a floor above the ceiling, you can't get at it (again this applies mainly to flats).

In the last two instances, if you intend the cable to run parallel to the joists, you may be able to fish it through. If not, you will have to treat the ceiling as if it were solid, and that means surface mounting the cable.

RUNNING CABLE UNDERGROUND

The most important part of taking power outside to a garden, a detached garage, or a workshop is running the electricity supply. An overhead cable run is a possibility, but taking it underground is the safer and more secure solution.

There are all sorts of reasons for taking a power supply out of doors. You may want to provide power to a garage so you can work on your car in light and warmth, or to transform your shed into an efficient workshop; you may require power sockets so you can use electrical power appliances in the garden, or a circuit to light your pool or garden fountain. Whatever you do involves running cable out of doors and this is bound to be the major part of any outside installation. There are three ways of running cable: overhead (for further details of overhead cable runs see pages 234–237), along a wall or underground. Running the cable underground is probably best, even if it involves the most installation work. That way it is concealed, cannot be disturbed and presents no danger whatsoever. But before you run the power supply, you'll have to decide which type of cable you want to use.

Underground cables

Three sorts of cable are suitable for running underground, and two of them can be laid directly in the ground without the need for further protection. PVC-covered mineral-insulated copper-covered cable (MICC) has a very small diameter and will pass conveniently through an airbrick, so avoiding the necessity of chopping a hole through the house wall. However, as the mineral insulation tends to absorb moisture, the ends of the cable have to be fitted with a special seal to prevent this. It is a complicated job for the do-it yourselfer to fit these seals and several special tools are required. The easiest thing to do is measure the cable run and ask your local electrical contractor for the length of cable with seals already fitted. This cable is usually two-core, as the copper sheathing provides adequate earth bonding and, as the cable run starts and ends in a metal conversion box (see below) which allows you to switch to ordinary PVC two-core and earth cable for indoor sections or for connection to accessories, each end should also be fitted with a screwed compression gland. These glands attach the cable to the box and provide the necessary earth continuity,. The cable usually has an outer

CABLE TYPES AND CONNECTIONS

Only PVC cable run in conduit (1) can be taken directly from the consumer unit to the switchfuse unit. If you use either PVC armoured cable (2) or mineral insulated copper cased cable (3) they must both be fitted with a gland and MICC with a seal and then run from a conversion box to another in the garage.

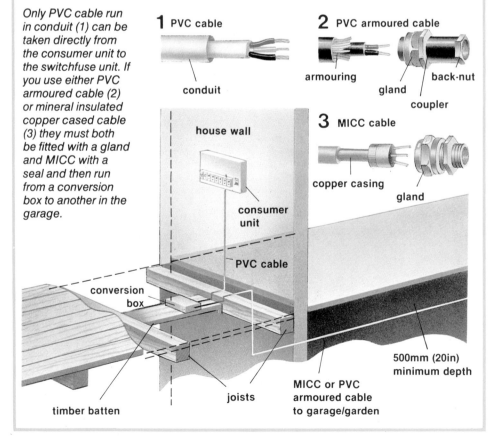

covering of PVC, often orange in colour, and is slim enough to be fairly unobtrusive – if run on the surface to wall-mounted light fittings, for example.

PVC-covered wire-armoured insulated and sheathed cable needs no seals, but has to have glands fitted at each end where it, too, enters the conversion box. This cable often comes with only two cores, in which case the armouring serves as an earth, but it may well be better to run three-core armoured cable. If you are using the three-core version, you'll find that the insulation colours will be slightly different to ordinary cable. Live is red, neutral blue, and earth yellow. The cable itself is usually black.

Both these types of cable are protected enough to allow them to be laid directly in the ground. But if you use PVC-sheathed two-core and earth cable then you'll have to run it in either heavy gauge galvanised steel or high impact rigid plastic conduit. You'll undoubtedly find it easier to use the plastic conduit as the steel sort requires stocks, dies and bending equipment that is not normally available to the householder. When using plastic conduit, however, do remember that it's likely to fracture in temperatures of −5°C or below, and also that fairly substantial holes will have to be cut in both the exterior wall and the garage wall to admit the cable.

The indoor section

All power supplies that are run outside are classified as sub-main cables and must originate from a spare fuseway in the consumer unit, or else from a new switchfuse unit. For further details on this and on the size of cable to use see page 234.

The section inside the home will normally be run in ordinary PVC-sheathed two-core and earth cable which will be taken to the exit point. Obstructions inside the home can alter the route of the indoor cable but there are a number of straightforward methods (for example, fishing cable through a ceiling void) which can be employed if you don't have access from above.

For further details on running cable inside the house see pages 226–229.

When the cable is being taken underground, the exit point is likely to be where the ditch in which it will run starts against the house wall. However, the presence of a concrete terrace or some other obstruction may mean you'll have to change the proposed exit point (although it may be possible to take other measures, such as chopping a chase to protect the cable). It is important to note that only if you're running the outdoor section in PVC two-core and earth cable will it run directly from the switchfuse unit to the outside installation. Otherwise the indoor section must be taken right inside the conversion box.

Laying cable underground

Having drilled the exit point in the house wall, if you are running the power to a garage in the outbuilding, you'll have to dig a ditch in which to lay the cable. This should be at least 500mm (20in) deep, and digging it will probably be the most tiring part of the job! Try to avoid taking the cable under vegetable plots and flower beds where it could be disturbed; and obviously you won't want to dig up your lawn. Probably the best place for a ditch is at the side of a concrete or gravel path; but if you're forced to run it at the edge of a flower bed, dig the ditch somewhat deeper to give the cable extra protection. If you're using either PVC-armoured cable or MICC cable, it's a good idea to place the cable on a layer of sand at the bottom of the trench and also to sift the soil before filling it in; that way you can avoid the slight risk of sharp stones damaging the cable. It's also wise to place a line of slates on top of the cable to give it extra protection, when you fill in the trench. If you're using PVC-sheathed two-core and earth cable, you should first lay the conduit in the trench and cut it to fit. You'll have to buy couplers for lengths that need to be joined; for vertical runs you'll have to fit elbows and you'll need a further elbow to take a short length of conduit into the wall so that the cable has complete protection. Do not use solvent-weld adhesive to assemble the conduit run at this stage, as you'll have to dismantle the fittings to thread in the cable. Start at the house end and, working in sections, thread through enough of the PVC cable to reach the mains switch in the garage to wherever you're running it. An alternative method is to attach the cable to a drawstring; thread it through the conduit and then pull the cable through after it. You can then start fixing the elbows and couplers permanently. Smear the solvent-weld adhesive over the end of the conduit and inside the elbows and couplers with the special brush provided before joining the sections together. Then place the assembled run into the trench, making sure that each elbow is correctly positioned. At the garage end push the end of the cable and the short length of conduit into the hole in the wall and then carefully fill in the trench. If you're using PVC-covered wire-armoured cable it should be laid directly in the trench and the ends passed directly into the house and garage. It will then be taken into a conversion box at each end.

Fitting a conversion box

Extending either PVC-armoured or MICC cable beyond the entry point to the house or garage is pointless. They are both relatively expensive cables, cannot usually be connected to a switchfuse unit and can be awkward to run. That is why you should fit what is called a conversion box. This allows

RUNNING CABLE UNDERGROUND

1 *After digging a ditch that is a minimum of 500mm (20in) deep, lay the conduit in it to give you an idea of what length you'll need.*

2 *Use a hacksaw to cut the conduit to length where necessary, and link it with special couplers; don't weld the joints yet.*

3 *Use an elbow fitting to join the vertical (above-ground) section of the conduit to the horizontal (underground) part next to the wall.*

4 *Fix a short section of conduit to the top elbow and check that it's long enough to take the cable completely through the garage wall.*

5 *Thread through the cable from the consumer unit. You can either dismantle the conduit or use a drawstring to pull through the cable.*

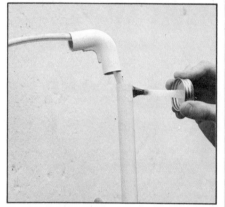

6 *With the cable in place, you should use special conduit adhesive to fix the couplers and elbows firmly in position. Then bury the conduit.*

you to change the type of cable in your sub-main circuit to ordinary PVC two-core and earth cable.

All that is required is a box containing three terminals and two entry holes. The correct one to use is an adaptable conversion box and lid or alternatively a standard one-gang metal mounting box fitted with a blanking-off plate as a cover. You can use a special three-way terminal block to make the connections, or else ordinary cable connectors. However, if you do use the cable connectors, you must make sure they are large enough for the current.

At the house end, the conversion box should either be fixed with wood screws to a timber batten fitted between the joists beneath the floor, or alternatively to the wall near the entry point of the cable. If you're running power to a garage or shed, the box at that end should be fitted to the wall near the cable entry point. You should remove two

knockout holes, one of which must be fitted with a PVC grommet while the other should be large enough to accommodate the PVC-armoured cable. Strip away the outer layer of PVC and slide a PVC sheath and gland nut onto the armoured cable. You should put a back-nut in the knockout hole without a grommet and then prepare the cable by clipping away the excess armouring, leaving enough to carry up to the end of the gland's thread. You can now slide on the gland which will screw into the gland nut and keep the armouring in place. It's a good idea to attach a coupler to the gland as this will allow you more room in the box for the connections. Then feed the cable into the box and attach the back-nut to the coupler. If you are using two-core cable the armouring will serve as the earth so the back-nut must be tightened by a spanner to provide good metal-to-metal contact. Then pull the PVC protective hood

over the whole assembly and remove the remaining PVC insulation to expose the red and black cores. If you are using two-core cable you'll now have to earth the box; it's a good idea to do this even if you're using three-core cable. You should link the earth screw on the box (which holds the earth connector) with a length of core that you have sleeved in green/yellow PVC. Feed in the PVC two-core and earth cable, which must be the same size as the sub-main cable, through the knockout hole previously fitted with a grommet, and prepare the ends of the cable in the usual way before joining the cores of the two cables together. From here the PVC cable will run to whatever appliance you want to supply. If it is a garage or workshop, it's likely to go to a switchfuse unit; if in the garden, it might be to well-protected sockets for lawnmowers, hedge trimmers, or lighting for an ornamental fountain.

FITTING A CONVERSION BOX

1 Use an adaptable mounting box to serve as a conversion box. Remove two opposite knockouts and fit a grommet to just one of them.

2 Remove two small knockouts at the back for the screws. Drill and plug holes in the corresponding spots on the wall, and position the box.

3 Fit a back-nut in the knockout hole, without a grommet, and then slide the PVC hood and gland nut onto the armoured cable.

4 Put on the gland and coupler and trim the armouring of the cable so that it ends at the bottom of the thread on the gland.

5 Feed the cable into the box and attach the back-nut to the coupler. Using a coupler allows you more room in the box for the connections.

6 The armouring serves as an earth but you should earth the box too by fitting an extra core to the box and connecting it to the terminal block.

7 Feed in the PVC two-core and earth cable that is to run to the switchfuse unit. Remember, this must be the same size as the armoured sub-main cable to which it is connected.

8 Using a block of three connectors, join the two cores of the armoured cable to their equivalents in the two-core and earth PVC cable and then connect the earth cores.

9 Finally screw on the lid of the conversion box. At the house end, the conversion box can be fitted safely to a timber batten that is fixed under the floorboards.

PROVIDING POWER IN THE GARAGE

If you add power and lighting to a garage, you can make it more than mere storage space for your car: your garage becomes a workshop. Connecting up the electricity supply is not difficult and sturdy accessories are produced specially.

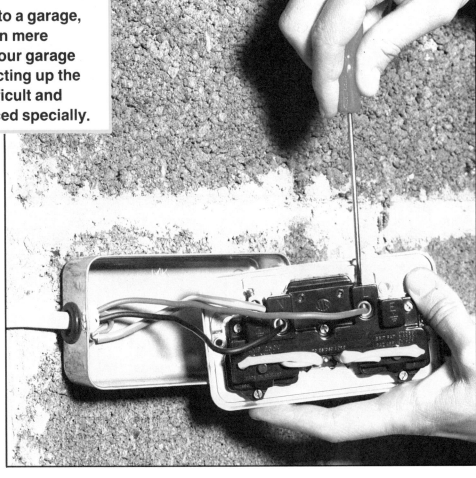

Installing electricity in a garage can completely transform it. No more fumbling in the dark for car keys; or flat batteries on a winter's morning; and car repairs will be carried out in the relative comfort of a well-lit and pleasantly heated garage. Indeed, a garage equipped with a number of power sockets, some lights and a couple of work surfaces can double as an extremely efficient workshop. If your garage is attached to your home, it is likely that it will already have a power supply; if it's detached, it's possible you'll have to install the supply yourself. But running electricity to a garage, or indeed to any other outside building, is not that difficult. It should be done in three stages: work inside the house; work outdoors, and finally the new circuitry in the garage itself.

Inside the home

If you're going to run a power supply to your garage you should remember that the electricity supply to any outbuilding, even if only for a lighting circuit, must be independent of the house circuits. Tempting though it may be, you're not allowed to run the supply in the form of a spur from a ring circuit in the house. The basic requirments are: a separate mains switch and fuse unit in the home, and an isolating switch and fuse unit in the garage. The mains switch at the house end will usually be a switchfuse unit that should be linked to the mains by the electricity board. If there is a spare fuseway in the main consumer unit obviously you can make use of it. However, it's probably better to leave the spare fuseway unit for another circuit within the house and install a new switchfuse unit for the circuit to the garage or outhouse. This must also contain a high-sensitivity RCD to protect socket outlets in the garage that will power outdoor electrical appliances.

The cable running from the new switch-fuse unit in the house to the garage is technically not a circuit cable and is classed as a sub-main cable. This is because it supplies a complete installation which has its own mains switch and fuse.

The section inside the house will normally be run in ordinary two-core and earth PVC sheathed cable, the size of which depends upon the circuit requirements in the garage.

The 2.5mm² size is suitable for a 20A supply; use 4mm² for a 30A supply, and 6mm² for a 45A supply. Do remember that if you are using the 4mm² cable for a 30A supply you must make sure that both switchfuse units are fitted with either a cartridge type fuse or MCB so that the circuit is uprated by one third. This is because 4mm² cable controlled by a rewirable fuse has a current-carrying capacity of only 27A and would consequently be a safety risk.

The outdoor section will either be in the same type of cable or else in special cable; which sort you use is determined by whether you run it overhead or underground, and if run underground, whether or not it is to be in conduit. More details about the underground cable runs can be found on pages 230–232.

It's best to make the outdoor section as short as possible, so the point at which the cable emerges from the house should be as near as practicable to the garage. This will obviously affect the section run in the home, as will obstructions inside. For further information on running cable procedure, take a look at pages 226–229.

Installing an overhead cable

Where the distance between the house and garage is no more than 5m (about 17ft), an overhead cable attached to a catenary wire is a practical alternative to an underground cable run. A catenary wire is merely a length of galvanised steel-stranded cable similar to that sometimes used for fencing and should be secured to an eye bolt or eye screw fixed into the wall of the house and of the garage. For spans larger than 5m, intermediate supports such as poles are required to prevent sagging. Apart from looking unattractive, there is always the risk of damage in high winds so you may find it better to take the cable underground for long runs.

In theory a span of less than 3.5m (11ft) need not be supported by a catenary wire. If you're running an overhead cable to your garage, you'll have to make sure that there is no danger of it being hit by anything passing underneath. For that very reason the regulation minimum height of an overhead cable run is 3.5m (11ft). However, when the cable is suspended across a driveway the minimum height is increased to 5.2m (17ft).

RUNNING CABLE OVERHEAD

Running power overhead keeps the cable out of harm's way provided you have the catenary wire at a minimum height of 3.5m (11ft). The cable should be taped and clipped and the catenary

wire itself should be bonded to earth. To gain extra height at the garage end use a length of 100x50mm (4x2in) timber which should be bolted securely to the wall with 150mm (6in) coach screws.

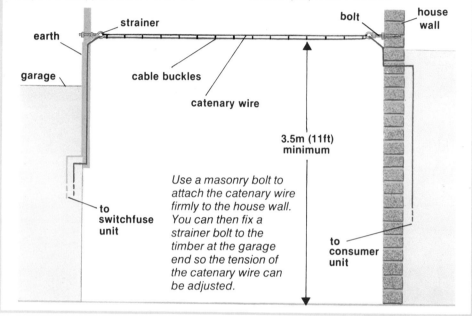

Use a masonry bolt to attach the catenary wire firmly to the house wall. You can then fix a strainer bolt to the timber at the garage end so the tension of the catenary wire can be adjusted.

THE GARAGE CIRCUITS

The lighting circuit can be either a loop-in or junction box system; the power circuit is wired as a radial circuit. Metal-clad sockets and switches are more robust

than plastic ones. Cable should be taken on the surface with vertical runs being clipped every 400mm (16in) and horizontal runs over 250mm (10in).

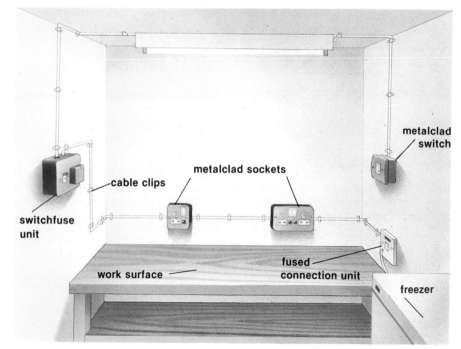

ATTACHED GARAGES
If your garage is attached to your home you can safely run the power as a spur from a ring circuit.

DETACHED GARAGES
If your garage is detached from your home then it is deemed a separate building and must be:
● supplied by a sub-main cable
● controlled by an isolating switch and fuse unit at each end.

TEMPORARY POWER SUPPLY
The only other form of power supply allowed to a detached garage, other than a sub-main cable, is an extension cable. This can be linked up temporarily while the actual appliance that it supplies is in use.

PERMANENT POWER SUPPLY
Power can be supplied permanently to a detached garage in three ways:
● by an overhead cable
● by an underground cable
● by a cable fixed along a wall. Cable should never be taken along a fence for reasons of safety.

OVERHEAD CABLE RUNS
Points to note:
● the minimum height for an overhead cable run is 3.5m (about 11ft)
● if the cable crosses a driveway the minimum height is increased to 5.2m (17ft)
● with a span of under 3:5m (11ft) the cable need not be supported
● if the span is between 3.5m (11ft) and 5m (about 17ft) the cable should be attached to a catenary wire
● for spans over 5m (17ft) there should be intermediate supports in addition to a catenary wire.

TIP: TAPE THE CABLE

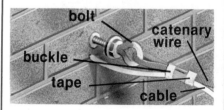

Attach the cable to the catenary wire with tape before fitting the buckle clips. That way the buckles will neither cut into the cable nor slide along it. It's also a good idea to leave a loop in the cable at each end to ease the strain and prevent water from entering the wall.

FITTING THE SWITCHFUSE UNIT

1 *If your garage is situated away from the house, it will need its own mains switch and fuses. Fix the unit to a sheet of treated chipboard.*

2 *Thread in the circuit cable and feed the red and black cores behind the switch so that they can connect to the unit's terminals.*

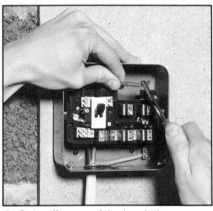

3 *Strip off some of the insulation from each core and make the connections. Sleeve the earth core in green/yellow PVC.*

4 *Then feed in the cables for the two circuits to provide power in the garage. Connect the lighting circuit to the fuseway nearest the switch.*

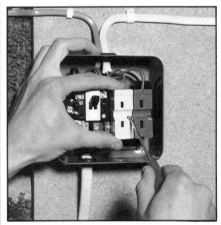

5 *When you have made all the connections fit the fuseway covers in the correct rating sequence, with the highest nearest the switch.*

6 *Finally fit the cover and shield and slot in the two MCB's. You can then turn on the power in both the house and garage.*

Running the cable

It's a good idea to insert an adjusting device at one end so that the catenary wire can be tightened once the cable has been attached to it. You'll probably have to fix a length of 100x50mm (4x2in) timber to the garage wall to obtain the necessary minimum height at that end. To fix the timber to the garage wall you'll have to drill and plug two holes and use 150mm (6in) coach screws. You should drill a hole in the house wall to serve as an exit point for the cable. This should be at about first floor level in a two-storey house and at eaves level in a bungalow.

You'll also have to drill a hole in the garage wall to enable the cable to enter and run to the mains switch. In addition, it's wise to run a length of green/yellow PVC insulated cable from the catenary wire to the mains switch to bond the catenary to earth. Measure the length of cable required to run from the switch-fuse unit in the house to the mains switch in the garage. Having fixed and tightened the catenary wire to the two eye bolts, pass the end of the cable through the hole in the house and then pull through sufficient to reach the mains switch in the garage. You should connect the bared end of the catenary wire to the bonding earth core by using a cable connector. After temporarily attaching the cable to the catenary wire (so you can make sure that there is sufficient to reach the garage) you can make a permanent attachment by using cable buckles every 250mm (10in). Both the supply and the earth cable should be fixed to the post with plastic cable clips that should be no more than 400mm (16in) apart. Alternatively, you can run the vertical section in metal or plastic conduit that is attached to the timber. You can now make the connections to the switchfuse unit in the house and in the garage.

An alternative method of running cable overhead is to carry it in an unjointed length of heavy gauge steel conduit; in this case the minimum height is reduced to 3m (10ft). You could also run it in rigid plastic conduit, but this will sag and is also likely to fracture at temperatures below –5°C. If you don't want to run the cable either overhead or underground then you may be able to take it along a boundary wall to the garage. Under no circumstances, however, may the outdoor section be fixed to a fence.

Inside the garage

Running cable to the garage is probably the most important and also the most difficult part of installing electricity there. There are, to begin with, certain precautions you must take with the work inside the garage. Remember that a detached garage is classed as a completely separate building and therefore must be fitted with a double-pole isolating switch, enabling the electricity to all circuits

FITTING POWER POINTS IN A GARAGE

1 *To provide current for a garage power point you should use 2.5mm² two-core and earth cable clipped firmly to the wall every 150mm (6in).*

2 *Fit a grommet on a knockout hole and fix to the wall the special metal box for surface mounting in garages and workshops.*

3 *Make the connections after sleeving the earth core in green/yellow PVC. It's a good idea to add an extra earth to protect the box.*

4 *Fit the faceplate with great care. This is necessary because its screws link the box into the earthing of the socket.*

Ready Reference

GARAGE ACCESSORIES

It's best to fit metal-clad switches and socket outlets in a garage or workshop. They are tougher than the plastic variety and last longer.

It's a good idea to choose versions which incorporate a neon indicator light. That way you can see at a glance if the power is on or off.

FIXING THE ACCESSORIES

These accessories are usually surface mounted. To install them:
● drill and plug the holes in the wall
● feed the cable into the surface mounting box
● fix the box to the wall with No 8 wood screws
● make the connections in the usual way
● attach the faceplate.

TIP: EARTH THE BOX

The circuit cable earth core protects the socket itself but it's wise to add extra protection for the mounting box. You can do this in two ways:

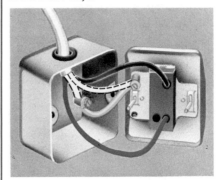

● loop the circuit earth core into the earth screw on the box and then take it onto the socket, or
● add an extra green/yellow sleeved earth core linking the box earth screw to the socket earth terminal.

and equipment to be completely cut off at the flick of a switch. If you're going to run more than one circuit within your garage, it's best to fit a switchfuse unit and the mains switch on this will serve as an isolating switch.

When you fit the new switchfuse unit, it's best to fix it as near as possible to the point where the incoming cable enters. It should be installed in the same way as inside the home and it's important to fit a sheet of fire-resistant material such as treated chipboard or asbestos to the wall beforehand.

You can obviously install as many circuits as you like, but for most garages two – one for power and one for lighting – should prove ample. Generally, you should fit the new switchfuse unit with a 5A and 15A MCB. If, however, you plan to have a number of power sockets, heaters and appliances, it is wise to fit a 30A fuse for the power socket. Cartridge fuses will also suffice but it's not advisable to

use rewirable fuses. You should run the lighting circuit in 1.0mm² or 1.5mm² two-core and earth PVC cable, fixed to the wall and roof surfaces, and you can install a loop-in or junction box system. The power circuit will have to be run in 2.5mm² two-core and earth cable and horizontal runs should be clipped every 250mm (10in), while vertical runs need to be clipped every 400mm (16in).

Although the standard plastic fittings can be used safely in a garage, it's probably best to use the special metal-clad versions. Although these are slightly more expensive, they are more robust and therefore safer in an environment where they could be subjected to the occasional knock or blow. It's also wise to choose versions with neon-indicators to show, at a glance, whether the socket is on or off. They are designed specifically for surface mounting and come complete with mounting boxes.

INSTALLING A LAMP AND SWITCH

1 If you're fitting a lamp to a beam, clip the cable along the middle of the beam so it runs to the centre of the battenholder.

2 You'll have to nibble out some plastic knockouts on the pattress block before offering it up to the beam or ceiling.

3 Clip the power and switch cables to the beam and run them into the pattress. Then sleeve and connect up the earth cores.

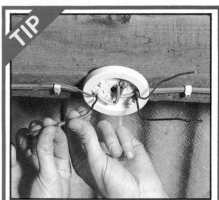

4 Before going any further make sure that you have flagged the black core of the switch cable with red PVC tape: this indicates that it's live.

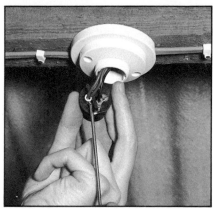

5 Make the connections. The two red cores go to one terminal; the flagged black core to another and the neutral to the third.

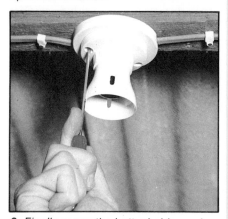

6 Finally screw the battenholder and pattress block to the beam after making holes with a bradawl. You can then connect up the switch.

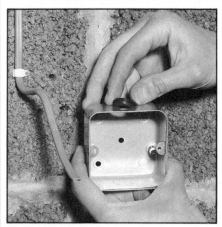

7 Clip the switch cable onto the wall and run it to the point where you'll mount the switch. Fit a grommet to the knockout hole.

8 Feed the cable into the box and make the connections. Remember to sleeve the earth in green/yellow PVC and also to earth the box itself.

9 Replace the switch in the mounting box and fit the faceplate. You can now switch on the power in the house and in the garage itself.

HOME
CARPENTRY

A GUIDE TO WOODWORK JOINTS

If there were no joints, there could be very little woodwork. They come in a great many varieties. This guide helps to remove the confusion from picking the right joint for the job.

Carpentry without joints is a miserable affair, depending solely on adhesive, nails, screws, bolts and other fittings.

Though all these have their places, and are often needed for reinforcement, proper joints provide a wholly different source of strength and stability. Made by shaping the pieces themselves, they frequently (and traditionally) need no fixing hardware at all. Because of this, they usually contribute neatness too, and sometimes save money. They can even supply ornament.

General principles

Accurate cutting is absolutely basic to good jointing. Apart from looks,

it's often vital for strength, since components which meet squarely and snugly help adhesives to do their work (especially PVA, which isn't much good at filling gaps).

Some joints, especially in building carpentry, need no adhesive, relying instead on weight and/or on being part of a large, solid structure. For the rest, the rule is that larger glued areas mean more strength. A mortise-and-tenon joint, for example, is stronger than a halving joint largely because it has two pairs of main meeting faces instead of one. Shoulders, too, aid location and rigidity.

Remember, however, that cutting any joint exacts its own price in

L-JOINTS FOR FRAMING

A mitred front (2) makes a halving joint (1) look neater; you can also include it in a corner bridle joint (3).

Haunches (4 and 5) stop a tenon piece from twisting.

A plain mitre (8) is quite weak. Keys (9) or a spline (10) reinforce it; both are planed flush after assembly. The spline can be of either thin plywood or solid timber. In the latter case the grain should run across it, for strength, instead of along it as you'd normally expect.

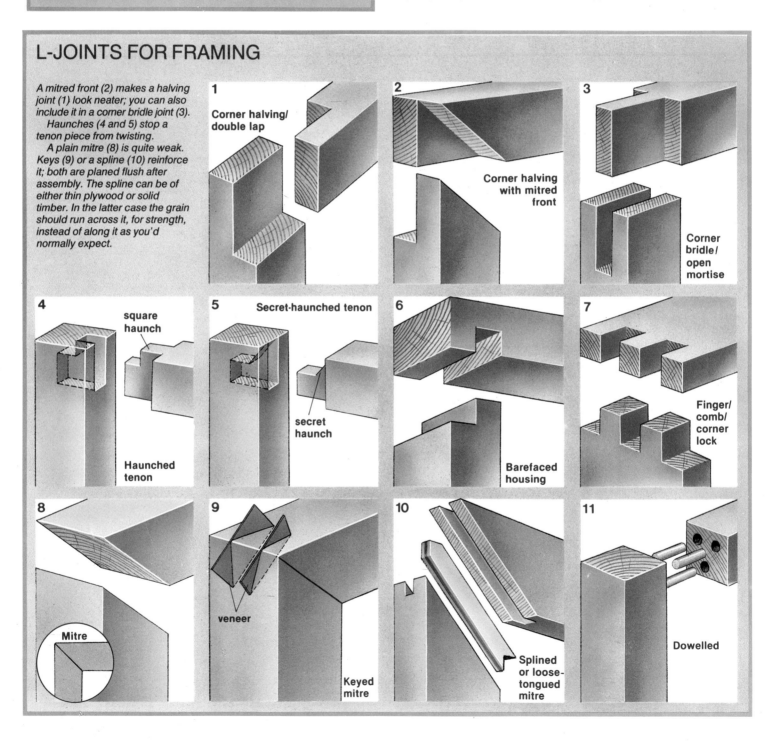

1 Corner halving/double lap

2 Corner halving with mitred front

3 Corner bridle/open mortise

4 Haunched tenon — square haunch

5 Secret-haunched tenon — secret haunch

6 Barefaced housing

7 Finger/comb/corner lock

8 Mitre

9 Keyed mitre — veneer

10 Splined or loose-tongued mitre

11 Dowelled

terms of strength. A halving effectively reduces (say) a 50x50mm (2x2in) piece to a 50x25mm (2x1in) piece. This point is often forgotten. The second piece, tight-fitting and well glued though that may be, won't lessen the fact. You must be sure your choice of joint justifies any overall reduction in size and therefore strength.

Choosing joints

Framing joints are used with lengths of timber, both softwood and hardwood. Board joints are for flat pieces, often of man-made materials. Broadly speaking, the two groups are separate, though

some joints (eg, the finger joint) can be used in either situation. Both groups include corner joints, T-joints and a few X-joints. Three-way framing joints are usually combinations of simple corner joints.

Note that there's another category we don't show, namely 'scarf' joints. These join timber end-to-end. Though many ingenious patterns have been devised, they take some cutting, and none is as strong as a piece of wood which is long enough to start with. In new work that's not hard to come by, and the scarf joint is usually used only for localised repair work where a complete length of timber cannot be easily replaced.

On the whole, the joints in common use – of which a good selection appears here – are popular for good reasons, and serve most purposes. Common sense and growing familiarity with them will reveal these in more detail. Very often, of course, there's more than one joint for a particular task – and different people have their own favourites. In many cases, further information about individual joints is given in other sections of this book.

But, whatever you do, don't think that these illustrations tell the whole story. Probably thousands of other joints have been used at one time and another – and there's still

nothing to stop you from inventing your own variants if you want and need to. But it's wise, first of all, to check that an ordinary joint won't do. This may save you trouble – and the search for one will concentrate your mind on the exact qualities you're looking for. Usually strength, appearance and ease of cutting are what it all boils down to.

Consider, too, exactly what you want the joint to do. In which direction, or directions, is each piece likely to sag, twist, be pushed or be pulled? Make sure you combat exactly the stresses you expect – and not others which are unlikely, or you risk making the joint unnecessarily complicated.

L-JOINTS FOR BOARDS

On wider pieces like these, the grain must always run the same way on both halves of the joint, so they can shrink and swell freely across it even when glued. For the same reason, use a glued spline (16) only with man-made boards.

Joints 12 to 16 are all best made with a router – or on a saw table, tilting the blade for the mitre cuts. You could use a rebate plane for the first four, but power tools are pretty well essential for 16 (a neat, strong joint).

20 represents the ultimate in Western joints. As its name implies, its complex innards are entirely hidden. Don't attempt to cut it unless you're very keen indeed – even many tradesmen would have difficulty.

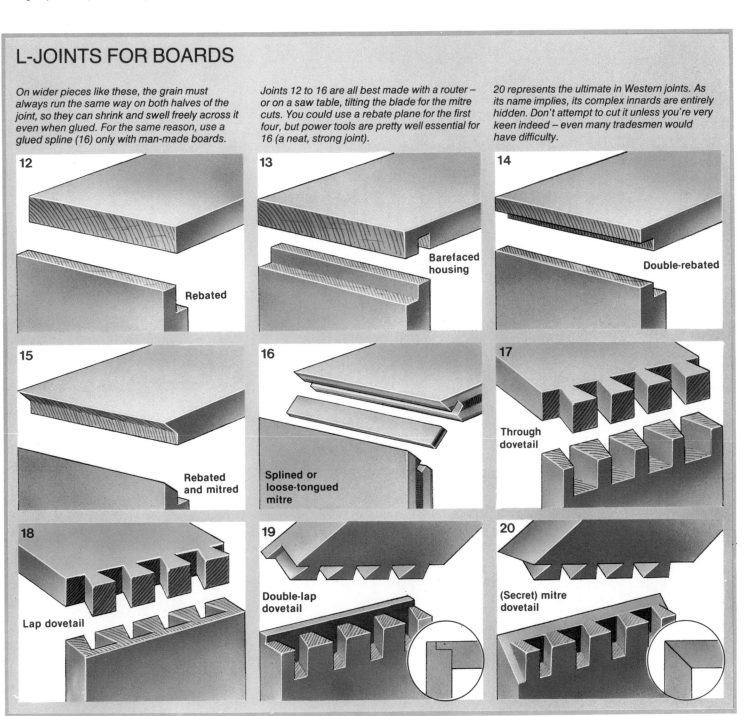

12 Rebated

13 Barefaced housing

14 Double-rebated

15 Rebated and mitred

16 Splined or loose-tongued mitre

17 Through dovetail

18 Lap dovetail

19 Double-lap dovetail

20 (Secret) mitre dovetail

T-JOINTS FOR FRAMING

There's a mortise-and-tenon joint for almost every purpose. Pegs and wedges (29 to 31) add strength and can be very attractive, especially in a contrasting wood. You can even wedge pegs. When using double wedges (30), drive them in with alternate strokes so that they enter the cuts evenly.

31 can be a knock-down joint if unglued.

As a general rule, make mortises one-third the thickness of the piece (24 to 31, 33, 34 – and see also 3, 4, 5). This avoids both weakening the tenon and splitting the mortise piece.

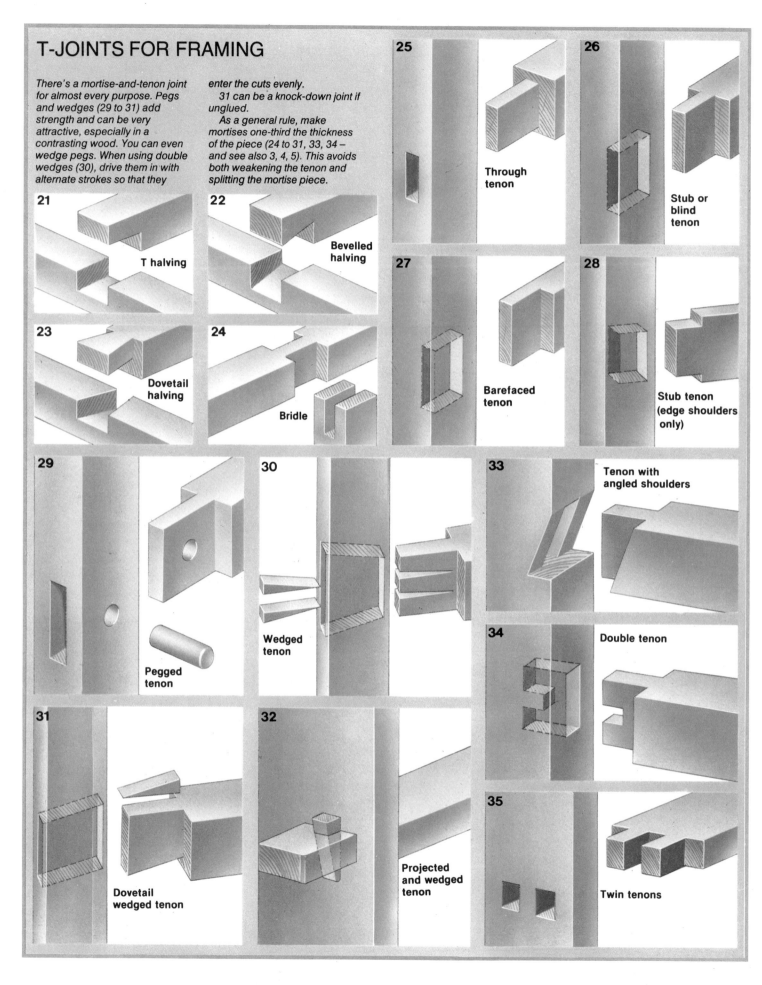

21 T halving

22 Bevelled halving

23 Dovetail halving

24 Bridle

25 Through tenon

26 Stub or blind tenon

27 Barefaced tenon

28 Stub tenon (edge shoulders only)

29 Pegged tenon

30 Wedged tenon

31 Dovetail wedged tenon

32 Projected and wedged tenon

33 Tenon with angled shoulders

34 Double tenon

35 Twin tenons

SIMPLE JOINTS

It's often thought that only elaborate joints give good results in woodwork. It isn't true. There are simple ways to join timber, and one of the simplest is the butt joint. It's easy to make, can be used on natural timber or man-made boards, and it's neat. What's more, given the right adhesive and the right reinforcement, a butt joint can also be strong enough for most purposes.

The great thing about butt joints is their simplicity. You can use them on any kind of timber or man-made board, provided it isn't too thin – not under 6mm (¼in). The only problem you will run into is where you are joining chipboard. A special technique is needed here to get the screws to grip, as is explained later.

Although it is possible simply to glue two pieces of wood together, unless you add some kind of reinforcement the result won't be very strong. So in most cases, the joint should be strengthened with either screws or nails. The question is which? As a rule of thumb, screws will give you a stronger joint than nails. The exception is where you are screwing into the endgrain of natural timber. Here, the screw thread chews up the timber to such an extent that it has almost no fixing value at all. Nails in this case are a much better bet.

Choosing the right adhesive
Even if you are screwing or nailing the joint together, it ought to be glued as well. A PVA woodworking adhesive will do the trick in most jobs, providing a strong and easily achieved fixing. This type of adhesive will not, however, stand up well to either extreme heat or to moisture; the sort of conditions you'll meet outdoors, or in a kitchen, for example. A urea formaldehyde is the glue to use in this sort of situation. It isn't as convenient – it comes as a powder that you have to mix with water – but your joints will hold.

Choosing the right joint
There are no hard and fast rules about choosing the best joint for a particular job. It's really just a case of finding a joint that is neat enough for what you're making, and strong enough not to fall apart the first time it is used. And as far as strength is concerned, the various kinds of butt joint work equally well.

Marking timber
Butt joints are the simplest of all joints – there's no complicated chiselling or marking out to worry about – but if the joint is to be both strong and neat you do need to be able

to saw wood to length leaving the end perfectly square.

The first important thing here is the accuracy of your marking out. Examine the piece of wood you want to cut and choose a side and an edge that are particularly flat and smooth. They're called the face edge and face side.

Next, measure up and press the point of a sharp knife into the face side where you intend to make the cut. Slide a try-square up to the knife, making sure that its stock – the handle – is pressed firmly against the face edge. Then use the knife to score a line across the surface of the timber. Carry this line round all four sides of the wood, always making sure that the try-square's stock is held against either the face edge or the face side. If you wish, you can run over the knife line with a pencil to make it easier to see – it's best to sharpen the lead into a chisel shape.

Why not use a pencil for marking out in the first place? There are two reasons. The first is that a knife gives a thinner and therefore more accurate line than even the sharpest pencil. The second is that the knife will cut through the surface layer of the wood, helping the saw to leave a clean, sharp edge

Ready Reference

MARKING AND CUTTING TOOLS

For butt joints:
measuring tape
sharp handyman's knife
try square
tenon saw

TIP: MARKING OUT

● use a try-square and sharp knife to mark cutting lines on all four faces
● press the stock of the try-square firmly against the wood, or the last line will not meet up with the first

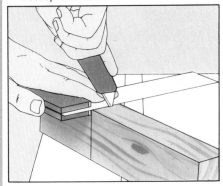

Sawing square

One of the most useful – and easiest to make – aids to sawing is a bench hook. It'll help you to grip the wood you want to cut, and to protect the surface on which you are working. You can make one up quite easily, by gluing and screwing together pieces of scrap timber (see *Ready Reference*).

You also need the ability to control the saw, and there are three tips that will help you here. Always point your index finger along the saw blade to stop it flapping from side to side as you work. And always stand in such a way that you are comfortable, well balanced, and can get your head directly above the saw so you can see what you are cutting. You should also turn slightly sideways on. This stops your elbow brushing against your body as you draw the saw back – a fault that is often the reason for sawing wavy lines.

Starting the cut

Position the piece of wood to be cut on the bench hook and hold it firmly against the block furthest from you. Start the cut by drawing the saw backwards two or three times over the far edge to create a notch, steadying the blade by 'cocking' the thumb of your left hand. Make sure that you position the saw so that the whole of this notch is on the waste side of the line. You can now begin to saw properly using your arm with sort of piston action, but keep your left (or right as the case may be) hand away from the saw.

As the cut deepens gradually reduce the angle of the saw until it is horizontal. At this point you can continue sawing through until you start cutting into the bench hook. Alternatively, you may find it easier to angle the saw towards you and make a sloping cut down the edge nearest to you. With that done, you can saw through the remaining waste holding the saw horizontally, using the two angled cuts to keep the saw on course.

Whichever method you choose, don't try to force the saw through the wood – if that seems necessary, then the saw is probably blunt. Save your muscle power for the forward stroke – but concentrate mainly on sawing accurately to your marked line.

Cleaning up cut ends

Once you have cut the wood to length, clean up the end with glasspaper. A good tip is to lay the abrasive flat on a table and work the end of the wood over it with a series of circular strokes, making sure that you keep the wood vertical so you don't sand the end out of square. If the piece of wood is too unmanageable, wrap the glasspaper round a square piece of scrap wood instead and sand the end of the wood by moving the block to and fro – it'll help in keeping the end square.

DOVETAIL NAILING

This is a simple way of strengthening any butt joint. All you do is grip the upright piece in a vice or the jaws of a portable work-bench, and glue the horizontal piece on top if it – supporting it with scrap wood to hold the joint square – and then drive in the nails dovetail fashion. If you were to drive the nails in square, there would be more risk that the joint would pull apart. Putting them in at an angle really does add strength.

The only difficulty is that the wood may split. To prevent this, use oval brads rather than round nails, making sure that their thickest part points along the grain. If that doesn't do the trick, try blunting the point of each nail by driving it into the side of an old hammer. This creates a burr of metal on the point which will cut through the wood fibres rather than parting them.

Once the nails are driven home, punch their heads below the surface using a nail punch, or a large blunt nail. Fill the resulting dents with wood stopping (better on wood than ordinary cellulose filler) and sand smooth.

1 *Drive nails at angle: first leans to left; next to right, and so on.*

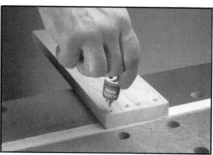

3 *Fill resulting dents with stopping compound to cover up nail heads.*

THE OVERLAP

This is the simplest of all and is one you can use on relatively thin timber. The example shown is for a T-joint, but the method is the same if you want to make an X-joint.

Bring the two pieces of wood together as they will be when joined, and use a pencil to mark the position of the topmost piece on the one underneath. To reinforce the joint, countersunk screws are best, so mark their positions on the top piece of wood, and drill clearance holes the same diameter as the screw's shank – the unthreaded part – right the way through. The screws should be arranged like the spots on a dice (two screws are shown here, but on a larger joint where more strength is needed five would be better) to help stop the joint twisting out of square. Enlarge the mouths of these holes with a countersink bit to accommodate the screw heads, and clean up any splinters where the drill breaks through the underside of the wood.

Bring the two pieces of wood together again using a piece of scrap wood to keep the top piece level. Then make

pilot holes in the lower piece using either a bradawl or a small drill, boring through the clearance holes to make sure they are correctly positioned. Make sure the pilot holes are drilled absolutely vertically, or the screws could pull the joint out of shape. Finally, apply a thin coating of adhesive to both the surfaces to be joined (follow the adhesive manufacturer's instructions), position the pieces of wood accurately and, without moving them again, drive home the screws.

3 *Reassemble joint and bore pilot holes in bottom piece with bradawl.*

2 With nail punch or large blunt nail, hammer nail heads below surface.

4 When stopping is dry, sand flush with surface of surrounding timber.

CORRUGATED TIMBER CONNECTORS

Another simple way of holding a butt joint together is to use ordinary corrugated timber connectors. Simply glue the two pieces of wood together, and hammer the connectors in across the joint. Note that they are driven in dovetail fashion – the fixing is stronger that way.

For strength, hammer in connectors diagonally rather than straight.

1 Bring pieces squarely together. Mark position of each on the other.

2 Drill and countersink (inset) clearance holes for screws in uppermost piece.

4 Apply woodworking adhesive to both pieces and press them together

5 Carefully drive in screws. If they're tight, remove and lubricate with soap.

Ready Reference

MAKING YOUR OWN BENCH HOOK

This a very useful sawing aid to help grip the wood when cutting. Hook one end over the edge of the workbench and hold the wood against the other end. Make it up from off-cuts and replace when it becomes worn.

You need:
● a piece of 12mm (½in) plywood measuring about 250 x 225mm (10 x 9in)
● two pieces of 50 x 25mm (2 x 1in) planed softwood, each about 175mm (7in) long. Glue and screw them together as shown in the sketch. Use the bench hook the other way up if you're left-handed.

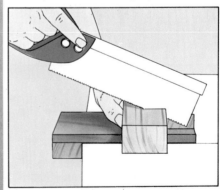

TIP: SAWING STRAIGHT

● hold wood firmly against bench hook and start cut on waste side of cutting line with two or three backward cuts
● decrease angle of the saw blade as cut progresses
● complete cut with saw horizontal, cutting into your bench hook slightly

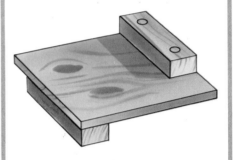

TIP: TO SMOOTH CUT END

● rub with a circular motion on glasspaper held flat on the workbench, so you don't round off the corners
● on large pieces of wood, wrap glasspaper round a block of wood and rub this across the cut end

FIXING INTO CHIPBOARD

Because neither nails nor screws hold well in chipboard, how do you hold a butt joint together? The answer is that you do use screws, but to help them grip, you drive them into a chipboard plug. Chipboard plugs are a bit like ordinary wall plugs. In fact, you can use ordinary plugs, but you have to be careful to position the plug so that any expanding jaws open across the board's width and not across the thickness where they could cause the board to break up.

The initial stages of the job are exactly the same as for the overlap joint – marking out, drilling the clearance holes, and so on. The difference is that instead of boring pilot holes in the second piece of wood, you drill holes large enough to take the chipboard plugs. Pop the plugs into the holes, glue the joint together and drive home the screws.

Incidentally, if you can't use any sort of plug at all – for example, when screwing into the face of the chipboard – the only way to get the screw to hold properly is to dip it in a little woodworking adhesive before you drive it home.

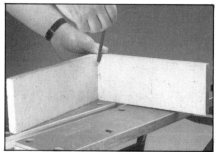
1 *Bring pieces together and mark position of overlap with a pencil.*

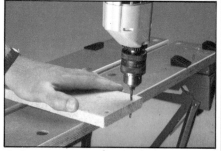
2 *Drill and countersink clearance holes in overlapping piece.*

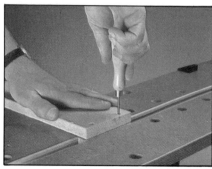
3 *Mark screw positions through holes onto end of second piece.*

4 *Drill chipboard to take plugs, then glue and screw joint together.*

REINFORCING BLOCKS

The joints described so far are fairly robust, but if a lot of strength is needed it's worth reinforcing the joint with some sort of block. The simplest is a square piece of timber.

First drill and countersink clearance holes through the block and glue and screw it to one of the pieces you want to join so that it's flush with the end. To complete the joint, glue the second piece in position, and drive screws through into that. You can arrange for the block to end up inside the angle or outside it. Choose whichever looks best and is easiest to achieve.

With the block inside the angle, you'll have a neat joint and the screw heads won't be openly on display. However, in most cases it means screwing through a thick piece of wood (the block) into a thin piece (one of the bits you want to join), so it's not as strong as it might be. If greater strength is needed work the other way round, driving the screws through the pieces to be joined, into the block. You can neaten the result to a certain extent by using a triangular rather than a square block.

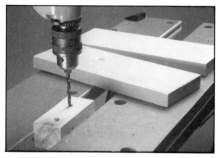
1 *Drill and countersink clearance holes through reinforcing block.*

2 *Glue and screw block in place level with end of one piece of wood.*

3 *Glue second piece in place and drive screws into it through block.*

4 *In some cases this joint looks better with block outside angle.*

JOINTING BLOCKS

Made from plastic, these are just sophisticated versions of the wooden blocks you can make yourself, and they're used in similar situations. Their only real advantage is that they tend to give a neater result when you're working with veneered or melamine covered chipboard, but only because they come in the right colours. There are basically two kinds to choose from.

The simplest is just a hollow triangular 'block' that comes with a snap-on cover to hide the screws. More complicated versions come in two parts. You screw one half of the block to each piece of wood, and then screw the two halves together using the machine screw provided. It's essential here that both halves of the block are positioned accurately, and since the blocks vary from brand to brand in the details of their design, you should follow the manufacturer's instructions on this point.

1 *Screw half of block to one piece of wood and mark position on other.*

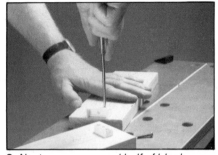

2 *Next, screw second half of block in place on second piece of timber.*

3 *Finally, connect both halves of block using built-in machine screw.*

4 *Treat blocks that come in one piece as wooden reinforcing blocks.*

ANGLE IRONS

If still greater strength is needed, use either an angle iron or a corner repair bracket to reinforce the joint. These are really just pieces of metal pre-drilled to take screws and shaped to do the same job as a reinforcing block (the angle irons) or to be screwed to the face of the two pieces of timber across the joint (the flat T-shaped and L-shaped corner repair brackets).

In either case, bring together the pieces of wood to be joined, position the bracket, and mark the screw holes. Drill clearance and pilot holes for all the screws, then screw the bracket to one of the pieces before glueing the joint together and screwing the bracket to the second piece. They don't look very attractive, so use where appearance isn't important, ie, at the back of a joint, or where the joint is going to be concealed in some other way.

1 *Corner joints strengthened with plywood and an angle repair iron.*

2 *T-joints can be simply made with angle irons or repair brackets.*

SKEW NAILING

There'll be some situations where you cannot get at the end of the wood to use dovetail nailing. Here you must use skew nailing instead. This means glueing the two pieces securely together and then driving a nail into the upright piece of wood at an angle so it also penetrates the horizontal piece. Put a couple of nails into each side of the upright so that they cross. To stop the upright moving, clamp a block of wood behind it or wedge it against something solid.

Stop movement while driving nails with scrap wood block and G-cramp.

HALVING JOINTS & simple mitres

Getting joints to fit snugly is one of the major objectives in carpentry, and nothing introduces the techniques so well as the halving joint. As for the perfect finish, that's the role of the mitre.

There are many situations in woodwork when you need a joint that's fast and simple, but also neat and strong. And this is where halving joints come into their own. Despite their simplicity, they're very effective joints because the two pieces of wood are cut so they interlock together, either face to face or edge to edge, making the joint as strong as — if not stronger than — the timber itself. They are used almost exclusively for building frameworks, joining the rails (side pieces) either at a corner or in a cross absolutely flush. You end up with a frame that's neat enough to be on show and sturdy enough to need no reinforcement.

Mitre joints, though not strictly speaking considered halving joints as there's no interlocking, are halved to make up a perfect 90° angle. In this section, only the simple mitre is dealt with — the more complicated forms (eg, mitred secret dovetails) are covered in another section.

Strength of joints

There are three things that affect the strength of a halving joint — the size of the timber, the quality of the timber, and any reinforcement you add.

The size of timber is important because it governs the amount of adhesive in the joint; the greater the areas glued together, the stronger the joint will be. Usually problems only arise when you are trying to join thin pieces of timber together — it's almost impossible to get the joint to stay rigid. Regarding timber quality, hardwoods rarely present a problem, but with softwoods, splitting can occur which will seriously weaken the joint. You should, therefore, reject timber containing knots, cracks and other potential weak spots.

In many cases, the correct adhesive is all the reinforcement you need — use a good quality PVA woodworking adhesive, or, if the joint will be subjected to heat or moisture, a urea formaldehyde woodworking adhesive. If still greater strength is required — this is more likely on corner halving joints than on cross halvings — you should drive screws through the overlaps, or, for a more natural look, drill a hole right through and glue in a length of dowel. Both the dowels and screws are set like the spots on a dice to stop the joint twisting.

Simple butt joints (see pages 109–113) must be reinforced in some way to have strength, but with mitred butt joints this would defeat the decorative aim. Because of this, they are normally reserved for situations where strength is not required — picture frames and decorative edgings, such as door architraves for example.

Marking corner halving joints

Having sawn the ends of the two pieces of wood to be joined perfectly square (see pages 110–111) place one piece on top of the other, and mark the width of the top piece on the one below. Carry this mark right round the timber using a knife and a try-square, then repeat the process, this time with the bottom piece of wood on top.

Next divide the thickness of the timber in two. You need a single-tooth marking gauge for this: it consists of a wooden shaft with a sharp metal pin called a spur near one end, and a block of wood (the stock) which can be moved along the shaft and be fixed at any point with the aid of a thumbscrew.

Position the stock so that the distance between it and the spur is roughly half the timber's thickness, and place it against one edge of the wood. Use the spur to dent the surface of the timber, then repeat with the stock against the other edge. If the dents co-incide, the gauge is set correctly. If they don't, reset the gauge. Don't try to make small adjustments by undoing the thumbscrew and moving the stock — you'll go on for ever trying to make it accurate. Instead, with the screw reasonably tight, tap one end of the shaft sharply on a hard surface. Depending which end you tap and how hard you tap it, the setting will increase or decrease by the merest fraction.

With the setting right, wedge one end of the timber into the angle of a bench hook, place the stock of the gauge firmly against the timber's edge and holding it there, score the wood from the width line to the end. You'll find this easier if, rather than digging the spur right into the wood, you merely drag it across the surface. Score identical lines on the other side and the end.

Use a pencil to shade the areas on each piece of wood that will form the waste (the top of one, the bottom of the other), then grip the first piece upright in a vice. The lower down you can get it the better. If you can't get it low, back it with a piece of scrap wood to reduce vibration. Using a tenon saw, carefully saw down until you reach the width line — the first one you marked. The golden rule of sawing any kind of joint is to saw on the waste side of the marked line (it's *always* better to saw or chisel off too little rather than too much since you can always take off a little more but you can never put it back). And remember that the closer the fit, the

MAKING A CORNER HALVING JOINT

1 *First mark the width of each piece of wood on the other. Then, using a knife and square, continue these width lines round all four sides of each piece.*

2 *To mark the thickness line, set a marking gauge to half the thickness of the wood and, holding the stock firmly against one edge, scribe the line.*

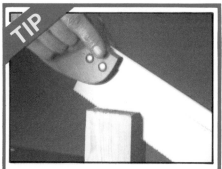

3 *It's easier to start sawing at an angle, then gradually bring the saw to the horizontal. Keep the wood gripped firmly in the vice until you're finished.*

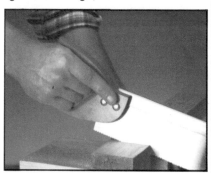

4 *Transfer the wood to a bench hook and cut down along the width line to remove the waste wood. Be sure to cut on the waste side of the guide line.*

5 *Smooth both parts to be joined with glasspaper and apply adhesive. Clamp together with a G-cramp until dry, protecting the wood with scrap timber.*

6 *When the adhesive has set, drill holes for reinforcing wood screws or dowels. If using screws, countersink the hole to take the screw head.*

stronger the joint will end up. Basically, it should fit like a hand in a glove.

Remove the wood from the vice, put it on a bench hook and cut down along the width line to release the waste wood. Again make sure you cut on the waste side of the line and be prepared to make final adjustments with a chisel. Treat the second piece of wood in exactly the same way, then bring the two together and check the fit.

You can use either a chisel or a piece of glasspaper to take off any unevenness in the timber, although it'll be quicker to use a chisel to clear out the edges so that the corners are absolutely square. When the pieces finally fit neatly, spread adhesive on both faces of the joint and hold them in place with a G-cramp (protecting the wood's surface with scrap timber) until the glue has set. Remove the cramp, and add any re-

Ready Reference

WHERE TO USE HALVING JOINTS

Halving joints are usually used for making frameworks. Here you can see which joint to use where, and how each one is assembled.

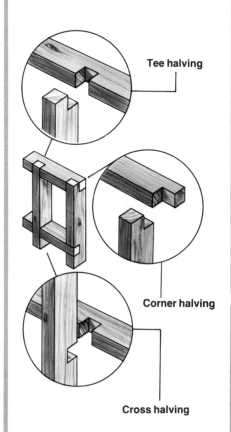

Tee halving

Corner halving

Cross halving

TOOLS FOR HALVING JOINTS

For measuring and marking: use a *handyman's knife* rather than a pencil for marking; use a *marking gauge* on each face of the joint – it'll be more accurate than using a tape measure; a *try-square* ensures accurate squaring off.
For cutting: use a *tenon saw* and a broad-blade *chisel* (25mm/1in) for cutting out cross halvings.

TIP: LABELLING JOINT PARTS

Avoid mixing up the pairs of joints by labelling the two parts with a letter and a number as soon as you cut them.

MAKING A CROSS HALVING JOINT

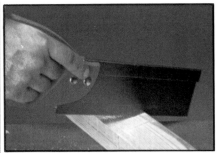

1 *First mark out the waste area to be removed, then cut down the width lines with a tenon saw.*

2 *Hold the timber in a vice or against a bench hook and remove the waste by chiselling at a slight upward angle.*

3 *Do the same on the other side until there's a 'pyramid' of waste in the middle. Gradually flatten this.*

4 *When nearing the thickness line, hold the cutting edge at an angle to the wood grain. Trim fibres in the corners.*

The next step is to turn the wood round and slope the other edge to leave a sort of pyramid of waste. With that done, pushing the chisel through the wood rather than hitting it, gradually flatten off the pyramid until you have brought it level with the half-way lines. You'll get a neater finish here if, in the final stages, you work with the chisel's blade flat but at an angle to the grain of the wood. Finally, again pushing the chisel, remove any ragged fibres lodged in the angles of the housing.

Once you've sawn and chiselled out the housing in the second piece of wood, the next step is to try fitting the two together. Don't try forcing them if they don't quite fit — you're in danger of splitting the wood. Instead, carefully chisel off a fraction more wood, bit by bit, until you can fit the pieces together without undue force. If, on the other hand, you've cut the housing too wide so the fit is very loose, you'll have to add some re-inforcement like screws or dowels, and fill in the gaps with a wood filler, stopping or a mixture of fine sawdust and PVA adhesive. It's not worth trying to add a wedge unless the gap is very wide (over 6mm/¼in) because the result can be very messy.

Making a mitre joint

With wood that's square or rectangular in section, the first job is to make sure that both pieces are absolutely squarely cut. Use the try-square to check this — if they're not, it's better to cut another piece of wood than attempt to make adjustments. Next, place one piece on top of the other to form a right angle. Mark an internal and external corner on both, then take them apart and carry the marks across the edge with a knife and try square. Join up the marks on each piece of wood — this will give sawing lines at 45° Mark the waste side of each with a pencil.

Wood that is raised on one side (eg, mouldings for picture frames) cannot be marked in the same way as the pieces won't sit flat on each other. The easiest way is to mark the

inforcing screws or dowels that may be needed, drilling pilot holes first.

Making cross halving joints

The difference between cross halving joints and corner halving joints is that you cannot remove the waste using only a saw. You have to make a 'housing' and for this you need a chisel (see pages 122–123 for more details of housing joints).

Saw down the width lines to the halfway mark and make additional saw cuts in between to break up the waste — these can

be the same width as the chisel blade to make chipping out easier. Grip the work in a vice, or on a bench hook, and now use the chisel to remove the waste. This is done in four stages. Guiding the chisel blade bevel uppermost with one hand and striking the handle with the palm of your other hand — for this job your hand is better than a mallet — reduce the edge of the timber nearest to you to a shallow slope ending a fraction above the halfway line. Don't try to remove all the wood in one go or it will split. Remove just sliver at a time.

MAKING MITRES

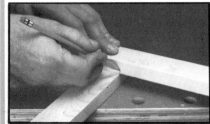

1 *With square or rectangular wood, cut ends absolutely square and stack to form a right angle. Then mark the inner and outer corners on both pieces.*

2 *Carry lines down each edge with knife and try square, and score a line between corner marks to create an angle of 45°. Shade waste in pencil.*

3 *Press the wood against the bench hook and keep the saw at a shallow angle. Cut the diagonal, using the line on the edge to keep the saw vertical.*

THE SIMPLE MITRE

1 *The ends of two battens are cut to 45° and, when fixed together, make a 90° angle in this simplest of mitre joints, ideal for picture framing.*

2 *With thick timber frames, use corrugated steel fasteners driven into the back of mitre joints, where they will not be seen from the front.*

3 *Another method of strengthening a fairly thick mitre joint from behind is to pin triangles of plywood across the corner, out of sight.*

4 *Ready-made angle brackets with pre-drilled, countersunk screw holes make a quick, rigid and hidden fixing for two mitred battens in a frame.*

Ready Reference

MAKING A MITRE BLOCK

Mitre blocks and boxes already have 45° angle cuts made as a saw guide. Rather than buying one, you can make one that's used in the same way as a bench hook. You'll need:
● a piece of 19mm (³⁄₄in) plywood measuring about 250 x 150mm (10 x 6in)
● a 250mm (10in) length of 50 x 50mm (2 x 2in) softwood – or hardwood such as beech if available
● a 250mm (10in) length of 50 x 25mm (2 x 1in) softwood.

Glue and screw together as shown in the diagrams, then
● use a combination square, or make a template by folding a square piece of paper in half diagonally, as a guide for the 45° angle saw cuts
● square the lines down both faces of the block, and cut the slots with a tenon saw.

MAKING A MITRE CRAMP

You can make a simple cramp for small mitred frames from 4 L-shaped softwood blocks. Drill holes through one leg of each block, thread string through holes and tie tightly to hold blocks against frame corners.

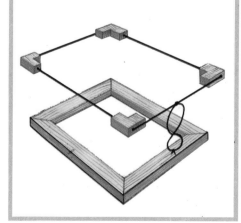

point of the mitre (the corner point) and then to use a simple *mitre block* to cut the angle. A mitre block not only helps you support the piece of wood (like a bench hook) but also has saw cuts at 45° in the back face to guide the saw. Then you only have to line up the mitre point on the wood with the saw now set at the correct angle. You can make a mitre block yourself — see *Ready Reference*.

Mitre aids

There are other devices available to help you cut mitres accurately. A proprietary *jointing jig*, for example, guides the saw either at right angles or at 45°; a *mitre box* is like a mitre block but has an extra side so that the whole length of the saw is kept in line.

Without these devices, getting the angles right isn't easy — but if necessary you can use a bench hook, driving in two nails so the wood is held against the block and the line of cutting is free of the bench hook. This is not as easy as using one of the other methods. Mark the wood so you know the sawing line, then place it in the mitre block , box or jig, to line up with the appropriate groove to guide the saw. If the wood you are cutting is very thin, put some blocks of scrap wood under the device to bring it up to a reasonable height. Insert a tenon saw into the guide slot and, holding it level, saw away.

There are only two things that can go wrong. If the block is old, the 'guide' cut may have widened, resulting in an inaccurate cut. A larger tenon saw may help, but really the only answer is to hold the saw as steady as possible. The other common error when cutting mouldings and the like is to cut two mitres the same — that is two right-handed or left-handed angles, instead of one of each. This can be avoided by always marking the waste on the wood, and checking that the saw is in the correct guide slot before you begin.

Clean up the cut ends with glasspaper, taking care not to alter the angle, and glue and cramp the joint together. For frames, special mitre cramps are available, but you again make up your own. From scrap wood, cut four L-shaped blocks, and drill a hole at an angle through the point of each L. Feed a single piece of string through the holes of all four blocks, position the blocks at the corners of the frame and tie the string into a continuous loop. To tighten up, twist the string around a stick, and keep twisting the stick to draw the blocks together. You can then wedge the stick against the frame to stop it untwisting until the adhesive has set.

There are three ways to strengthen mitres — with timber connectors, plywood triangles or metal angle repair irons. For frames they should be fitted from behind, either by glueing, or glueing and pinning (see the photographs above).

MAKING JOINTS WITH DOWELS

Called wood pins or pegs, dowels are lengths of hardwood with an important role to play in simple carpentry. They can be a decorative part of joints made with them, or be there for strength alone. Few tools are needed but the secret of success lies in using them accurately.

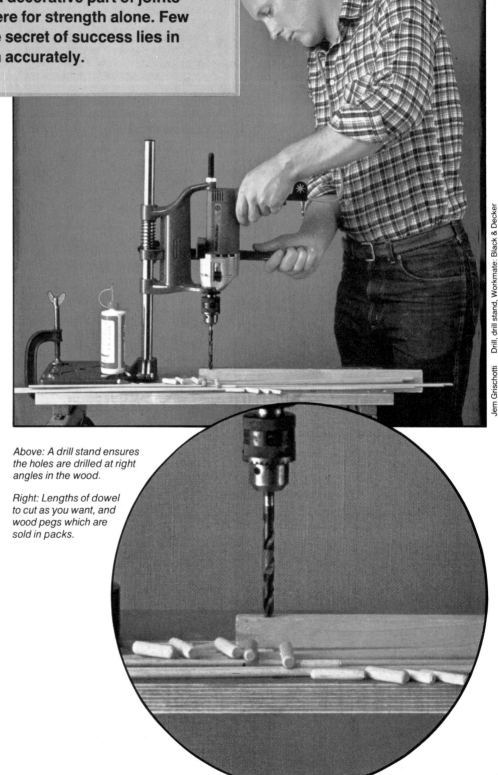

Jem Grischotti   Drill, drill stand, Workmate: Black & Decker

There are two basic ways in which you can use dowels in woodworking joints. You can drive a dowel through such joints as a half lap instead of using a nail or screw, or you can use them to make joints in their own right by drilling holes in one piece of wood, glueing in dowels, and then slotting these into corresponding holes in the second piece.

The dowel joint proper is used mostly in furniture making where it provides a neat joint of great strength without intricate cutting and without the need for unsightly reinforcement. Dowels can also be used to repair furniture.

In any joint, the size of the dowel is very important. Use a small one in a big joint and it won't have sufficient strength; use one that's too large and the holes you drill to accommodate it will weaken the wood. Ideally you should choose dowels which are no more than one third the thickness of the timber into which they will be fixed.

The thickness of the wood must be considered, too, for the dowels must have sufficient space between them and at each side otherwise when they're hit home or pushed into their corresponding holes the wood will split. So follow the carpenter's 'one third rule' and mark the width as well as the thickness into three (ie, a 9mm/³⁄₈in dowel will need at least the same amount on both sides of it). And don't forget that planed wood can be up to 5mm less all round than the dimensions you ordered, and three into this size might not give you enough room for a successful joint.

Types of joints

There are different types of dowel joint. The simplest and easiest to make is the *through* dowel joint in which the dowel peg passes right through one piece of timber and into the other, sometimes passing through this as well if it's thin enough. Because in either case the ends of the dowels show, they are often used as a decorative feature of the article you're making.

If you don't want the ends of the dowels to be seen, you must make a *stopped* joint. In

Above: A drill stand ensures the holes are drilled at right angles in the wood.

Right: Lengths of dowel to cut as you want, and wood pegs which are sold in packs.

JOINTS MADE WITH DOWELS

The through dowel joint ready for assembly. The dowels are firmly embedded in one piece and will pass right through the other.

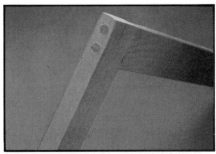

When assembled the through joint shows up the dowels. Cut them a little longer so after cramping they can be planed flush with the wood.

The stopped joint has dowels in one piece which will go into the other far enough to ensure rigidity but won't be seen on the other side.

A close fit for the finished stopped joint. When drilling the holes they should be slightly deeper than the dowel to hold any excess adhesive.

Mitred dowel joints can be tricky to make as you can't use the 'pin' method (see next page) for marking up because of the 45° angle.

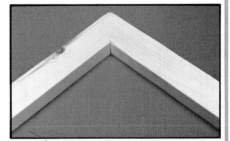

The hidden strength in this joint is the two different lengths of dowel. Very effective for frames where you don't want reinforcement to be seen.

A halving or half lap joint made at a corner can either be glued and screwed or, if it will be on show, made secure with dowels which fit into holes placed like spots on a dice.

Jem Grischotti

The completed dowelled halving joint gives one overall look of wood. The same effect can be achieved by topping countersunk screws with dowel pellets cut from an offcut of the wood.

Jem Grischotti

Ready Reference

BUYING DOWELS

Dowel lengths from timber merchants are sold in these diameters:
● 6mm (1/4in)
● 9mm (3/8in)
● 12mm (1/2in)
Larger diameters – 16mm (5/8in) and 19mm (3/4in) – can be softwood rather than hardwood.

TIPS TO SAVE TIME

● Buying grooved dowel saves you having to groove it yourself.
● **Pre-packed dowels** are bought in packs containing short lengths of diameters such as 4mm, 8mm and 10mm. They are fluted (finely grooved) and the ends are chamfered.
● **Dowel pellets** finish woodwork where screws have been countersunk. They should fit the hole exactly but be fractionally deeper so they can be planed back when the adhesive has set. Buy pre-packed, or cut your own from offcuts using a special plug attachment for an electric drill.

TOOLS

● **try-square and marking gauge** are essential for accurate marking up
● **electric drill** held in a drill stand for perfectly plumb holes
● **mallet** for tapping in the dowels
● **block or ordinary plane** for finishing a through joint
● **cramp** to hold the joint until the adhesive has set

CHAMFER DOWEL ENDS

If cutting your own dowels rub the cut ends with medium-grade glasspaper to give a gentle chamfer (it makes the dowel go in more easily).

Apply woodworking adhesive to the meeting faces of the wood as well as brushing or squirting it into the holes.

MARKING UP

1 *With wood that's rectangular or square in section, use a marking gauge to make the central line on the edge where the dowels will go.*

3 *Lightly tap small panel pins into the wood at the two centre points. Snip off their heads leaving about 3mm (¹/8in) protruding.*

2 *Divide this central line into three, then draw two lines at right angles.*

4 *Holding the second piece of timber firmly against a bench hook or edge of the try-square, press the pins in to mark the drill positions (inset).*

Jem Grischotti

Leave the pins slightly proud of the surface and snip off their heads with pliers. Bring the two pieces of wood together in the correct joint position, and the heads of the pins will mark where the holes are to be bored in the second piece of timber. Remove the pins with pincers before drilling.

Where you are joining two horizontal rails to an upright at a corner, you should stagger the holes, otherwise the dowels will clash inside the upright.

Cutting holes
Holes for the dowels can be made either with a hand drill or an electric drill. In each case, obviously, the bit used must match the diameter of the dowel. The main difficulty is that you must ensure the bit is truly at right angles to the timber you are drilling, or a dowel that protrudes from one hole will not fit snugly into the hole in the matching timber.

You can use an electric drill held in a drill stand to guarantee that the bit is truly at right angles to the timber. Or where the timber is too large for this you can use a dowelling jig to ensure accuracy. Where you are cutting a through dowel joint, you can avoid this problem by cramping both pieces of wood together in a vice and boring through both.

For stopped joints, the hole you bore should be slightly deeper than the depth to which the dowel penetrates, to leave a small reservoir for any excess glue that is not squeezed out along the groove. A depth gauge ensures this. Various types for both hand and electric drills are available but you can improvise by making your own. Either stick a bit of tape on the bit's shank, carefully positioned so that the distance between its lower edge and the end of the drill exactly equals the depth of the hole required. Or you can take a length of timber – 25mm (1in) or 38mm (1½in) square according to the diameter of the dowel – and bore a hole right through its length. Cut this timber to length so that when it is slipped onto the bit's shank, the part of the bit left protruding will cut a hole of the right depth. In both cases you should take your measurement to the cutting end of the drill only – not to any threaded or shaped lead-in point.

For a stopped dowel joint, drill holes so the dowels will penetrate each piece of timber by between one-half and two-thirds of the timber's thickness.

Fixing and finishing dowels
Always check first that the joint is a good fit and is accurately square before applying PVA adhesive. You can then squirt adhesive into the holes, but since you risk applying too much this way, it is better to brush the

this the peg doesn't go right through either piece of timber. This is perhaps the most common dowel joint.

Joint shapes
Dowels can be used to make joints of various types, including L-joints, T-joints and X-joints between rails or boards, and three-way joints between rails and posts, as in furniture-making. They can also be used to reinforce edge-to-edge joints between boards, for example when making a drawer.

Cutting dowels
Cut dowels to length with a fine-toothed tenon saw, holding the dowels in a bench hook or a vice. For through joints, cut one dowel slightly longer than the combined thicknesses of the timbers, so that the ends can be trimmed flush after the joint is assembled. For stopped joints, cut the dowels slightly shorter than the combined depths of the holes into which they fit, and lightly chamfer the ends using glasspaper, a chisel or a proprietary dowel sharpener (which works just like a pencil sharpener).

Dowels need a shallow groove cut in their sides to allow excess adhesive to squeeze out as the joints are assembled. With much

practice you can do this with a chisel or tenon saw (having cramped it lengthways in a workbench), but it is probably easier to buy grooved dowel in the first place – in lengths you cut to size yourself, or for small jobs as pre-packed pegs. If buying pegs make sure you choose ones that correspond with the bit size for your drill.

Marking hole positions
First, use a try-square to check that the meeting faces or ends of the timber to be joined are cut perfectly square and are of the same thickness. You can then mark the positions for the dowel holes. Set a marking gauge to half the width of the timber, and mark a line down the middle of the end of one length of timber. Determine exactly where on this line the centre of the holes will be – the ideal is that they should be from 25mm (1in) to 50mm (2in) apart and never nearer than 19mm (¾in) from the edges. Using a try-square, draw lines across the gauge line to mark the exact centres of the holes.

To mark matching holes in corresponding positions on the second piece of timber use the following method to ensure accuracy. Drive small panel pins into the first piece at the positions you've marked for the holes.

DRILLING HOLES

1 *To ensure that holes will be in exactly opposite positions on a through joint, drill both pieces of wood at the same time.*

2 *The depths you have to go to for a dowel joint can be marked on the bit with a piece of tape, allowing a little extra at both ends for glue.*

3 *Another way of making sure you don't go too deep is by making a depth gauge from a scrap of timber. Or you can buy a proprietary gauge.*

4 *A dowelling jig has holes for different sized bits. When you cramp it over the wood use spare timber to prevent the screw marking the wood.*

adhesive onto the dowel before tapping it into place with a mallet — you can use a hammer but you should protect the dowel with a block of wood. You should also apply adhesive to the meeting faces of the timber.

The glued joints should be cramped until the adhesive has set.

With through joints and halving joints, you now saw off the bulk of the protruding dowel

and use a block plane to trim the end flush. You can use an ordinary plane for this, but it must be set for a very fine cut. Smooth off any remaining roughness with glasspaper.

If using dowel pellets, hit them into place over the countersunk screws (with the ones you've cut yourself make sure the grain follows that of the wood). Plane off excess after the adhesive has dried.

MAKING THE JOINT

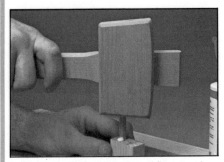

1 *First check that the dowel fits snugly, but not too tightly. Then apply adhesive and gently tap it into place with a mallet.*

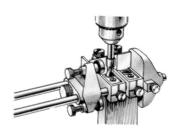

2 *After cramping to allow the adhesive to set, finish off a through joint by planing away the excess along the side of the wood.*

Dowelling jig: Buck & Ryan   Jem Grischotti

Block plane: Stanley Tools   Jem Grischotti

Ready Reference

RULES FOR DRILLING HOLES
● make them the same diameter as the dowels
● they should be a little deeper than the dowel's length
● slightly countersink these where the pieces of wood meet

TIP: DOWELLING JIG
With a drill use a dowelling jig so the holes will be straight and square.

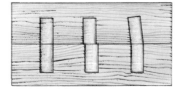

WHAT CAN GO WRONG?
The most common problems are:
● the dowels being too tight. Forcing the joint together causes the wood to split – so always check the fit first
● the joint being forced out of alignment because the holes were drilled out of line with one another – always check the alignment before finally applying the adhesive

MITRED DOWEL JOINTS
● use a mitre box for accuracy
● place mitred pieces together in a cramp and mark them at the same time
● the dowel at the outer corner should be shorter than the one at the inner corner

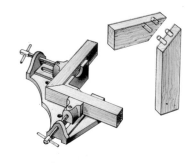

HOUSING JOINTS

If you're putting together a bookcase or installing shelves in any other sort of furniture, then housing joints are the ones to use for attaching the shelves to the uprights. Here's how to make them.

Jem Grischotti

Housing joints are very useful in constructing drawers, door frames and partition walls, among other things: but they're indispensable for fixing shelves neatly into uprights. The joint gets its name because the end of the shelf fits into a square-bottomed channel or 'housing' across the upright. A basic housing joint is as simple as that, and very easy to cut and assemble. What's more, it's ideal for supporting the weight of a shelf and its contents – it resists twisting, and it looks much more professional than the metal brackets or other fittings which can do the same job.

Such fittings are readily available and often easy to use, but if your design is modern, they'll tend to spoil its clean lines; and if it's traditional, they'll naturally be inappropriate. They will never give the unobtrusive and craftsmanlike finish which you can obtain from carefully designed and made housing joints.

Types of housing joint
There are a few variations, and each has its own purpose. A 'stopped' housing joint is completely invisible; you can't see the connection between shelf and upright at all, because (unlike the basic 'through' housing joint) its housing stops about 20mm (3/4in) short of the front of the upright. You can also cut out a step in the front of the shelf to allow it to fit flush with the upright just as in a through housing joint, and so get the best of both worlds.

A 'barefaced' housing joint is a little more complicated. You still slot the shelf into the upright – but this time you also cut away a step or 'rebate' across the end of the shelf to form a sort of tongue (with one 'bare face'). So the housing into which it fits has to be correspondingly narrower than the shelf thickness. This type of joint is used at corners, where you can't cut an ordinary housing; and its stepped shape helps to keep the structure rigid. It can also be used with the rebate in the upright where you want unbroken woodgrain across the top surface of the horizontal.

Strongest of all is the dovetail housing joint. For this one, the housing has sloping (undercut) sides, and the end of the shelf is shaped to fit – which means it can't be pulled out sideways. This is an attraction where you expect furniture to come in for rough treatment, (eg, being dragged across the floor). However, it's tricky to cut without power-tool assistance, and in practice the do-it-yourselfer will seldom find it really necessary.

It's worth saying here that even the best-made housing joint is only as strong as the shelf. If you're planning shelf storage, you have to think about what the shelf is made of, its thickness, its length and how much weight you want it to carry. A thin shelf bends easily, and it's unwise to try to span a gap of more than 1,200mm (4ft), at the very most, without some support in the middle. Even then, a full load of books will cause sagging.

Making a housing joint
Even with hand tools, housing joints are among the easiest to cut. For a basic through housing joint, you don't need to touch the shelf at all. You just mark out the position of the housing in the upright, cut down the housing sides with a tenon saw, and pare

away the waste with a chisel and wooden mallet (see pages 123–125 for details). The only difficulty, as in all carpentry, is to make sure that your marking, sawing and chiselling are always careful and accurate.

A stopped housing takes a little longer to cut, but only because you need to hollow out its stopped end first, to make sawing easier. You may also need to remove a small notch or 'shoulder' from the shelf, which is easily done with a tenon saw and perhaps a chisel too.

For a barefaced housing joint, the housing is cut in the same way as a basic housing. Cutting the rebate in the shelf is another job for tenon saw and chisel.

Using power tools
A power router is an integral tool with a chuck that accepts a wide range of special bits for cutting grooves and mouldings quickly and accurately. It saves a lot of time when making housing joints, and eliminates both sawing and chiselling. Or you can use a circular saw, setting it for a very shallow cut and running it across the upright where you want the housing to be – first clamping on a batten to act as a guide. Because the saw-

BASIC HOUSING JOINT

1 Use your knife and try-square to square a mark across the inner face of the upright where the top of the shelf is to go.

3 Mark this distance on the upright, working down from the first line to give the housing width; square the mark across in pencil only.

5 Use a rule to set your marking gauge to 1/3 the thickness of the upright, which is the usual depth of a housing for a strong and rigid joint.

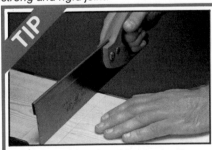

7 When cutting the sides to depth, cramp on a batten to prevent the saw from wandering sideways.

2 Measure up the full shelf thickness with a carpenter's rule or a flexible tape measure. As always, try for absolute accuracy.

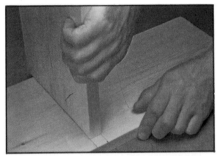

4 Place the shelf between the two lines to check them. If necessary, re-draw the second. When that's right, go over it with knife and try-square.

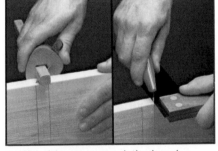

6 With the gauge, mark the housing depth on the upright's edges. Then use a knife to square the marks for the housing sides to depth across the edges.

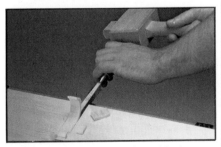

8 Remove the waste with a chisel, working from both ends on long housings. Pare along the sides if necessary to clean them up.

Jem Grischotti

Ready Reference

WHICH HOUSING GOES WHERE

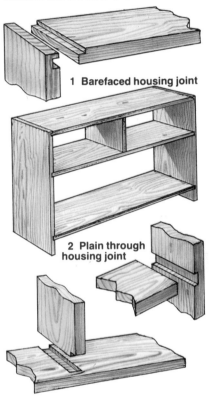

1 Barefaced housing joint

2 Plain through housing joint

3 Stopped housing joint with shoulder

THE TOOLS YOU'LL NEED

A tenon saw: for cutting the sides of housings, rebates and shoulders.
A bevel-edged chisel: the same width as the housing, plus a wooden mallet.
A hand router: is useful for smoothing the bottom of the housing.
Marking gauge, knife, pencil and try-square: for accurate setting-out.

POWER TOOL OPTIONS

A power router: ideal for cutting all types of housing quickly and easily.

A circular saw will cut an ordinary housing very well – but you'll need to make several passes with it across the timber to cut the housing.

STOPPED HOUSING WITH SHOULDER

1 After marking out the housing on the upright (except on the front edge), mark where it stops, about 19-25mm (3/4-1in) inside the front edge.

2 With the marking gauge still at the same setting, mark the shoulder depth across the shelf end and a little way down each of its faces.

3 Set the gauge to 1/3 the thickness of the upright, and mark the housing depth on its back edge only. Bring the side marks down to meet it.

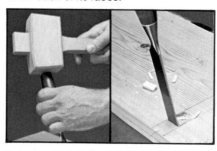

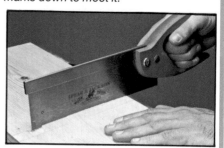

4 Use the same setting to mark the shoulder width on the front edge and both faces of the shelf, meeting the marks you've made for the depth.

5 Roughly chisel out the first 25mm (1in) or so of the stopped end of the housing – across the grain and up to the sides, then back towards the end.

6 Cut the sides of the housing with a tenon saw. You'll need to use short careful strokes so as not to bang against its inner end.

7 Clear out the housing with a mallet and chisel, inching forwards at an angle if the chisel won't reach all the way in when held flat.

8 Saw down into the front edge of the shelf until you reach the marked depth of the shoulder, being careful not to overshoot.

9 Chisel into the endgrain to remove the waste and complete the shoulder; or you can use a saw – but again, don't cut too deep.

blade is narrower than the housing you're cutting out, you'll need to make several parallel, overlapping cuts.

Putting it together
When you assemble the joint before glueing, to see if it fits, you may think that it's too tight and you need to pare away wood from the housing or the shelf.

But be sure not to overdo this – and be careful where you remove it from. A shaving off the wrong place can allow the end of the shelf to rise or fall so that it's no longer level.

If, on the other hand, the joint turns out to be very loose, you'll need thin slivers of wood or veneer to pack it out.

For maximum tightness, strength and squareness, a housing joint should really be glued, then cramped together while the adhesive sets. Where a shelf or shelves fit between a pair of uprights, as usually happens, your best plan is to glue and cramp the whole structure up at once, so as to get it all square in one go. Use sash cramps (long bars of steel with two adjustable jaws) and simply place the structure between them, with the shelf running along their length, and blocks of scrap wood positioned on the outside of the uprights to protect them from the pressure of the jaws. You'll probably have to borrow or hire the sash-cramps. When using them, you need to

check the structure constantly for squareness, as cramping, unless done correctly, can cause distortion.

You can always reinforce a housing joint by nailing through the outside of the upright and into the endgrain of the shelf, concealing the heads by punching them in and plugging the holes with wood filler.

On the whole, screws are best avoided, since they grip badly in endgrain; but for a chipboard shelf you can use special chipboard screws – or ordinary wood screws each driven into a special plastic plug, or 'bush', which is pressed into a pre-drilled hole in the end of the shelf. You can disguise screwheads with plastic covers.

BAREFACED HOUSING JOINT

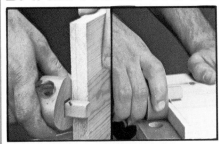

1 At ⅓ the shelf thickness, mark the rebate depth along its end and across its edges; likewise mark across the upright's edges and inner face.

2 At ⅓ the upright thickness (very likely the same as the shelf thickness), mark your rebate width across the top face and both edges of the shelf.

3 Saw out the rebate depth across the shelf with a tenon saw, using careful strokes to keep it the right side of the line.

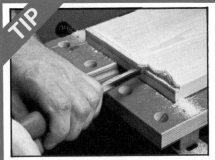

4 Chisel out the rebate width along the endgrain. You'll get a more accurate result if you do it in several goes rather than all at once.

5 Measure the full shelf thickness and set your marking gauge to that measurement by holding it against the rule.

6 Pressing the gauge against the end of the upright, mark across its face and edges where the bottom of the shelf will be positioned.

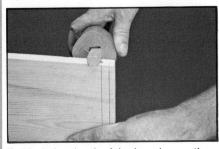

7 Mark the depth of the housing on the back edge of the upright, only ⅓ of the way across: any further and you'll weaken the joint.

8 Cut the housing just like the basic one, taking care not to break off the end. After glueing, nail through into the tongue for extra rigidity.

Ready Reference

TIPS FOR BETTER HOUSINGS
- a cramped-on batten is useful as a saw guide
- a third saw-cut down the centre of a wide housing will help the removal of waste

- for short housings in narrow wood, set the piece on edge and chisel vertically for greater accuracy

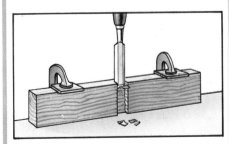

- use a rule or try-square to check that the housing has a level bottom

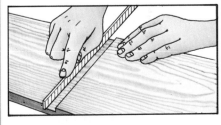

- for pairs of uprights, use the housings in the first to mark out those in the second; this will ensure a level shelf

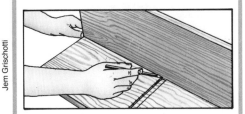

- a chipboard shelf can be secured with chipboard screws driven into special plastic plugs.

Jem Grischotti

HOME
CARPENTRY

Basic Projects

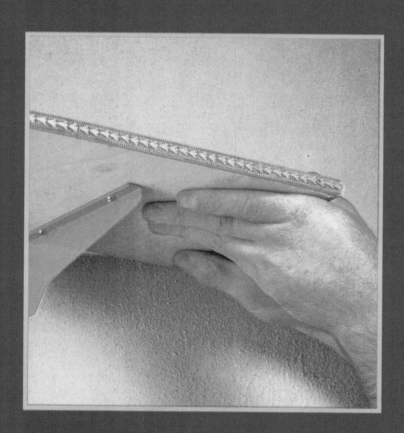

HANGING A DOOR

Ill-fitting doors are irritating to use, ungainly to look at, and ineffective at keeping out draughts. Knowing how to adjust the frame, straighten the door, or, if need be, how to replace it entirely, may sound complicated. In fact, the techniques required – planing, chiselling and sawing – are nothing more than basic carpentry.

Replacing old doors that squeak, stick or let in draughts is one of the quickest ways of improving your home. And whether you're changing a bedroom door, cupboard door or front door, large or small, the techniques are the same. They involve nothing more complex than planing, chiselling and sawing.

Recently there has been greater awareness of how doors can make or mar a house, and there are now many different styles to choose from. There are, however, only two basic types for rooms or entrances to houses: the traditional panelled door, and the flush door. Though plain, the flush offers a wide choice of finishes – including adding your own mouldings to make up panels!

Doors described as external are thicker, heavier and tougher, more resistant to weather and burglars. Unless you want to soundproof a room, you'll only waste money if you buy an external door for use inside the house where a lighter one will do – and you might even damage a light partition wall by overloading it with a door that's too heavy.

Sometimes local building regulations insist on a fire-resistant internal door: normally where it opens onto the stairwell of a modern three-storey building (or an old two-storey one with a loft conversion), and where it separates your home from a built-on garage. If you have to put these in you have to make adjustments to the frame and change the hinges as well.

Look first at the frame

Before you do anything at all about a new door, you should take a long hard look at the frame in which you intend hanging it. If it's badly damaged or out of square by more than 25mm (1in) you should consider replacing it altogether. This is not as difficult as it sounds, for if you shop around you can find sections of framing, and even complete frames, ready shaped to blend with every style and accommodate every type of door.

On the other hand, the frame may only need surface blemishes repaired to be in good enough shape to take the new door. Taking off the old door may prove tricky if the screws are stuck fast; but, once it's done,

you can make good the frame with wood or cellulose filler so it will look as good as new when painted. It makes life easier if you can reuse the old hinge recesses, but if they're too chewed-up you'll need to pin and glue in bits of wood (as with other large holes) before filling them.

You may have to renew the doorstop – (draught-excluder) the part which the front of the door actually hits when it closes – if the new door is a different thickness from the old or won't lie flush with the outside frame. You can buy suitable planed wood in various thicknesses. If the old doorstop isn't

removable (it may be made all in one with the frame) you'll need to add another piece, flush with it, before attaching a new doorstop bead. This should only be lightly nailed until the door is hung, for its position may have to be altered.

The hanging process

Even once you've got the frame right, and you've chosen your new door for the exact size of opening, it may still not quite fit. This could mean offering it up to the door-frame, marking it with a pencil and planing or sawing it down to make adjustments. As this can be time-consuming, and demanding on the arms, it's best to work on it next to the place where it'll be hung. Panel doors, especially, are heavy; and another pair of hands can be very useful at strategic points – for example, when the hinges need to be held exactly in the right place to be screwed in.

Chocks and wedges are also very handy for holding the door steady when planing and chiselling, and for supporting the door in the opening when you're marking it so the clearance is right above and below. Luckily these are made from scraps you'll probably have around – small pieces of 3mm (1/8in) hardboard, for example, can be stacked to give the right thickness for the space that should be above and below the door.

Jem Grischotti: Sapele plywood door: W H Newson

HANGING A DOOR

1 To check the height, wedge the door against the hinge side of the frame using an offcut that gives the correct clearance at the bottom.

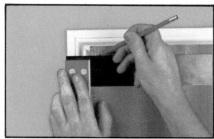

2 Mark the area that has to be removed using a try-square for accuracy, then saw off. On a panel door, take equal amounts from top and bottom.

3 To check the width, offer the door to the frame against the hinge side and wedge with offcuts that give the correct clearance top and bottom.

4 Hold the door steady when planing: saw and chisel a housing in scrap wood and press in a wedge.

5 On the latch edge hold your finger under the side of the plane to prevent it rocking. On top and bottom, plane inwards so end grain doesn't splinter.

6 When the door hangs properly, put in the handle. Rub the tongue with chalk, then open and shut it till the frame is marked with keep plate's position.

Jem Grischotti

Plane: Stanley Tools

Altering dimensions

Enlarging a door, by adding a strip of wood, carries the risk both that it will be too obvious and that it will eventually fall off. But the job can be tackled fairly easily if you first plane the edge of the door straight – keeping your finger at the side of the plane will prevent it falling off the narrow surface. Next, cut your strip to length and plane it to the exact extra size you require – making sure it's a little proud of the door thickness on both sides. Glue and nail it on, and lastly plane it flush with the door face so that when painted it makes an inconspicuous join.

More commonly, however, you'll have to make your door smaller. To take off large amounts you'll need a ripsaw or a powered circular saw; guide it along a batten firmly cramped to the door. After sawing, plane the edge smooth.

Alterations like this are relatively easy on panel doors – but remember to saw similar amounts off both opposite edges to avoid lopsidedness, and be careful not to destroy the joints. A flush door, unless the core is solid, is a very different proposition. A cellular core (made of wood strips laminated together or a honeycomb of kraft paper), a narrow timber frame, and the hardboard or plywood faces are all there to

make the door lightweight. And you risk mutilating any or all of them if you try to alter the width (the height's all right, for you can make a new piece to glue and nail in at the top or bottom if you need to).

So, if you need to take off more than a little, buy a panel door. If you must have a flush door and you can't get one that fits or is about 10mm (³⁄₈in) larger, buy one slightly undersize and add lippings all round to make up the extra height and width.

A fitting finish

Once the door fits the frame you can add the hinges. If you're re-using the existing hinge recesses in the frame, support the door in the opening parallel to the upright and mark on it where their tops and bottoms are. If you're cutting new ones, mark their positions on both door and frame.

Remove the door and, using a try-square and marking-gauge, mark out all new recesses – a hinge should fit flush with both the door edge and the edge of the frame. Carefully chisel out the recess and screw one side of the hinges to the door, checking that they lie neatly in place.

The standard steel or brass butt hinges you need can be bought anywhere. Another option is self-closing 'rising butts' which will

carry the door clear of the floorcovering as it opens, and enable it to be lifted off if necessary without unscrewing them – good if you're redecorating. If the door's not going to have a lot of weight put on it (eg, on a cupboard) light and shorter hinges are best. Choose those that can be surface-mounted and you won't have to chisel out recesses.

Support the door in position again, and fix the hinges to the frame with one screw each. See whether the door swings and closes properly; if not, you can take it off again and make various adjustments to the way the hinges sit in the frame.

The final step is to fill any defects, to sand the door down, and to paint or varnish it. On an external door in particular, make sure you include the top and bottom edges in your treatment (the bottom will have to be dealt with before the door is hung) so that damp cannot penetrate and swell or rot the door.

Hinges should not be painted as this can interfere with the pivot action – and the constant friction of the door will cause the paint to chip anyway. If made of ferrous metal, they can rust, so they should either be primed with a metal or rust-inhibitor primer or coated with a clear lacquer. A non-ferrous metal like brass won't rust but it can tarnish, so clear lacquer is a good idea in this case.

PUTTING ON THE HINGES

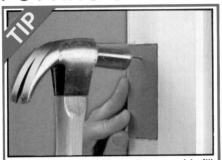

1 If old hinge positions are unusable fill in with 3mm (⅛in) hardboard or ply. Nail in place, fill with wood filler.

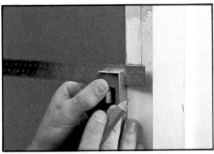

2 Mark up the new hinge positions on the frame using a combination square to get the width measurement right.

3 Make the first shallow cut with the chisel bevel down. Turn it bevel up to smooth the recess.

4 Wedge the cut-to-fit door in the frame with correct clearance at side, top and bottom. Mark hinge positions.

5 With the door held in the block cramp, use a marking gauge, then a try-square to mark recesses.

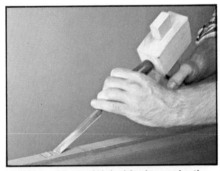

6 Use a 25mm (1in) chisel to make the recess (the hinge must lie flush). Drill holes, screw hinges to door.

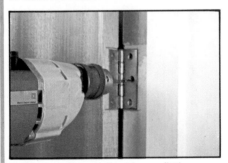

7 Wedge door so the hinges fit the recesses in the frame. Mark, then drill the central holes only.

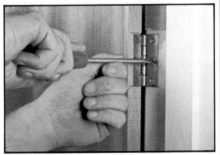

8 Put screws in central holes, then check that the door closes properly. Adjust if necessary, add other screws.

Ready Reference

TIPS: REMOVING OLD SCREWS
● use a screwdriver that fits the slot exactly (scrape out any paint first)
● if the slot is damaged make a new one with a hacksaw at right-angles to the old
● if the screw won't budge put the screwdriver in the slot and tap it with a hammer or mallet; or heat the screw with a blow-torch, then leave to cool and contract before trying to remove
● the last resort is to drill out the screw using a power drill.

PROBLEM CHECKLIST
If the door swings open or closed by itself the hinges are not taking the weight equally. To do this they must be vertically above each other, so you'll have to move one of them either backwards or forwards across the frame.

If the door sticks at the lock edge you can either deepen the hinge recesses in the frame or shave a little off the lock edge.

If the door springs open when you shut it the hinge recesses are too deep. Pack the back of the hinge with a piece of cardboard cut to the shape of the recess.

If the bottom of the door isn't parallel with the floor glue and pin on a wedge-shaped lipping. When planed flush and painted it should not be seen.

Remember to make all the adjustments while each hinge is held only by its central screw. Only when the door fits well should you drive in the rest.

Jem Grischotti

FITTING FRONT DOOR FURNITURE

A door looks naked without the right fittings. These make it attractive, and help it do its job. Installing them requires few special skills – just some careful planning and accurate workmanship.

When you buy a door, it comes without 'furniture' – as tradesmen call handles, letter plates, street numbers, knockers and the rest. You'll have to obtain and fit these yourself; there is an immense variety of styles available.

But the most important items, though they don't strictly come under the same heading, are of course locks and latches. First of all, let's run over the most important difference between the two. A latch has a bolt which is kept closed – ie, protruding – by a spring. It's opened by turning a handle, but closes again the instant this is released. A lock, on the other hand, has no spring, and is both opened and closed by a key or handle, or both.

A mortise lock (or latch) is so called because it fits into a deep mortise which you cut in the edge of the door. This far-from-impossible task is the most demanding you're likely to face when fitting out a door: if you can tackle it successfully, you should certainly be equal to the others.

It involves carefully marking the position of the mortise, drilling out the bulk of the waste to the right depth, cleaning up the hole with chisels, and chiselling a larger shallow recess to take the 'forend' of the lock or latch (plus the faceplate which is screwed over it).

You'll also need to cut a hole for the handle spindle, or for the key – drilling in either case, and elongating the keyhole with a padsaw. In the case of a 'sashlock', which combines a lock with a latch, you'll need both these holes.

Moreover, some types of mortise lock have a cylinder mechanism (round, oval or 'dual-profile' – pear-shaped) which passes through the door, so you need a hole for that instead of a keyhole. An ordinary round cylinder needs a sizeable hole, which – like a mortise – will require a bit and brace, or a spade bit in a power drill. Pear-shaped and oval holes can also be made with twist bits; enlarge them with a padsaw or chisel.

The body of a rim lock (or latch), on the other hand, is screwed to the inside of the door. It doesn't require a separate hole for a key or handle. But all except the cheapest rim locks have a cylinder mechanism, which again needs a hole through the door face.

Choosing and fitting locks and latches

For internal doors, a mortise latch – or even just a catch – is usually enough, and it's unobtrusive. An external door needs a latch, too, so you can open it from inside without a key. But, of course, it also needs at least one lock.

In many homes, it carries a cylinder lock called a 'nightlatch', which is halfway to being a latch. A rim nightlatch (the usual type) opens from inside with an integral handle as well as from outside with a key.

Though sprung, it can be retained in the open or closed position with a locking knob on the inside called a snib. However, a nightlatch isn't secure unless it's a 'deadlatch': that is, unless the bolt can be 'deadlocked' immovably in the closed position from outside. This is either done with a key – a procedure usually known as double-locking – or else happens automatically as you close the door. Often the handle can be deadlocked too.

A nightlatch, therefore, should be accompanied by a good mortise lock – preferably a five-lever model.

All locks and latches also have a part which goes on the door jamb – see *Ready Reference*. In the case of mortise fittings, it's a 'striking plate' (usually flat, with a rectangular hole in the centre) which is screwed into a recess cut to fit. More secure types have a sort of box on the plate, which is mortised

into the timber of the door frame. Rim fittings have a 'staple' or 'keep', which again incorporates a box for the tongue, and is usually partly recessed. In both cases, you fit these components after the main lock – closing the door and using the lock itself to mark the right position on the jamb with the aid of a square.

Apart from security and convenience, there's one thing to bear in mind when choosing locks and latches: the construction of the door they are fitted to. A panel door should present no problem unless its stiles (uprights) are exceptionally narrow, in which case you need a special narrow-stile lock or latch. It's wise, too, not to cut mortises in or near timber joints.

A flush door, unless it's solid throughout, will have at least one solid 'lock block' in its largely hollow core – the position or positions of which should be indicated on the door itself. For a secure fixing, it's important that the lock or latch should be sited there and nowhere else.

Fitting a letterplate

Apart from locks and latches, the only item of door furniture whose installation could remotely be described as complicated is a letterplate.

This consists of a metal surround with a hinged and sometimes sprung flap to cover the hole, plus maybe a knocker and/or a handle. Its siting demands some thought.

On a flush door, it too will have to be placed over a special block. A panel door usually affords more choice – but, if there's no rail (cross-member) at a height which is suitable from the point of view of looks and the postman's comfort, you may have to position it vertically.

If the rear of the plate lies flat against the door and the flap opens outwards, your best plan is to position the plate accurately, lift the flap and draw round the inside to give the outline of your intended hole. Otherwise, you'll have to rely on careful measurement to determine the hole's size and position.

If you have a jigsaw with a blade long enough to pass through the door, cutting the hole is straightforward. If not, you'll probably have to resort to a wide, robust chisel and mallet, perhaps after drilling a series of holes closely spaced round the edge. A padsaw is an alternative, but cutting the hole with it will be a long, hard job.

Finish the inside of the hole (and any mortises) in the same way as the rest of the door to stop moisture from penetrating.

The actual fixing of the plate will be via bolts or machine screws which pass through holes drilled right through the door. If these are overlong, shorten them with a junior hacksaw.

A useful accessory for the inside of the door is a letterbox to catch your post – thus protecting it from children, pets and feet, and saving you from stooping.

Other items

Handles are fitted (and usually sold) separately from the mortise latches which they operate, and almost always in pairs. They're simply screwed to the door face in the same way as the escutcheon plates which cover keyholes. A square-sectioned steel spindle, cut to length if necessary with a hacksaw, passes through the door between handles.

For a sashlock, you can use the type of handle which incorporates a keyhole as well.

A common adjunct, especially for internal doors, is a finger-plate – often decorative – which prevents dirty finger-marks on the door itself. It too is screwed on. Knockers and house numbers are bolted, screwed, nailed, self-adhesive or secured by spikes protruding from the back.

A door viewer – the wide-angle lens which enables you to eye callers without their seeing you – comes in two halves, which are simply screwed together through a single pre-drilled hole.

For doors by which you don't leave the house, such as most back doors, bolts are an extra security measure. The mortise bolt, a simple type of mortise lock usually operated by a serrated key, is better than the traditional 'barrel' or 'tower' bolt, which can be more easily forced open.

FITTING A CYLINDER RIM LOCK

1 *Drill a hole for the cylinder after marking its position from the lock's mounting plate, or with a template if one is supplied by the manufacturer.*

2 *Fit the cylinder and 'rose' through the hole, and mark where to cut off the connecting bar (including any extra length required). Cut with a hacksaw.*

3 *Screw on the mounting plate, after marking the screw positions (from the fitting or template) and making pilot holes with a drill or bradawl.*

4 *Insert the cylinder and rose through the hole again, and make sure the connecting bar engages in the slotted pivot in the mounting plate.*

5 *Insert the connecting screws through the mounting plate and into the threaded lugs in the back of the cylinder, and tighten them to hold it in place.*

6 *Screw the main body of the lock to the mounting plate via the screws in the case. Fit the keep to the door jamb.*

FITTING A LEVER MORTISE LOCK

1 Decide the height at which you want the lock to go, place it on its side on the door edge, get it square, and mark the height of the casing.

2 Set a mortise gauge to the thickness of the casing, centre it on the door edge, and score along. Alternatively, use an ordinary marking gauge.

3 Choose a spade or auger bit that matches the thickness of the casing, and use tape to mark on it the lock's depth from the front of the faceplate.

5 Using chisels, turn the row of holes into a clean, oblong mortise. Insert the lock to test the fit, and shave the mortise further if necessary.

6 Insert the lock casing fully into the mortise (being careful that it doesn't jam) and mark all round the fore-end with a sharp pencil.

7 To chisel the recess for the fore-end and faceplate, first make a series of cuts across the grain. Work very carefully while doing this.

9 Position the faceplate and fore-end back to front, to check whether your recess is the right depth. Chisel it a little deeper if necessary.

10 Position the lock accurately against the face of the door, and mark through the keyhole (plus the spindle hole, if there is one) with a bradawl.

11 Drill the hole (or holes) right through the door, and enlarge the keyhole with a padsaw. Fit an escutcheon plate (keyhole plate) over it.

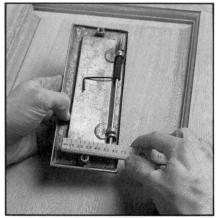

1 *Measure the size of the cutout you'll need to make in the door. It may have to be off-centre – for example, if it must include room for the flap mechanism.*

LETTERPLATES

4 *Drill a row of holes to depth, being sure to stay exactly between your height and thickness marks. At all costs, you must keep the drill vertical.*

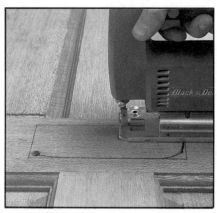

2 *Mark your measured rectangle on the door, drill a hole inside the line, and cut it out – using a jigsaw for speed if you have a long enough blade.*

8 *Chisel vertically along the sides of the recess (gently, so as not to split the timber) and then remove the waste with the chisel bevel-upwards.*

12 *Insert the lock again, position the faceplate and drive in the screws. Sometimes the lock and faceplate each have a separate pair of screws.*

3 *Finish the hole neatly, and cut out recesses for the threaded lugs if necessary. Then drill holes for the bolts, fit the plate and tighten the nuts.*

Ready Reference

DOOR JAMB FIXINGS

For a **mortise** fitting: extend the bolt (if any), push the door to, and mark where each tongue comes on the frame (A). Then square the marks across to the doorstop, position the striking plate, mark round it, and chisel a shallow recess plus one or two mortises (B). Screw the plate on.

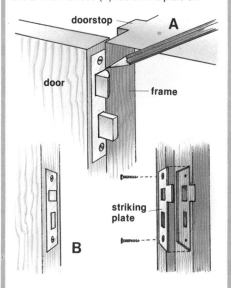

For a **rim** fitting: mark the frame opposite the edges of the case (C). Position the keep, mark round it, chisel a recess and screw it on (D).

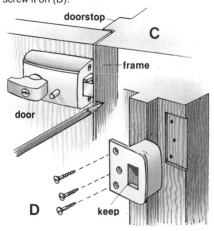

TIP: BEWARE 'HANDING'

Latches (and some handles) only fit one way round. Before buying, know which 'hand' you want. A door that's hinged on your **left** and opens towards you ('anti-clockwise closing') takes a **left-hand** latch with a **left-hand** handle on your side, and a right-hand latch and handle on the other.

SHELVING: THE BASICS

There are lots of ways of putting up shelves. Some systems are fixed, others adjustable – the choice is yours. Here's how both types work, and how to get the best from each.

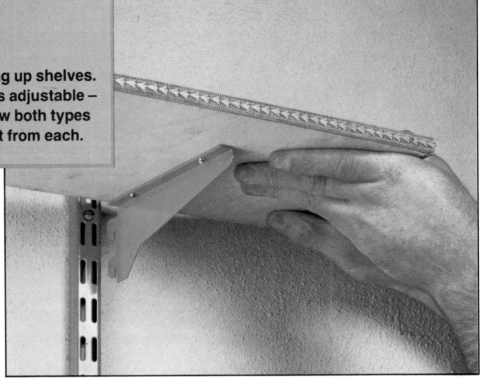

Deciding how much shelving you'll need is always tricky – because, the more shelves you have, the more you'll find to go on them! So it's always wise to add an extra 10 per cent to the specification when you start planning.

Think carefully about what you want to store and display, and try to categorise it by size and weight. The size part is fairly easy. Concentrate first on the depth (from front to back) and length; a collection of paperback books, for instance, might need 3.5m (10ft) of 150mm (6in) deep shelves. Having the shelves a bit deeper than you really need is always worthwhile, and if you add 10 per cent the length should look after itself.

Next, the heights in each grouping will tell you roughly how far apart the shelves must be. Most paperbacks are 175mm (7in) high – allow an extra 25mm (1in) for easy access and removal.

Finally, weight. The trouble here is that, even if you weigh what you'll be storing, you can't translate the result into shelf, bracket and fixing materials or sizes. Instead, think in terms of light, moderately heavy and very heavy. Items such as the TV and stereo, while not especially weighty, are best treated as very heavy, because it would be nothing short of disastrous if a shelf did give way under them!

Shelf design

Where you put the shelves affects the amount of storage you can gain, how you build them, and the overall look of the room itself. This last may not be important in a workshop, for instance, but in a living room, where the shelves may well be the focal point, a bad decision can be serious.

The obvious spot for shelving is against a continuous wall. This offers most scope to arrange the shelves in an interesting and attractive way. An alcove is another possibility. Shelving here is neat, and easily erected; it is a very good way of using an otherwise awkward bit of space. A corner has similar advantages if you make triangular shelves to fit – though they're really only suitable for displaying plants or favourite ornaments.

Planning it out

If appearance matters and you're putting up a lot of shelves, a good way to plan is by making a scale drawing of the whole scheme to see how it looks. Then check for detail. If your TV has an indoor aerial, make sure you have room to adjust it. With stereo systems, ensure the shelf is deep enough to take all the wiring spaghetti at the back. And do think about the heights of the shelves from the floor (see *Ready Reference*).

Finally, make sure you provide adequate support for the shelves and the weight they'll be carrying. There is no very precise method of gauging this, but you won't go wrong if you remember that for most household storage a shelf needs support at least every 750mm (30in) along its length. This will usually be enough even with chipboard, which is the weakest of shelving materials. But bowing may still be a problem, so for items in the 'very heavy' category it's advisable to increase the number of supports by reducing the space between them.

Which material?

Chipboard is usually the most economical material, and if properly supported is strong enough for most shelving It can be fairly attractive, too, since you can choose a type with a decorative wood veneer or plastic finish. These come in a variety of widths – most of them designed with shelving in mind.

Natural timber, though more costly and sometimes prone to warping, is an obvious alternative. You may have difficulty obtaining some timber in boards over 225mm (9in) wide, but narrower widths are readily available. For wider shelves, another way is to make up the shelf width from narrower pieces. An easy method is to leave gaps between the lengths and brace them with others which run from front to back on the underside, forming a slatted shelf.

Blockboard and plywood are also worth considering when it comes to building shelving. They are both a lot stronger than chipboard and have a more attractive surface which can be painted or varnished without trouble. However, in the thickness you need at least 12mm (½in) – plywood is relatively expensive; blockboard is cheaper, and chipboard cheaper still. All these man-made boards need to have their edges disguised to give a clean finish. An easy yet effective way to do this is just to glue and pin on strips of timber moulding or 'beading'. Also remember that the cheapest way to buy any of these boards is in large sheets (approximately 2.4m x 1.2m/8ft x 4ft), so it's most economical to plan your shelves in lengths and widths than can be cut from a standard size sheet.

Shelves needn't be solid, though. If you want them extra-thick, for appearance or strength, you can make them up from a timber frame covered with a thin sheet material. Hardboard is cheap, but thin plywood gives a more attractive edge; alternatively use a timber edging strip.

BRACKET SHELVING

1 *If your shelves are of man-made board, a good way to give them neat edges is to pin on decorative 'beading', mitred at the corners.*

2 *Begin by screwing the shorter arm of the bracket to the shelf. Position it squarely and in such a way that the shelf will lie snugly against the wall.*

3 *Using a spirit level as a guide, mark a pencil line along the wall at the height where you want the top of the shelf to be positioned.*

4 *Hold the shelf, complete with brackets, against this line, and mark with a pencil through the screw holes in the brackets, so you know where to drill.*

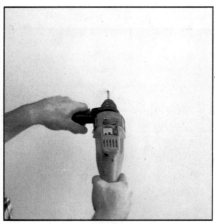

5 *Drill holes in the wall with a power drill, using a masonry bit if necessary, and being sure to keep the drill straight. Then insert plastic plugs.*

6 *Hold the shelf in position, insert one screw in each bracket and tighten it halfway; then insert the others and tighten the whole lot up.*

Ready Reference

PLANNING SHELVES

When you design storage, plan ahead and think about *how* you're going to use it.

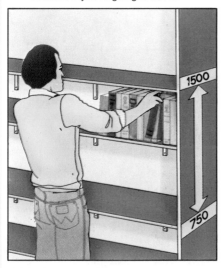

Height. Keep everyday items well within reach. That means between 750 and 1500mm (30 and 60in) off the ground.
Depth. Shelves that are deepest (from front to back) should be lower, so you can see and reach to the back.
Spacing. An inch or two over the actual height of the objects means you can get your hand in more easily.

HOW TO SPACE BRACKETS

Space brackets according to the shelf thickness. Heavy loads (left) need closer brackets than light loads (right).

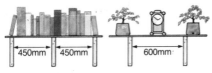

450mm   450mm   600mm

12mm (½in) chipboard

600mm   750mm

12mm (½in) plywood
19mm (¾in) chipboard

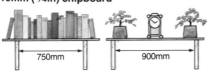

750mm   900mm

19mm (¾in) plywood

ADJUSTABLE SHELVING

1 Metal uprights come in a range of sizes, but occasionally they may need shortening. If so, you can easily cut them down with a hacksaw.

2 After using your level to mark the height for the tops of the uprights, measure along it and mark out the spacings between them.

3 Hold each of the uprights with its top at the right height, and mark through it onto the wall for the position of the uppermost screw hole only.

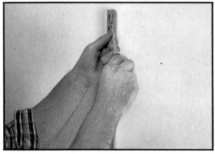

4 Remove the upright, drill the hole and plug it if necessary. Then replace the upright, and fit the screw – but don't tighten it completely.

5 With the upright loose, hold a level against it and adjust it till it's vertical. Then mark through it for the other screw positions.

6 Hold the upright aside and drill the other holes. Plug them, insert the screws and tighten them all up – not forgetting the topmost one.

7 Now you can screw the bracket to the shelf, aligning it correctly and taking particular care over how it lines up at the back edge.

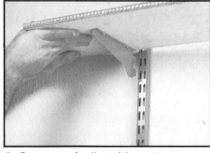

8 One type of adjustable system uses brackets with lugs at the back. It's easiest to let these lugs project behind the shelf when screwing on brackets.

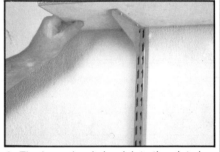

9 The lugs simply hook into the slots in the uprights. Changing the shelf height is just a matter of unhooking them and moving them up or down.

10 If you want the back edge of the shelf right against the wall, notch it with a tenon saw and chisel to fit round the upright. Inset the bracket on the shelf.

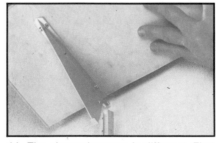

11 The channel system is different. First of all, you engage the bracket's upper lug in the channel and slide it down, keeping the lower one clear.

12 When you reach the position you want, level the shelf and the bracket, so as to slide its lower lug into one of the pairs of slots down the upright.

Fixing shelves

The simplest method of fixing shelves is directly to the wall, using brackets. L-shaped metal brackets of various sizes and designs are available everywhere – some plain and functional, some with attractive lacquered or enamelled finishes. It's just a question of choosing ones about 25mm (1in) less than the shelf depth, spacing them the right distance apart and screwing them to both shelf and wall.

If you're filling up your shelves with books, the support brackets won't be seen. But if you're using the shelves for ornaments, the brackets will be visible, so choose a style that blends. Alternatively, you can make up your own brackets from two pieces of timber butt-jointed into an L shape and braced with a diagonal strut or triangular block.

The fixing technique is the same either way. First you draw a line on the wall where the shelf is to go, using a spirit level. Next, fix the brackets to the shelf and put the whole assembly up against the line. Mark on to the wall through the pre-drilled screw holes in the brackets; then take the shelf away and drill holes in the wall, filling each with a plastic plug. Lastly, drive in one screw through each bracket; then insert the rest and tighten them all up.

Because the accuracy of this method relies largely on your ability to hold the shelf level against your line, you may find it easier to work the other way round. By fixing the brackets to the wall along the guide line, you can then drop the shelf into place and screw up into it through the brackets. This works, but you must position the brackets with great care, and avoid squeezing them out of position as you screw them into the wall. That isn't always easy. For one thing, many brackets don't have arms which meet at a neat right angle. They curve slightly, which makes it hard to align the top of the shelf-bearing arm with the line on the wall.

Making a firm fixing

Remember that the strength of all brackets depends partly on the length of their arms (particularly the one fixed to the wall) and partly on the strength of your fixing into the wall. The longer the wall arm in proportion to the shelf arm, the better; but it's also important to use adequate screws – 38mm (1½in) No 8s or 10s should do – and to plug the wall properly. In a hollow partition wall you really must make sure you secure the brackets to the wall's wooden framework and not just to the cladding. Even if you use plasterboard plugs or similar devices, a lot of weight on the shelf will cause the brackets to come away from the cladding and possibly damage the wall.

Of course, there is a limit to how much weight the brackets themselves will take.

Under very wide shelves they may bend. With shelves that have heavy items regularly taken off and dumped back on, and shelves used as desk-tops, worktops and the like, the movement can eventually work the fixings loose. In such cases it's best to opt for what's called a cantilevered shelf bracket. Part of this is set into the masonry to give a very strong fixing indeed. Details of its installation vary from brand to brand, but you should get instructions when you buy.

Alcove shelving

All proprietary brackets are expensive. However, for alcove shelving there's a much cheaper alternative, and that is to use battens screwed to the wall. All you do is fix a 50 x 25mm (2 x 1in) piece of softwood along the back of the alcove, using screws driven into plastic plugs at roughly 450mm (18in) centres. Then screw similar ones to the side walls, making sure that they line up with the first. In both cases, getting the battens absolutely level is vital. In fact, it's best to start by drawing guidelines using a spirit level as a straight edge.

A front 'rail' is advisable where the shelf spans a wide alcove and has to carry a lot of weight. But there's a limit to what you can do. With a 50 x 25mm (2 x 1in) front rail and battens, all on edge, 1.5m (5ft) is the safe maximum width.

A front rail has another advantage because, as well as giving man-made boards a respectably thick and natural look, it also hides the ends of the side battens. So does stopping them short of the shelf's front edge and cutting the ends at an angle. The shelf can be screwed or even just nailed to the battens to complete the job.

Movable shelves

Unfortunately, both brackets and battens have one big drawback: once they're fixed, they're permanent. So you might consider an adjustable shelving system which gives you the chance to move shelves up and down. Such systems consist of uprights, screwed to the wall, and brackets which slot into them at almost any point down the length.

There are two main types. In one, brackets locate in vertical slots in the uprights. The other has a continuous channel down each upright. You can slide brackets along it and lock them at any point along the way, where they stay put largely because of the weight of the shelf. With both types, brackets come in standard sizes suitable for shelf widths, and there's a choice of upright lengths to fulfil most needs.

Many proprietary shelving systems of this sort include a number of accessories to make them more versatile. These include book ends, shelf clips and even light fittings.

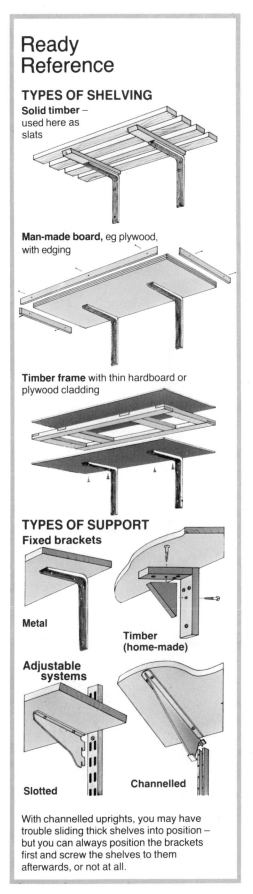

Ready Reference

TYPES OF SHELVING

Solid timber – used here as slats

Man-made board, eg plywood, with edging

Timber frame with thin hardboard or plywood cladding

TYPES OF SUPPORT

Fixed brackets

Metal

Timber (home-made)

Adjustable systems

Slotted

Channelled

With channelled uprights, you may have trouble sliding thick shelves into position – but you can always position the brackets first and screw the shelves to them afterwards, or not at all.

HOME DECORATING

Painting and Wallpapering

PAINTING WALLS AND CEILINGS

The quickest and cheapest way to transform a room is to paint the walls and ceiling. But, for a successful result, you have to prepare the surfaces properly and use the correct painting techniques.

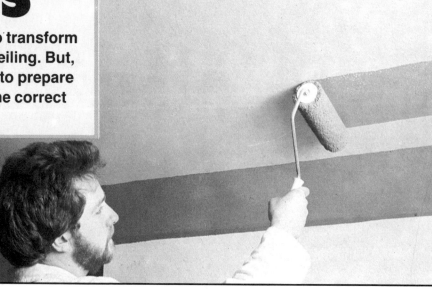

Dulux Russet over Dulux Cameo

Paint is the most popular material used to protect and decorate walls and ceilings in the home. Whereas many people hesitate before hanging wallpaper or sticking more permanent wall and ceiling coverings in place, few would worry about wielding a paint brush for the first time.

One of the chief advantages of painting a room is that it doesn't take much time; large areas can be given two or even three coats of emulsion paint in a day. The paints now available are hardwearing and totally unlike earlier distemper and water paints. They are easy to apply by brush, roller or pad and can be safely washed at frequent intervals to keep them looking fresh.

Any drawbacks are usually caused by faults in the wall or ceiling surface, rather than by the paints. A standard paint alone cannot cover up defects in the same way that some other wallcoverings can, so a surface which is to be painted usually needs more careful preparation than one which is to be papered.

The majority of walls and ceilings are plastered and this type of surface, when in sound condition, is ideal as a base for emulsion and other paints. But it is not the only surface finish you are likely to come across.

Previous occupiers of the house may well have covered the walls with a decorative paper and even painted on top of that. At the very worst there may be several layers of paper and paint, making it very difficult to achieve a smooth paint surface. In this situation it is invariably better to strip the surface completely down to the plaster and to start again from scratch.

This does not mean that no paper should be overpainted. Certain types such as plain white relief wallcoverings and woodchips are intended to be so treated, and actually look 'softer' after one or two redecorations. In short, most wall or ceiling surfaces you are likely to encounter will be paintable. All you have to do is select the right paint for the job and get the surface into as good a condition as possible.

Choosing paints

Vinyl emulsion paints are the most commonly used types of paint for painting walls and ceilings. They are easy to apply and come in a wide range of colours. You will usually have a choice of three finishes: matt, silk, or gloss.

There are also textured paints which are increasing in popularity, particularly for ceiling use. These are vinyl emulsion paints with added 'body' so they can be applied more thickly and then given a decorative textured finish.

Oil-based eggshell paints can be used where a more durable surface is needed or where you want to use the same colour on both walls and woodwork. Resin-based gloss paint is used occasionally also on walls and ceilings, particularly in humid rooms like kitchens and bathrooms.

You should choose paint carefully. The fact that one make is half the price of another may indicate that it has only half the covering power and you would therefore need to apply two coats of the cheaper paint. Also, if you're using white paint, you may find that one brand is noticeably 'whiter' than another.

Tools and equipment

Few specialised tools are needed for wall and ceiling paintwork. If you are content to work with only a brush you will require two sizes: one larger one for the bulk of the work, and a smaller brush for working into corners. It is worth decanting quantities of paint into a paint kettle which is easier to carry around than large heavy cans.

Rollers make the job of painting large areas of wall or ceiling much quicker and also help to achieve a better finish. But you will still need a small brush for working into corners and for dealing with coving, cornices etc.

To prepare a new fibre roller for painting, soak it in soapy water for 2 to 3 hours to get rid of any loose bits of fibre, then roll it out on the wall to dry it off. One point to remember: if you intend using silk vinyl emulsion paint, it's best not to use a roller as this tends to show up as a stippled effect on the silk surface.

Large paint pads will also enable you to cover big expanses of wall or ceiling very quickly. You can use a brush or a small paint pad for work in corners.

Apart from these paint application tools you'll need a variety of other items for preparing the surfaces so they're ready for the paint. The walls must be cleaned, so you'll need washing-down equipment: sponges, cloths, detergent, and a bucket or two of water.

You'll need filler for cracks and a filling knife about 75mm (3in) wide. When any filler is dry it will need to be sanded down, so have some glasspaper ready for wrapping round a cork sanding block. A scraper will also be needed if old wallpaper has to be stripped from the walls.

Finally, because of the height of the walls and ceiling, you'll need access equipment, such as a stepladder, to enable you to reach them safely and comfortably.

Preparing the surface

No painting will be successful until the

PAINTING THE CEILING WITH A ROLLER

1 *Use a brush to paint a strip about 50mm wide round the outside edge of the ceiling; a roller cannot reach right into angles or corners.*

2 *Pour paint into the roller tray; don't put in too much at a time or you risk overloading the roller and splashing paint out of the tray.*

3 *Dip the roller in and pull it back so there is paint at the shallow end of the tray. Push the roller back and forth in the paint at the shallow end.*

4 *Run the roller over the ceiling so there is a band of paint next to the strip of paint you have brushed along the edge of the ceiling.*

5 *Reverse the roller's direction so you join up the two strips of paint into one band. Then finish off by running the roller over the band.*

6 *Now start the next section by running the roller alongside the completed band. Work your way round the ceiling in bands.*

Ready Reference

LINING WALL SURFACES
You can use lining paper to do the same job for paint as it does for wallpapers, covering minor cracks and defects on the wall or ceiling and providing a smooth surface for painting.

TIP: SEAL STRONG COLOURS
Wallcoverings with strong colourings, and particularly those tinted with metallic inks, will almost certainly show through the new paint. To prevent this they should be stripped off, or sealed with special aluminium spirit-based sealer.

FILLING HAIRLINE CRACKS
You may not be able to push enough filler into hairline cracks to ensure a good bond:
● it is often better to open the crack up further with the edge of an old chisel or screwdriver so the filler can penetrate more deeply and key better to both sides of the crack
● when using a textured vinyl paint there is no need to fill hairline cracks, but cracks wider than 1mm ($^1/_{32}$in) should be filled.

DEALING WITH FITTINGS
Protect electrical fittings so paint or water can't enter them during cleaning and decorating:
● ideally, power to these fittings should be cut off and the fittings removed
● if items cannot be removed, use masking tape to protect them.

SELECTING PAINTS
When choosing paints, remember that:
● emulsion paints are quicker to apply, dry more quickly and lack the smell of resin- or oil-based paints. They are also cheaper and can be easily cleaned off painting equipment with water
● non-drip paints are best for ceilings and cover more thickly than runny ones, cutting down on the number of coats
● a silk or gloss finish will tend to highlight surface irregularities more than a matt finish
● textured paints are suitable for use on surfaces which are in poor condition since they will cover defects which a standard emulsion paint cannot.

PAINTING THE WALL WITH A BRUSH

1 *Use a small brush to cut in at the wall and ceiling join and in corners. With a larger brush paint the wall in bands. First, brush across the wall.*

2 *Move the brush across the wall in the opposite direction. The bands of paint should be about 1m wide and you should be working downwards.*

3 *When you are working at the top of the wall your next strokes should be downwards to complete the area you have covered with crossways strokes.*

4 *At the bottom two-thirds of the wall continue working in crossways strokes, but this time finish off each section by brushing upwards.*

USING PAINT PADS

1 *Thin the paint a little (with water for emulsions, turps for oil-based ones). Cut in with a small brush or pad and use a larger pad to paint in bands.*

2 *For precise work you can use a small pad like this. Ensure that you cover areas you don't want painted with masking tape.*

surface beneath has been properly prepared. Unless wallpaper is of a type intended for painting it is usually better to strip it off, and walls which have been stripped of their previous wallcoverings need a thorough washing to remove all traces of old paste. Make sure the floor is protected against debris by covering it with a dust sheet or sheets of old newspaper. Emulsion-painted walls also need washing to remove surface dirt. In both cases, use warm water with a little household detergent added. Then rinse with clean water.

If you decide to leave the wallpaper on the walls you will have to wash it down before you paint. Take care to avoid overwetting the paper, particularly at joins. When the surface is dry, check the seams; if any have lifted, stick them down with a ready-mixed paste.

Ceilings should be washed in small areas at a time and rinsed thoroughly before you move onto another section systematically.

If the surfaces are left in perfect condition, they can be painted as soon as they are dry.

It's possible that walls or ceilings may have been painted with distemper, which may only become apparent after you have removed the existing wallcovering. Unless it is the washable type, you will have to remove it completely since emulsion paint will not adhere well to it. Use hot water, detergent and a scrubbing brush to soften and get rid of the coating; this is hard work, but you could use a steam stripper to speed up the process.

With all the surface cleaned, the next job is to fill any cracks and repair defects such a as indentations caused perhaps by knocks or the blade of a carelessly handled wallpaper scraper (see *Ready Reference*).

Whenever a filler has been used it should be sanded down flush with the wall surface, once dry, and the resulting dust should be brushed away.

If the plaster is in bad condition and obviously covered in cracks you should consider covering it completely with liningpaper, woodchip or other relief wallcovering before painting it. The paper will provide a good base for redecoration, and will save a great deal of preparation time. However, this can only be done if the plaster itself is still bonded securely to the wall. If it is coming away in chunks or sounds hollow behind the cracks, then the wall should be replastered

Cracks which have developed round door and window frames are best filled with a flexible sealant, which will be unaffected by movement of the frames. Acrylic-based sealants are available for this purpose and they can be easily overpainted.

After all the preparation work has been

PAINTING PROCEDURE

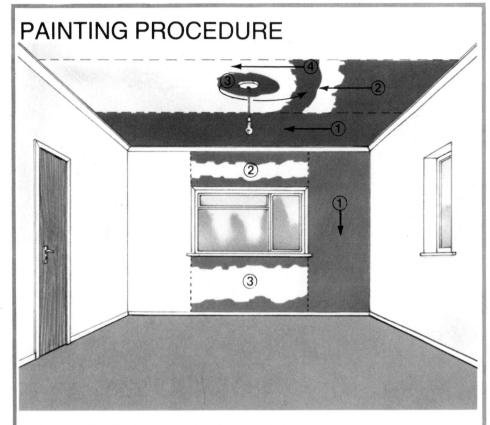

Paint the ceiling first in 1m-wide bands (1 & 2). Paint round a ceiling rose (3), then complete the rest of that band (4). On walls work downwards (1). At a window, paint along the top band (2) and repeat the process at the bottom (3). Work from right to left unless you are left-handed.

completed, have a good clear-up in the room so that when you begin painting you do not stir up dust and have to work around numerous bits and pieces scattered over the floor space.

Re-lay dust sheets and set up your access equipment before even opening the first can of paint. Make sure your brushes or rollers are clean and ready for use.

Painting sequences
If possible, do all your painting in daylight hours. Artificial light is less easy to work by and can lead to small areas being missed.

Painting is always done from the highest point downwards, so ceilings are the first areas to be tackled. The whole ceiling will be painted in bands across the room no wider than you can easily reach without stretching on your stepladder or platform. This generally means that at any one time you will probably be painting a band no wider than 1m and less than 2m long unless you are using scaffolding boards to support you.

You start at the edges first and then work into the main body of the room.

Linking one section to another is seldom difficult with emulsion paint and is simply a matter of blending the paint from the new section back into the previous one.

Walls are treated similarly, starting at the top and working downwards in sections about 1m wide, cutting in at the ceiling and at return walls.

Painting tips
The number of coats required will depend on the previous colour and condition of the surface and the type of paint. If another coat has to be applied, be sure that the previous one is fully dry first. With modern vinyl emulsion paint it may be that because the paint is water-based it will cause the paper underneath to swell and bubble; however, you shouldn't worry about this because as the water in the paint dries out the paper and paste behind the paint surface will begin to flatten again.

If the paper is badly hung with a lack of adhesive at the edge, seams may lift as the paint dries. They will have to be stuck down in the same way as if they had lifted during washing. Careful preparation would prevent this problem anyway.

STRIPPING WOOD

Wood has a natural beauty, but it's often a beauty concealed by layers and layers of paint. Doors, window frames, even skirting boards and architraves can all become attractive features in themselves when stripped back to reveal the wood. Even if you prefer to repaint, using the right techniques to strip off the old will give the best possible surface on which to work.

Stripping wood of old paint or layers of ancient varnish isn't the easiest of jobs. It's usually only done because you're after a natural finish, or because the painted surface has degenerated to such an extent that further coats of paint simply can't produce a smooth finish. Either way, once wood has been stripped back to its natural state, it then has to be sealed again – to protect it from moisture which can cause cracking, warping and ultimately decay. Both varnishes and paints act as sealants, giving a durable finish. But which one you choose might depend on the wood itself – and you won't know what that's like until you've stripped it. If you're unsure of its quality, it's advisable to strip a test area first.

Some of the timber used in houses is of a grade that was never intended for a clear finish – large ugly knots, cracks, splits or even an unattractive grain are some of the signs. In cases like this it is probably better to treat the problems (eg, applying 'knotting' – a special liquid sealer – to make the knots tight and prevent them 'bleeding', filling cracks and splits to give a flush surface) and then paint to seal.

If you are set on having the wood on show and don't want to paint it – because it wouldn't fit in with a colour scheme or make the feature you want – you can give it a better appearance and extra protection with stain or coloured varnish.

Stripping with abrasives

For dry stripping there are several different kinds of powered sanders available, all of which use abrasive papers of some kind to strip the surface off wood. On large areas such as floors it is best to use a purpose-made power sander which you can hire. A drill with a sanding attachment, however, is useful for getting small areas smooth after paint has been removed by other methods.

One such attachment is a 'disc sander' and is quite tricky to use effectively without scoring the wood surface. Hold it at a slight angle to the wood and present only half the disc to the surface. Work in short bursts and keep the disc moving over the surface – if it stays too long in one place it can damage the wood.

A 'drum sander' attachment has a belt of abrasive paper stuck round the edge of a cylinder of foam, and if used along the grain only is rather easier to handle than a disc

USING SCRAPERS

1 A triangular shavehook needs two hands when paint is thick. Hold the blade at an angle to the wood so it doesn't cause gouges.

2 A combination shavehook has round, straight and pointed edges to help remove paint and varnish from mouldings round windows and doors.

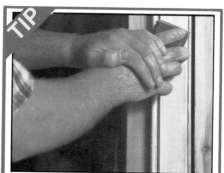

3 A special hook scraper has a sharp replaceable blade suitable both for scraping paint off flat surfaces and for getting into awkward crevices.

sander. Whichever type is chosen, a fine grade abrasive should be used for finishing stripped wood.

Orbital sanders (which are also known as finishing sanders) usually come as self-powered tools – although attachments are available for some drills. These have a much milder action and as long as the spread of wood isn't interrupted by mouldings they smooth well and are useful for rubbing down between coats. These sanders are rectangular and should be moved over the surface in line with the grain. Make sure you choose the right type of sander, depending on the work in hand.

For sanding by hand – hard work, but much better for finishing – there are many grades of glasspaper from the coarse to the very fine. On flat surfaces it's best to wrap the paper round a small block of wood. As an alternative to glasspaper, there's also steel wool, which is most useful when you're trying to smooth down an intricate moulding. Always sand backwards and forwards *with the grain of the wood*, not across it. Scratches across the grain will always be highlighted by a clear finish. To remove remaining bits of paint use medium grade glasspaper; for finishing, a fine grade is better. Renew the glasspaper frequently as the paint will clog the surface,

although a useful tip is to try cleaning clogged paper with a wire brush. It'll work once or twice, but after that the abrasive surface is usually lost. Alternatively pull the sheet backwards and forwards, abrasive side uppermost, over a table edge to dislodge paint particles.

A useful tool for cleaning paint from corners and mouldings is a hand scraper with replaceable blades. These 'hook' scrapers are also used for 'smoothing' and often need two-hands – they slightly raise the surface of a clear run of wood, giving an attractive finish under a clear seal. Use with the grain.

Heat stripping

Heat stripping is the quickest way to remove paint or varnish, but it needs a lot of expertise if you are to avoid charring the wood. So it is best reserved for stripping out of doors where a less-than-perfect surface will be less noticeable. A gas blow-torch is used along with metal scrapers to lift the finish off the wood while it's still warm. Blow-torches with gas canister attachments are light to use and a flame spreader nozzle makes the job easier (it can be bought separately).

Where there's no glass, it's a two-handed operation. Light the blow-torch and hold it a

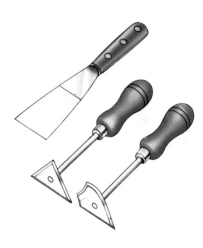
HEAT STRIPPING

1 *Play the blow-torch onto the paint and when it begins to bubble, start to scrape. Protect floor and sills with a sheet of non-flammable material.*

2 *When stripping paint near windows one hand must hold protection for glass. When paint hardens again, return the flame to the area.*

3 *Working overhead can be tricky if using a blow-torch. Protect your hands with gloves, your eyes with safety goggles and cover surfaces below.*

4 *To strip paint overhead, remove torch (be careful where it points), blow out flames and scrape quickly. As the paint loses heat it hardens.*

little way from the surface. Move it back and forth, going nearer and withdrawing, till the paint starts to wrinkle and blister. Now begin to scrape – be careful where you point the flame at this stage or you may damage other surfaces. As soon as the paint is hard to move return the flame to the area. Wear gloves to save your hands from being burnt by the falling paint, and cover areas below where you are working with a sheet of non-flammable material to catch the scrapings. In awkward areas, especially overhead, you should wear protective goggles for safety's sake.

Chemical stripping

Chemical strippers are probably the easiest way to strip wood. Available in liquid, gel and paste forms, their methods of application and removal vary, so always remember to read the manufacturer's instructions before you begin. Though all of them will remove paint and varnish, if you are dealing with a large area of wood they can work out to be very expensive – they're also very messy.

Liquid and gel strippers, decanted if necessary into a more convenient-sized container (read the instructions as to whether it can be heavy gauge plastic or should be glass or metal), are stippled onto the surface with a brush and left till the paint bubbles

before scraping. Usually these strippers will work through only 1 layer of paint at a time so several applications can be necessary. If stripping a chair or table, stand the legs in old paint cans or jam jars so that any stripper which runs down the legs can be recycled. Artists brushes rather than paint brushes are useful when applying these strippers to mouldings or beading in windows and No 2 steel wool is useful for removing it.

After liquids or gels have been used, the surface must be cleaned down with white spirit or water (it depends on the stripper used) to remove any trace of chemical and must be left till completely dry before any stain or seal is applied.

Pastes are mostly water soluble and manufacturers stress important conditions for using them safely (eg, not in direct sun, in well ventilated rooms, the wearing of protective gloves, etc). Bought in tubs ready-mixed or in powder form to be made up, they are spread in thick (3-6mm) layers over the wood which must then be covered with strips of polythene (good way of using up plastic carrier bags) or a special 'blanket' (supplied with the tub) which adheres – when you press it – to the paste. They have to be left for between 2 and 8 hours after which the paste can be scrubbed off (with a firm brush) or washed down. Frequent changes of water

are needed; follow manufacturer's advice about additives (eg, vinegar). Pastes are particularly effective with extraordinarily stubborn paint or varnish in very awkward places (eg, windows, bannisters etc); or where using a scraper might damage old wood. Some pastes are unsuitable for certain types of wood and can stain it – so read instructions carefully. Washing down should not be done, for example, with valuable furniture for. this can raise the grain of the wood.

Bleaching

If the wood is discoloured once stripped (either from the stripper used or from some other source) you can try and achieve an overall colour with bleach – the household type, used diluted 1:3 with water to begin with and more concentrated if necessary, or better still a proprietary wood bleach.

Clean the surface of the stripped wood with paint thinner and steel wool and leave for 15 minutes to dry. Cover areas you don't want bleached with polythene, then brush bleach on generously. Work it into the wood *with the grain* using medium steel wool.

Leave for 2-4 minutes, then wipe off with rags. Leave to dry (up to 5 hours) before sanding after which you can finish the surface as desired.

CHEMICAL STRIPPING

1 *Liquid strippers are stippled onto wood with a brush. First pour the liquid into a smaller container — but remember it will dissolve light plastic.*

2 *When paint is bubbling use a scraper to remove it. Work upwards and be careful not to gouge the wood with the blade.*

3 *Several applications of liquid may be needed as chemicals often only eat through one layer at a time. Use gloves to protect your hands.*

4 *After all paint has been stripped off, wipe the wood down with white spirit or water so that the chemicals are neutralised.*

TIP

5 *A good way to deal with mouldings is to apply a thick layer of stripping paste. This needs to be covered while it works, but is very effective.*

6 *After leaving for the specified time (can be several hours) wash the paste off with sponge or a scrubbing brush, changing the water often.*

COLOURING WOOD

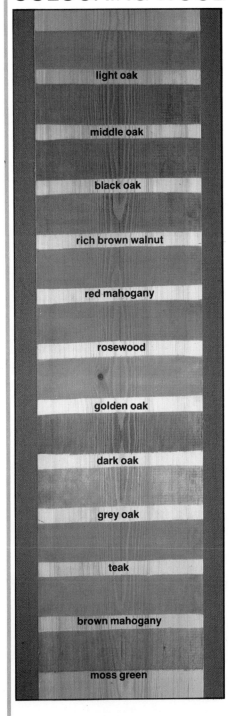

light oak

middle oak

black oak

rich brown walnut

red mahogany

rosewood

golden oak

dark oak

grey oak

teak

brown mahogany

moss green

On a plank of freshly planed wood the colours of different stains highlight the grain attractively (results will differ according to the age and condition of the wood). Stains don't seal and so they need a finishing coat of clear varnish — either gloss, satin or matt.

There are several different ways of altering the look of stripped wood.

● *Wood stains* are based on water, white spirit, alcohol, lacquer thinner or oil. Named after the wood whose colour they resemble, these penetrate the wood permanently. To give an even staining, the trick is to apply several thin coats — work from top to bottom on vertical surfaces to prevent drips and overlap marks. Use a pad (not a brush) made with cotton wool wrapped in a lint-free cloth and work backwards and forwards along the grain. When completely dry, seal with a clear varnish that is compatible with the stain. If applying more than one sealing coat, rub down the surface each time with fine glasspaper.

● *Coloured varnishes* both seal and 'stain' the wood surface and are removeable. They are also named after natural timber and are applied like ordinary clear varnish to sanded-smooth wood. You just go on applying the coats till you get the colour you want — rubbing down between each. Varnishes are oil (interior and exterior grades), spirit (not suitable for outdoors) or polyurethane based. Polyurethane varnishes can also be non-wood colours (such as red and green) and are especially useful if you want inexpensive wooden furniture to fit in with a colour scheme.

When using varnishes remember:
○ Never use a cellulose filler for it will always remain as a white mark. Choose a wood filler of similar colour to the stripped wood.

○ They have to be applied to perfectly smooth surfaces with all dust, grit and paint particles removed — wipe down with white spirit first, then leave to dry.

○ Don't attempt to apply them in dusty or windy conditions — the merest speck will spoil the finish and to be truly effective, stripped and sealed wood has to be beautifully smooth to the touch. A spray will give a more even finish than a brush.

● *Stained oils* both colour and seal. They are particularly suited to wood exposed to the elements (eg, outside doors and window sills) or wood that isn't in very good condition. Choose from a range of natural timber colours and apply several coats to give the wood 'depth'.

Ready Reference

WHAT TO USE WHERE

For large flat areas such as flush doors and skirting boards, use a
● blow-torch for speedy stripping if you're going to repaint it
● powered sander if you're going to varnish.

For **intricate mouldings** and **awkward areas** such as staircases, panelled doors and window frames, use
● a blow-torch and a shavehook if you're repainting
● chemical strippers if varnishing (remember they're relatively expensive).

For **fine finishing** use
● glasspaper and sanding block or an orbital (powered) sander.

Caustic soda
This is used for 'immersion' stripping of doors and other fairly durable pieces of furniture. If you have a suitable old galvanised iron tub or water tank, remember to put the water in first then add the crystals. BUT remember that
● caustic soda is a powerful chemical: handle with care
● immersion stripping can loosen old joints and peel off veneers
● you must wash down the wood with water after stripping
● you'll have to finish the wood with glasspaper or a powered sander.

DOS AND DON'TS

● DO leave a freshly lit blow-torch to stand for a few minutes or it may flare dangerously when moved
● DO wear gloves if you're using a blow torch OR chemical strippers
● DO wash splashes of chemical strippers off your skin immediately
● DON'T use a blow-torch to strip wood you intend to varnish – scorch marks are almost impossible to avoid
● DON'T work in a very confined space with chemical strippers.

STAINING AND VARNISHING WOOD

If you want to decorate and protect the woodwork around your home without obliterating its grain pattern with paint, wood stains and varnishes offer a wide choice of finishes. Here's how to get the best results.

When it comes to giving wood a clear finish, you can choose from a variety of traditional and modern materials, including oils, wax, French polish and different types of varnish. Some are suitable for exterior use, others for interior use only. The degree of skill you need to apply them varies; some are quite simple to use, whereas others, like French polish, require special techniques acquired only by patient practice. The type of wood may affect your choice of finish; for example, open-textured woods like teak, iroko and afrormosia are best treated with an oil finish – they don't take varnishes well.

You may decide to change the colour of the wood before you finish it. You can use a varnish which incorporates a colour or apply a wood stain and then coat the wood with clear varnish or another clear finish.

If you don't wish to change the colour of the wood, but want to restore it to its natural colour – for example, where the wood has been slightly darkened by the action of a paint stripper – you can use a proprietary colour restorer.

Types of varnish and stains
Clear varnishes are like paint without the pigment. They contain a resin carried in a drying oil or spirit and it is the resin which gives a hard protective finish to wood. Traditionally, the resins used were like copal, natural and obtained from various tropical trees, but in modern varnishes they are synthetic, for example alkyd or polyurethane.

While other varnishes are available, by far the easiest to obtain and most widely used are those containing polyurethane resin. Polyurethane varnish is available in gloss, satin or matt finishes and for interior or exterior use. A non-drip variety is particularly suitable for vertical surfaces, ceilings and hard-to-get-at areas.

There are polyurethane varnishes which have added pigments and are known as coloured sealers. It's quicker to use one of these rather than to apply a wood-stain followed by a clear finish but you won't get the same depth of colour, and if the coloured varnish chips in use, timber of a different colour will show through.

Wood stains are colouring pigments suspended in water, oil or spirits. Some come ready-mixed; others in powder form to be mixed up. Oil-based stains tend to be more difficult to obtain and are not as widely used as the other two types.

Preparing the surface
Before staining, bleaching, varnishing or using other types of finish you should ensure that the surface is clean, dry, smooth and free from any old paint or varnish.

To smooth down a flat surface you can use glasspaper wrapped around a sanding block. On small curves and fiddly bits wrap small strips of abrasive round a pencil. For larger curves use a sanding glove which you can make yourself (see *Ready Reference*).

A powered sander is a boon on large surfaces; use an orbital sander rather than the disc type which is tricky to use without causing scratches across the grain.

Besides getting rid of shallow scratches, sanding will also get rid of cigarette burns and similar marks on the wood surface. However, make sure you don't sand for too long in one place or you will leave a depression that will show up after finishing.

Large cracks and dents can be filled with wax (from a crayon of a suitable colour, for instance) or with a proprietary wood filler. But since stains don't hide fillers in the same way as paint would, you may decide not to carry out such treatment and to leave the blemishes for an authentic 'old wood' look. If you do decide to use a filler, don't try to smooth it flat as you apply it with the knife or you'll risk spreading it round – it tends to show up in the nearby grain if it is rubbed in when wet.

Finally, you should make sure the surface is dust-free by wiping it with a clean, dry cloth or a fine brush. It's a good idea, too, to wipe it with a cloth soaked in turpentine to remove any greasy fingermarks you may have left while preparing the surface.

Bleaching wood
One of the snags with staining wood is that you cannot make the surface lighter; you can only make it darker. A light-coloured stain on a darkish piece of wood just won't work. The way round this problem is to bleach the wood before you start sealing it – and for this proprietary wood bleaches are available at most hardware stores.

Some bleaches are applied in one stage and others in two stages. The wood is washed with a neutralizing agent afterwards so the bleach doesn't carry on working when the finish is applied. Follow the manufacturer's instructions when applying the bleach, particularly concerning the time you should allow for each stage of the treatment. Usually, bleach is applied with a sponge or brush; make sure you use a white fibre brush or the dye in the brush may come out onto the wood.

Staining wood
You can apply the stain with a brush or a folded lint-free rag. Aim to get the colour you want in one coat; a second coat can be applied if needed to get a darker finish, but too many coats will result in the stain lying on the surface, lengthening the time it takes for the subsequent coat of varnish to dry and even preventing it from bonding properly to the surface. With water-based types, if overlaps show when the first coat dries you can add about 20 per cent more water to a mixed-up solution of stain and apply a second coat over the whole surface, brushing it out well.

After the stain has dried (usually about 24 hours after application), you should rub the surface thoroughly with a dry cloth to remove excess stain.

Filling the grain
It's not necessary to fill the grain of soft-woods, but for a good finish on open-grained hardwoods like oak, mahogany and walnut you will have to apply a grain filler

BLEACHING WOOD

1 In a two-stage bleaching process, apply the first solution liberally and leave it to work for the recommended time – usually 10 to 20 minutes.

2 Brush on the second solution, leaving it to work. If the wood is very dark or stained, reapply both solutions. If a crust forms, wipe it off with a damp rag.

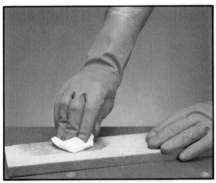

3 Wash the wood with a solution of acetic acid (white vinegar) and water to neutralise the bleach. Allow it to dry completely before staining it.

STAINING WOOD

1 Shake the can well and then pour the stain into a dish wide enough for you to dip in a cloth pad. Avoid plastic dishes; some stains may attack them.

2 Apply the stain liberally using a cloth pad. If you apply it too sparingly you run the risk of getting light and dark areas instead of even coverage.

3 For greater grain contrast, wipe over each strip with a rag after allowing a minute or so for penetration. Leave to dry for 24 hours before varnishing.

VARNISHING WOOD

1 *After you've made sure the surface is clean and dry, use a clean cloth pad to apply the first coat. Rub it well into the wood along the grain.*

2 *Leave the first coat to dry and then brush on the next coat. Make sure the brush is really clean, with no paint particles or loose bristles to mar the finish.*

3 *When brushing, it is important to work with the grain and brush out fully. On a narrow surface like a shelf upright, first apply the varnish in one stroke.*

4 *Then work the brush out towards the edges of the upright, working first to one edge and then to the other, using gentle but firm strokes.*

5 *To complete coating the upright, again move the brush in one upward stroke. This technique will ensure that there are no ugly 'runs' at the edges.*

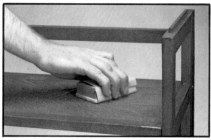

6 *Leave each coat to dry for the recommended time (approx 12 hours) before re-coating. Rub down between coats with flour-grade glass paper.*

to the wood surface before using varnish.

There are various proprietary fillers available in either a paste or liquid form; choose one to match the wood or stain you are using. Follow the manufacturer's instructions for applying it; normally, you work the filler over the wood with a brush or cloth, wipe off the excess and then sand the surface lightly down with fine glasspaper.

Varnishing wood

Polyurethane varnish is easy to apply; you simply brush it on, taking care to work with the grain of the wood. Follow the manufacturer's instructions as to the number of coats you should apply and the time

allowed between each coat – at least 12 hours. You should sand down the surface lightly with flour-grade glasspaper between coats to provide a key for the next coat, and remove any dust that's accumulated during application with a damp cloth.

As with paints, it's advisable to stir the contents of any can of varnish that's been stored for a while. This ensures an even distribution of the solvents so that the varnish dries evenly when it is applied. Although the varnish will be touch-dry in about 4 hours, it may take as long as 7 days before the surface reaches full hardness – so avoid standing anything on the newly-decorated surface for a week or so.

Ready Reference

SAFETY FIRST
Varnishes, bleaches and stains can be flammable. Always work in a ventilated area away from the naked flames and don't smoke when applying them.

PROTECT YOUR SKIN
Bleach can burn skin and clothing so you should wear rubber gloves and an apron or old clothes when applying it.

AVOID SCRATCHES
When sanding take care not to leave scratches on the wood which will be highlighted by the finish. Always work in the direction of the grain, not across it, and finish off with the finest grade of glasspaper. If you are using power tools, never press too hard.

MAKING A SANDING GLOVE
For sanding large curves, staple two ends of a sheet of glasspaper together so it forms a 'glove' when you put your hand through the middle.

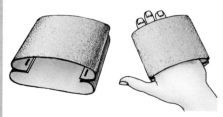

TIP: HOW TO REMOVE STAINS
Place a damp cloth over the dent, then apply a warm iron on top of the cloth so the wood swells up and fills out the hollow.

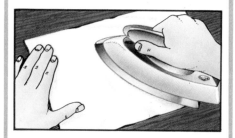

WORKING WITH VENEERS
● never use a bleach on a wood veneer; the bleach has to be washed off and water can loosen the veneer and cause it to swell
● take special care when sanding a veneer; it's easy to go right through it, especially at the edges, and expose the timber underneath. Such damage is very difficult to repair.

PAINTING WOOD

Painting is the most popular way of decorating and protecting much of the wood in our homes. As with so many do-it-yourself jobs, getting a good finish depends on your skill. Here's how to paint wood perfectly.

Wood is used extensively in every part of our homes — from roof trusses to skirting boards. Structural timber is usually left rough and unfinished, while joinery — windows, doors, staircases, architraves and so on — is usually decorated in some way. Wood has just one drawback; as a natural material it's prone to deterioration and even decay unless it's protected. Painting wood is one way of combining decoration and protection, and the popularity of paint is a testimony to its effectiveness. Properly applied and well looked after, it gives wood a highly attractive appearance and also provides excellent protection against dampness, dirt, mould, insect attack, and general wear and tear.

Of course, paint isn't the only finish you can choose for wood. If its colour and grain pattern are worth displaying, you can use

PREPARING WOOD FOR PAINT

1 Before you can apply the paint you must fill any cracks or holes with wood filler (applied with a filling knife) and leave to dry.

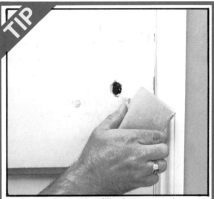

2 Sand down the filled areas using medium-grade glasspaper. Wrap the abrasive around a sanding block or wood offcut so it's easier to use.

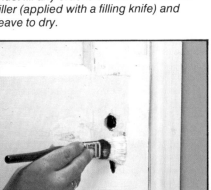

3 Where paint has been chipped off, sand down the area and apply an ordinary wood primer to the bare wood using a small paintbrush.

4 When the surface of the wood is smooth, apply undercoat (as the maker recommends) and leave to dry before you put on the top coat.

PREPARING PAINT

1 *Remove the lid from the paint can using the edge of a knife as a lever – don't use a screwdriver or you'll damage the lip of the lid.*

2 *Stir the paint (if recommended by the maker) using an offcut of wood, with a turning, lifting motion, or use an electric drill attachment.*

3 *Decant some paint into a paint kettle, which you'll find easier to carry than a heavy can. Top up the kettle from the can as you work.*

4 *To load the brush, dip the bristles into the paint to one-third of their length and wipe off excess on a string tied across the kettle rim.*

oils, stains or varnishes to enhance the overall effect and protect the surface. But as most of the wood used in our houses is chosen more for performance and price rather than looks, bland and uninteresting softwoods are generally the order of the day for everything from windows and door frames to staircases, skirting boards and door architraves. And painting them offers a number of distinct advantages.

Firstly, paint covers a multitude of sins — knots and other blemishes in the wood surface, poorly-made joints patched up with filler, dents and scratches caused by the rough and tumble of everyday life — and does it in almost every colour of the spectrum. Secondly, paint provides a surface that's hard-wearing and easy to keep clean — an important point for many interior surfaces in the home. And thirdly, paint is easy to apply ... and to keep on applying. In fact, redecorating existing paintwork accounts for the greater part of all paint bought.

What woods can be painted?

In theory you can paint any wood under the sun. In practice, paint (solvent-based or emulsion, see *Ready Reference*), is usually applied only to softwoods — spruce (whitewood), European redwood (deal), pine and the like — and to man-made boards such as plywood, blockboard, hardboard and chipboard. Hardwoods and boards finished with hardwood veneers can be painted, but are usually given a clear or tinted finish to enhance their attractive colour and grain pattern.

Paint systems

If you're decorating new wood, there's more to it than putting on a coat of your chosen paint. It would just soak in where the wood was porous and give a very uneven colour — certainly without the smooth gloss finish expected. It wouldn't stick to the wood very well, nor would it form the continuous surface film needed for full protection. All in all, not very satisfactory. So what is needed is a paint system which consists of built-up layers, each one designed to serve a particular purpose.

The first in the system is a primer (sometimes called a primer/sealer) which stops the paint soaking into porous areas and provides a good key between the bare wood and the paint film. Next, you want another 'layer' — the undercoat — to help build up the paint film and at the same time to obliterate the colour of the primer, so that the top coat which you apply last of all is perfectly smooth and uniform in colour. With some paints — emulsions and non-drip glosses — an undercoat is not always used and instead several coats of primer or two

HOW TO APPLY PAINT

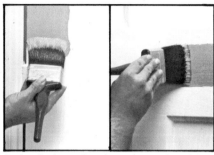

1 *Apply the paint along the grain; with non-drip paint (left) you can apply a thicker coat in one go without further spreading (brushing out).*

4 *Now you must 'lay off' the paint with very light brush strokes along the grain to give a smooth finish that's free from brush marks.*

top coats are applied with the same result.

The general rule to obey when choosing primer, undercoat and top coat is to stick with the same base types in one paint system, particularly out of doors and on surfaces subjected to heavy wear and tear (staircases and skirting boards, for example). On other indoor woodwork you can combine primers and top coats of different types.

If the wood you are painting has been treated with a preservative to prevent decay (likely only on exterior woodwork) an ordinary primer won't take well. Instead use an aluminium wood primer — not to be confused with aluminium paint — which is recommended for use on all hardwoods too. Oily woods such as teak must be degreased with white spirit and allowed to dry before the primer is applied.

As far as man-made boards are concerned, chipboard is best primed with a solvent-based wood primer to seal its comparatively porous surface. Hardboard is even more porous, and here a stabilising primer (a product more usually used on absorbent or powdery masonry surfaces) is the best product to use. Plywood and blockboard should be primed as for softwood. There's one other

2 Still working with the grain and without reloading the brush, paint another strip alongside the first one and blend the two together.

3 Reload the brush and apply strokes back and forth across the grain over the area you've just painted to ensure full, even coverage.

5 Paint an area adjoining the first in the same way, blending the two sections together by about 50mm (2in) and laying off as before.

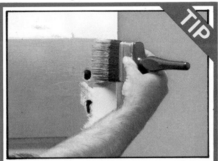

6 Brush towards edges, not parallel with them or onto them, as the paint will be scraped onto the adjacent face, forming a ridge.

WHAT CAN GO WRONG WITH PAINT

Left: Lifting and flaking occurs if paint is applied over a surface that is damp or powdery.

Right: Crazing is caused when paint is applied over a previous coat that was not completely dry.

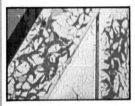

Left: Blistering occurs when damp or resin is trapped beneath the paint film and is drawn out by heat.

Right: Cratering results from rain or condensation droplets falling onto the wet paint surface.

Left: Running, sagging or 'curtaining' happens when paint is applied too thickly on vertical surfaces.

Right: Wrinkling or shrivelling can occur on horizontal surfaces if paint is applied too thickly.

Ready Reference

HOW MUCH PAINT?

Large areas – in all cases coverage per litre depends on the wood's porosity and the painter's technique:
Wood primer 9-15 sq metres (95-160 sq ft)
Aluminium primer 16 sq metres (170 sq ft)
Primer/undercoat 11 sq metres (120 sq ft)
Undercoat 11 sq metres (120 sq ft)
Runny gloss or satin 17 sq metres (180 sq ft)
Non-drip gloss or satin 13 sq metres (140 sq ft)
Runny emulsions 15 sq metres (160 sq ft)
Non-drip emulsions 12 sq metres (130 sq ft)

Small areas – add up all the lengths of wood to be painted. One sq metre is equivalent to:
● 16m (52 ft) of glazing bars
● 10-13m (33-43 ft) of window frame
● 6m (20 ft) of sill
● 10m (33 ft) of narrow skirting
● 3-6m (10-20 ft) of deep skirting

CHOOSING BRUSHES

The best brushes have a generous filling of long bristles and are an even, tapered shape. Cheaper brushes have short, thin bristles and big wooden filler strips to pack them out. The ideal sizes for wood are:
● 25mm (1in) or 50mm (2in) for panel doors, skirtings
● 50mm (2in) or 75mm (3in) for flush doors, skirting, large areas
● 25mm (1in) cutting-in brush for window glazing bars
● 12mm (½in), 25mm (1in) or cheap paintbox brush for spot priming, applying knotting

Alternative to brushes
Paint pads are more widely used on walls than on woodwork, but the crevice or sash paint pad will do the same job as a cutting-in brush. It should be cleaned with white spirit or hot water and washing-up liquid (paint solvents might dissolve the adhesive between the mohair pile and foam).

TIP: PREPARING A BRUSH

Before using a new (or stored) brush work the bristles against the palm of your hand to remove dust and loose hairs.

thing you need to know. If the wood you want to paint has knots in it you should brush a special sealer called knotting over them to stop the resin oozing up through the paint film and spoiling its looks. If the knots are 'live' — exuding sticky yellowish resin — use a blow-torch to draw out the resin and scrape it off before applying knotting.

Paint on paint

You'll often want to paint wood that has already been painted. How you tackle this depends on the state of the existing paintwork. If it's flaking off and is in generally poor condition, you will have to remove the entire paint system — primer, undercoat and top coat — by burning off with a blow-torch,

applying a chemical paint stripper or rubbing with an abrasive. You then treat the stripped wood as already described for new wood.

Where the paintwork is in good condition, you simply have to clean it and sand it down lightly to provide a key for the new paint and to remove any small bits that got stuck in the surface when it was last painted. Then you can apply fresh top coat over the surface; the paint system is already there. You may, of course, need two top coats if you add a light colour to a dark one to stop the colour beneath from showing through.

If the paintwork is basically sound but needs localised attention, you can scrape or sand these damaged areas back to bare wood and 'spot-treat' them with primer and

undercoat to bring the patch up to the level of the surrounding paintwork, ready for a final top coat over the entire surface.

Painting large areas

Though the same principle applies to wood as it does to any other large surface area — ie, you divide it into manageable sections and complete one before moving on to another — if you're using an oil-based gloss paint you have to make sure that the completed area hasn't dried to such an extent that you cannot blend in the new. On the rare occasion that you might want to paint a whole wall of wood you should make the section no wider than a couple of brush widths and work from ceiling to floor.

With emulsions there isn't the same problem for although they are quick drying the nature of the paint is such that brush marks don't show.

You might think that a wide brush is the best for a large area but the constant flexing action of the wrist in moving the brush up and down will tire you out fast. Holding a brush is an art in itself and aches are the first indication that you're doing it wrongly. A thin brush should be held by the handle like a pencil, while a wider brush should be held with the fingers and thumb gripping the brush just above the bristles.

You'll find a variety of paint brushes on sale — some are designed to be 'throwaway' (good if you only have one or two jobs to do), others will stand you in good stead for years. But remember before using a new brush to brush the bristles back and forth against the palm of your hand — this is called 'flirting' and will dislodge any dust or loose hairs that could spoil your paintwork.

It is wise to decant the paint to save you moving a heavy can from place to place — a paint kettle which resembles a small bucket is made for the purpose. Plastic ones are easier to keep clean than metal ones.

Never be tempted to dip the bristles too far into the paint and always scrape off excess from both sides. Paint has the habit of building up inside the brush and if this happens on overhead work, you risk it running down the handle and onto your arm.

Painting small areas

These tend to be the fiddly woodwork on windows, around doors and lengths of stairs or skirting boards — and the hardest bit about all of them is working out how much paint you'll need (see Ready Reference).

Special shaped or narrow brushes can make painting these areas easier — for example, they prevent you 'straddling' angles in wood (like you find on mouldings) which damages the bristles in the middle of the brush. With windows and panelled doors you should also follow an order of working to

ORDER OF PAINTING

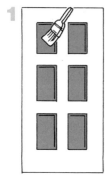 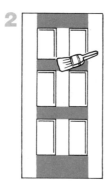 

Panel doors: *tackle any mouldings first, then the recessed panels, horizontal members, vertical members and lastly the edges.*

Casement windows: *start with any glazing bars, then paint the opening casement itself (the hinge edge is the only one which should match the inside); lastly paint the frame.*

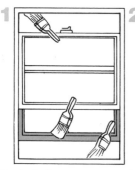 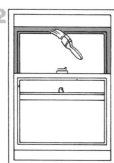 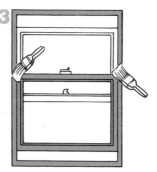

Sash windows: *paint the inside top and bottom and a little way up and down the sides of the frame first. Then paint the bottom of the outer sash. Move the sashes and do the rest of the outer sash, the inner sash and finally the frame.*

avoid causing overlap marks on the parts you've already painted.

Fiddly or not, they are the jobs you have to do first if you are putting up wallcoverings (if you're painting a room, the walls should be done before the woodwork) so that the drops can be placed against finished edges. If you want to touch up the paint without changing the wallpaper, it's best to use a paint shield.

Getting ready to paint
Ideally, before painting doors and windows you should remove all the 'furniture' — handles, fingerplates, keyholes, hooks etc — so you can move the brush freely without interruption. You should also take time to read the manufacturer's instructions on the can. If, for example, they tell you to stir the paint, then stir it for this is the only way of distributing the particles which have settled.

If you open a can of non-drip paint and find a layer of solvent on the top, you should stir it in, then leave it to become jelly-like again before painting.

All your brushes should be dry — this is something to remember if you are painting over several days and have put them to soak overnight in white spirit or a proprietary brush cleaner. If you don't get rid of all the traces of the liquid it will mess up your paint-work. They should be rinsed, then brushed on newspaper till the strokes leave no sign.

Cleaning up
When you've finished painting clean your brushes thoroughly, concentrating on the roots where paint accumulates and will harden. They should be hung up, bristles down, till dry, then wrapped in aluminium foil for storage. Don't ever store them damp for they can be ruined by mildew.

If there's only a small amount of paint left, you can either decant it for storage into a dark glass screw-topped jar so you can use it to touch up damaged spots — it's important to choose a suitable sized jar so there's very little air space. Air and dust are both potential paint spoilers and there are two ways to keep them out if you're storing the can. Either put a circle of aluminium foil over the paint surface before putting the lid on securely, or — and this is the best way if the lid is distorted — put on the lid and then invert the can to spread the paint round the inner rim to form an airtight seal. Set it back the right way for storage.

If despite these safeguards a skin forms on the paint (usually over months of storage) you have to cut round the edge of it with a sharp knife and carefully lift it off.

PAINTING WINDOWS

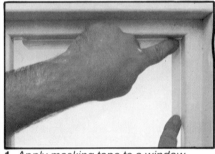

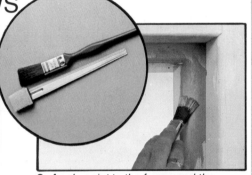

1 Apply masking tape to a window pane to prevent paint getting onto the glass – leave 3mm (^{1}/$_8$in) of glass exposed so the paint forms a seal.

2 Apply paint to the frame and the glazing bars using a small brush, or (inset) a cutting-in brush or a sash paint pad.

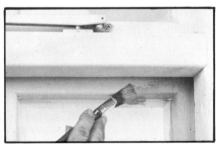

3 Apply the paint along the grain; remove the tape when the paint is almost dry – if it dries completely you might peel it off with the tape.

4 An alternative way of keeping paint off the glass is to use a paint shield or offcut of plywood but, again, leave a paint margin on the glass.

PAPERING WALLS
the basics

No other wall covering can quite so dramatically alter the look and feeling of a room as wallpaper. Correctly hung paper makes the walls sharp and fresh, and to achieve this finish there are important things to know. What do you do if the walls are out of true? Where's the best place to start? How do you prevent bubbles and creases? The answers are here.

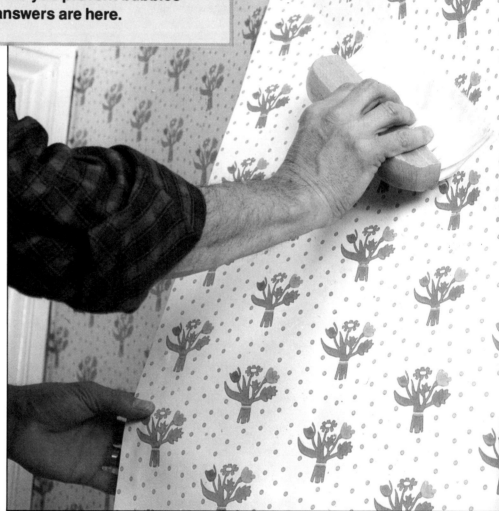

Wallpapering isn't so much an art, it's more a matter of attention to detail. And perhaps the first mistake that's made by many people is expecting too much of their walls. Rarely are walls perfectly flat, perfectly vertical and at right angles to each other. So the first and most crucial part of hanging wallpaper is to prepare the walls properly. Obviously you can't change their basic character – if they're not entirely flat or vertical, you're stuck with them – but you can make sure that the surface is suitably prepared so that the new paper will stick.

This means that any old wallpaper really should come off before you do anything else. Papering on top of old wall coverings won't *always* lead to disaster, but it will quite often simply because the new adhesive will tend to loosen the old. The result will be bubbles at best and peeling at worst.

Adhesives
Always use the correct adhesive for the wallcovering and follow the manufacturers instructions for mixing. Using the wrong paste can result in the paper not sticking, mould growth or discoloration of the paper.

A cellulose-based adhesive is used for all standard wallcoverings. There are two types, ordinary and heavy-duty which relates to the weight of the paper being hung. Heavy-duty pastes are for heavyweight wallcoverings. Certain brands of paste are suitable for all types of wallcoverings – less water being used for mixing when hanging heavy papers.

Since vinyls and washable wallcoverings are impervious, mould could attack the paste unless it contains a fungicide. Fungicidal paste is also needed if the wall has previously been treated against mould or if there is any sign of damp.

Some wallcoverings (like polyethylene foam, some hessians and foils) require a specially thick adhesive which is pasted onto the wall. Follow manufacturers' instructions.

Ready-pasted papers are exactly that and require no extra adhesive – although it's useful to have a tube of latex glue handy for finishing off corners and joints which mightn't

have stuck. (The same applies to all washable wallpapers).

Glue *size* (a watered down adhesive). is brushed over the walls before papering to seal them and prevent the paste from soaking in to the wall. It also ensures all-over adhesion and makes sliding the paper into place easier.

Although size can be bought, most wallpaper pastes will make size when mixed with the amount of water stated in the instructions.

If you buy a proprietary size and the wallcovering you are using needs an adhesive containing fungicide, make sure that the size you buy also contains a

fungicide. Use an old brush to apply and a damp cloth to clean off any that runs on to paintwork. It can be difficult to remove after it has dried. Sizing can be done several days or an hour before.

Where to begin
The traditional rule is to start next to the window and work away from it, but that is really a hangover from the days when paper was overlapped and shadows showed up joins. Today, papers butt up, so light isn't the problem. But as inaccuracies can occur with slight loss of pattern, you have to be able to make this as inconspicuous as possible. In

an average room, the corner nearest the door is the best starting point. Any loss of pattern will then end up behind you as you enter the room. In a room with a chimney breast, hang the first drop in the centre and work outwards from both sides of the drop

Problem areas in a house (recesses, arches, stairwells) are dealt with later in this chapter.

Measuring and cutting

Measure the height of the wall you want to paper using a steel tape measure and cut a piece of paper from the roll to this length, allowing an extra 50mm (2in) top and bottom for trimming. This allowance is needed for pattern matching, and to ensure a neat finish at skirting board and ceiling.

Lay the first drop — that's the name given to each length of paper — pattern side up on the table and unroll the paper from which the second drop is to be cut next to it. Move this along until the patterns match, then cut the second drop using the other end of the first as a guide. Subsequent lengths of paper are cut in exactly the same way, with each matching the drop that preceded it.

Remember some wallpapers have patterns that are a straight match across the width, while others have what is called a drop pattern that rises as it extends across the width. With drop match papers the second length will begin half a pattern repeat further along the roll. Length 3 will match length 1, length 4 will match length 2 and so on.

For things to run smoothly, you should establish a work routine when paper hanging. Cut all the wall drops first (so you only have to measure once) and cut bits for papering above windows and doors as you come to them. If you paste say 3 drops, the first will have had its required soaking time

HOW TO CUT AND PASTE

1 *Mark the pasting table with lines at 150mm (6in) and 300mm (1ft) intervals. Measure wall drop and use guidelines to cut your first length.*

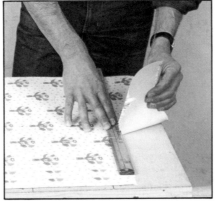

2 *Use the first length as a guide for the other drops, matching the pattern carefully. Tear off the waste against a wooden rule.*

3 *Lay all the drops pattern down, overhanging the far edge of the table. Pull the first drop to the near edge and paste it from centre to edges.*

4 *Fold pasted end, paste the rest and fold in. Now fold up the whole drop and leave it to soak. The top of the longer fold always goes to the top of the wall.*

Ready Reference

STRIPPING OLD WALLPAPER

Never hang new coverings over existing wallpaper – the old may lift and bring the new with it.

Ordinary wallpaper:
● use hot water with washing-up liquid or proprietary wallpaper stripper to soak the surface
● scrape off old paper in strips with broad-bladed scraper, re-soaking stubborn areas; wash surface down to remove bits

Washable or painted wallpaper:
● always score surface coating with serrated scraper before soaking and scraping
● for large areas a steam stripper (from hire shops) is a real time-saver

Vinyl wallcovering:
● lift corner of vinyl coating at skirting board level and peel away from backing paper by pulling steadily up and away
● then soak and scrape off backing paper

WHERE TO START

Room with a chimney breast: start at its centre and work outward to each end of the chimney wall, then on down the two side walls towards the door. Any loss of pattern will be least noticed in the short lengths hung over the door.

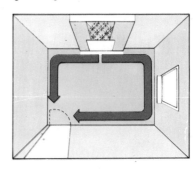

Room without a chimney breast: start at one corner of the room – ideally near the door – and work around continuously until you return to your starting point.

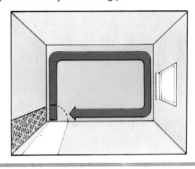

PAPER HANGING TECHNIQUES

1 Place chosen pattern on ceiling line with waste above. Align side edge with vertical and turn waste onto adjacent wall. Brush up to ceiling first, then corners and edges, and then down. Open out short fold last.

2 Mark cutting line for waste at ceiling and skirting board with a pencil — ends of scissors won't fit creases neatly and can give a thick line which causes you to cut the paper inaccurately and will give an uneven look at ceiling and skirting.

3 To cut waste, pull short length of paper away from wall so pencil line catches the light. Cut using full length of blades — hurried, short cuts can make the edges jagged. Brush paper back on wall so that it is perfectly flat.

4 Reduce waste on adjacent wall to 6mm (¼in) to lessen bulk when paper overlaps from other direction.

5 Continue along wall matching the pattern horizontally. Press drop onto wall so long edges butt.

6 As each drop is hung, brush up first, then to edges and finally down to remove any trapped air.

7 To turn a corner, measure between hung paper and corner at the top, middle and bottom of wall. Add 6mm (¼in) to widest width, then use this measurement to cut the pasted and folded drop into two. Set aside offcut for new wall.

8 Hang drop to complete wall, brushing the waste round the corner. Find the new vertical and mark the line the width of offcut from the corner. Check this measurement at the top, middle and bottom of wall. If the same, hang offcut.

9 If corner is out of true, offcut and wall measurements will differ. To disguise pattern loss, hang the offcut so waste laps onto completed wall. Brush into corner, run pencil down crease line and cut waste.

(with medium weight paper) by the time the third is pasted and folded and is ready to be hung. With heavy papers paste, fold and soak 6 drops at a time as extra soaking time is needed.

Avoiding bubbles

The purpose behind soaking time (apart from making paper supple enough to handle) is to give it time to expand to its natural limit. On the width this can be 6mm-12mm (¼in-½in) and the average wall-size drop will gain 24mm (1in) on the length – this explains why you have more to cut as waste than you started with.

If you haven't given paper the time it needs, it will expand on the walls – but its spread will be contained by adjoining drops and so you get bubbles in the central part.

Soak medium weight papers for 3-4 minutes, heavy weights for about 10. Ready-pasted papers don't need too long a soaking, but to ensure they get wet all over, roll drops loosely and press into water till they are completely covered.

Pasting and soaking

Position the paper with its top edge at the right-hand end of the table (or at the other end if you're left handed). Paste it carefully to ensure that all parts, the edges especially, are well covered. Work from the centre outwards in herring-bone style using the width of the brush to cover the drop in sweeps, first to the nearest edge, then the other – excess paste here will go onto second drop, not the table. Cover two-thirds of the drop, then fold the top edge in so paste is to paste. Move the drop along the table and paste the remainder, folding bottom edge in paste to paste. Because the first folded part is longer than the other, this will remind you which is the

top. Fold the drop up and put aside to soak while you paste the others.

This technique will give you a manageable parcel of paper to hang no matter what length the drop – but always remember to make the first fold longer – this is the one offered to the ceiling line. If in doubt mark the top edge lightly with a pencil cross.

Hanging pasted paper

Wallpaper must be hung absolutely vertical if it is to look right, so always work to a vertical line (see *Ready Reference*).

Position your step ladder as close as possible to where you want to work, and climb it with the first length of paper under or over your arm. Open out the long fold and offer the top edge up, placing the pattern as you want it at the ceiling with waste above. Align the side edge of the drop with your vertical guide line, allowing the other side edge to turn onto the adjacent wall if starting at a corner. Smooth the paper onto the wall with the paperhanging brush, using the bristle ends to form a crease between wall and ceiling, and at corners. When brushing paper into place, always work up first then to the join, then to the side edge, then down. This will remove trapped air.

As soon as the paper is holding in place, work down the wall, brushing the rest of the drop in position, opening out the bottom fold when you reach it. Again use the bristle ends to form a good crease where paper meets the skirting board.

The next step is to trim off the waste paper at the top and bottom. Run a lead pencil along the crease between the ceiling or skirting and the wall — the blades or points of scissors wil make a line that's too thick for accurate cutting. Gently peel paper away from the wall and cut carefully along the line with your scissors. Finally brush the paper back in place.

Hanging the second drop is done as the

Estimator

Most wallpaper is sold in rolls 10.05m (11yds) long and 530mm (21in) wide. Calculate rolls needed by measuring perimeter of the room and height from skirting board to ceiling.

WALLS	Distance around the room (doors and windows included)										
Height from skirting	10m 33'	11m 36'	12m 39'	13m 43'	14m 46'	15m 49'	16m 52'	17m 56'	18m 59'	19m 62'	20m 66'
2.15–2.30m (7'–7'6")	5	5	5	6	6	7	7	8	8	9	9
2.30–2.45m (7'6"–8')	5	5	6	6	7	7	8	8	9	9	10
2.45–2.60m (8'–8'6")	5	6	6	7	7	8	9	9	10	10	11

The number of rolls needed can be greatly affected by the frequency of pattern repeat. With a large pattern repeat, buy an extra roll.

first except that you have to butt it up against the edge of the first length, matching the pattern across the two. The secret here is not to try and do it all in one go. Get the paper onto the wall at the right place at the ceiling join but just a little way away from the first length. Now press against the paper with the palms of your hands and slide it into place. Using well-soaked paper on a wall that's been sized makes this easy, but if you're using a thin wallpaper press gently as it could tear. Butt the paper up after pattern matching and brush into place.

When trimming waste from drops other than the first, cut from where the lengths butt to ensure even ceiling and skirting lines.

Hanging ready-pasted wallpaper

With these you won't need pasting table, bucket and pasting brush but you will need a special light plastic trough made for the purpose. Put it below where the first drop is to be hung and fill with water – covering the floor with layers of newspaper will soak up accidental spillages. Don't try to lift the trough; slide it along the floor as the work progresses.

Cut each drop so patterns are matching, then roll the first one loosely from the bottom up with the pattern inside. Place it in the trough and press it down so water can reach all the parts covered with paste. Leave for the required soaking time (check manufacturers' instructions but, it's usually between 30 seconds and 2 minutes), then pick the drop up by the two top corners and take it to the ceiling line. Press onto the wall using an absorbent sponge to mop up and push out air bubbles. Press firmly on the edges with the sponge or a seam roller, then trim waste.

COPING WITH WALL FITTINGS ... AND CREASES

Few walls present a perfectly clear surface for paperhanging. Almost all will contain such small obstacles as light switches and power points, while some may carry wall-mounted fittings such as curtain tracks and adjustable shelving. Small obstacles can be papered round with some careful trimming, but larger obstacles are best taken down from the wall and replaced when you have finished decorating. That way you will get a really professional finish.

Creases can also spoil the look of your work. If they occur, take steps to remove them before the paste dries. Here's how.

1 *To cut round light switches, mark centre of plate, insert scissor tips and cut out towards plate corners.*

1 *Creases are a common fault where the wall is out of true or if you haven't brushed the paper out properly.*

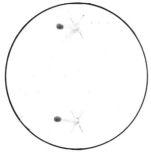

1 *Use matchsticks, pushed head out into wall plugs, to show where wall fittings have been taken down.*

2 *Crease tongues of paper against edges of plate, lift away from wall, trim along line and brush back into place.*

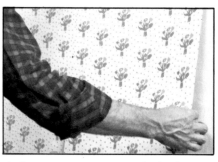

2 *To remove the crease, peel the paper from the wall to a point above the crease – to the ceiling if necessary.*

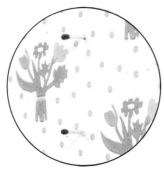

2 *Brush paper firmly over match heads so they pierce it. With hanging complete remove matches and replace fittings.*

3 *With washable and vinyl papers push a strip of rigid plastic against plate edges and trim with a sharp knife.*

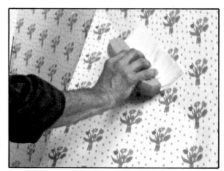

3 *Brush the paper back into position – across towards the butt join, then to the other edge and down to the bottom.*

PAPERING AWKWARD AREAS

The techniques for papering round tricky areas like corners and reveals are quite basic. But care and patience is required if you are going to get really professional results from your paperhanging.

Although the major part of wallpapering, hanging straight lengths is fairly quick and straightforward. The tricky areas – corners, doorways and so on – which call for careful measuring, cutting and pattern matching are the bits that slow the job down. There's no worse eye-sore than a lop-sided pattern at a corner; but if you use the right techniques you can avoid this problem.

You have to accept in advance that the continuity of a pattern will be lost in corners and similar places; even a professional decorator can't avoid this. However, he has the ability to match the pattern as closely as possible so that the discontinuity is not noticeable, and this is what you have to emulate.

Things would, of course, be a lot simpler if all corners were perfectly square, but this is rarely the case. When you wallpaper a room for the first time you are likely to discover that all those angles that appeared to be true are anything but.

You can, however, help to overcome the problem of careful pattern matching at corners by choosing a paper with the right design (see *Ready Reference*). The most difficult of the lot to hang are those with a regular small and simple repeat motif. The loss of pattern continuity will be easy to spot if even slight errors are made. The same is often true of large, repeat designs. With either of these types, a lot more time will be involved and it could well take a couple of hours to hang a few strips around a single window reveal.

Sloping ceiling lines are another problem area and certain patterns will show it up clearly. You can understand the nuisance of a sloping ceiling by imagining a pattern with, say, regular rows of horizontal roses. Although the first length on the wall may be hung correctly to leave a neat row of roses along the ceiling line the trouble is that as subsequent lengths are hung and the pattern is matched, you will see less and less of that top row of roses as the ceiling slopes down. And, conversely, if the ceiling line slopes upwards, you will start to see a new row of roses appearing above. So, despite the fact that each length has been hung

vertically, the sloping ceiling will make the job look thoroughly unsightly.

Internal and external corners

Before you begin papering round a corner, you must hang the last full length before the corner. Your corner measurement will be done from one edge of this length. You can use a steel tape or boxwood rule to measure the gap to the corner (see *Ready Reference*) and then cut the piece required to fill it, plus a margin which is carried round onto the new wall. Since it's likely that the walls will be out of square and that the margin taken round the corner will not be exactly equal all the way down, it's obvious you would have a terrible job hanging the matching offcut strip to give a neat butt join.

For this reason you must hang the matching offcut which goes on the 'new' wall to a true vertical and then brush it over the margin you've turned onto this wall. You should aim to match the pattern at the corner as closely as possible. Since the paper overlaps, the match will not be perfect, but this is unavoidable and will not, in any case be noticeable as the overlap is tucked into or round the corner out of sight (see *Ready Reference*).

Papering round window reveals

Unless you intend to paper just one or two walls in a room you will eventually have to cope with papering round a window. Pattern matching is the problem here, but you should find cutting the paper to fit above and

below a window is not too difficult provided you work in a logical order (see box opposite). But you may have to be prepared for lots of scissor work when you cut out strips of paper for the two sides and top of the reveal to ensure the pattern matches the paper on the facing wall. (It's worth getting into the habit of marking some sort of code on the back of each piece of paper before it's cut up so you will be able to find matching pieces quickly.)

Make sure that you don't end up with a seam on the edge of the reveal, where it will be exposed to knocks and liable to lift. Before you begin work on the window wall, take a roll of wallcovering and estimate how many widths will fit between the window and the nearest corner. If it looks as though you will be left with a join within about 25mm (1in) of the window opening you should alter your starting point slightly so that, when you come to the window, the seam will have moved away from the edge of the reveal.

Where the lengths of paper are positioned on the window wall obviously depends on the position of the window, its size and the width of the wallpaper. But the ideal situation occurs when the last full length before you reach the window leaves a width of wall, plus window reveal, that measures just less than the width of the wallpaper. You can then hang the next length so its upper part goes on the wall above the window, the lower part on the wall below it and (after making two scissor cuts) turn the middle part to cover the side of the window reveal. The edge of

PAPERING ROUND A WINDOW

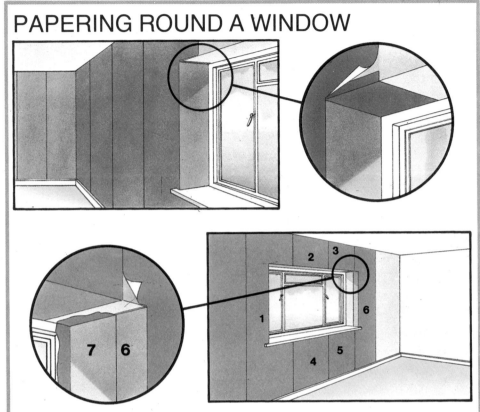

Top: Fill the narrow gap left on the underside of the reveal with a small offcut.
Above: The papering sequence; piece 7 fills the gap left on the reveal by piece 6.

the middle part can then be creased and trimmed so it fits neatly up against the window frame.

Go on to hang short lengths of wallpaper above the window, cutting them so their lower parts can be taken on to the underside of the top window reveal, and again trim them so they fit neatly up against the window frame. When you reach a point where the reveal on the opposite side of the window is less than the width of the wallpaper away from the last edge hung, you should stop and repeat the papering process below the window between the sill and skirting board, trimming as you go.

You can then hang the next full length in the same way as the one you hung on the first side of the window. You should, first, however, hang a plumbline over the pieces in place above the top and bottom of the window then hang the full length to the plumb-line, trimming any slight overlap on the new length if necessary. (By doing this, you will ensure that the lengths to be hung on the rest of the wall will be truly vertical.)

Often, however, the position of the last full length at the window will fall so that the paper does not cover the reveal at the side of the window, and in this case you will have to cut matching strips to fill the gap. Similarly, you

will have to cut strips to fill the gaps on the underside of the reveal at the top of the window.

Dormer windows

In attics and loft rooms there will be sloping ceilings and dormer windows with which you will have to contend. If you decide to paper rather than paint the sloping ceiling, then you treat it in the same way as you would a vertical wall; there are no unusual problems involved, other than the peculiar working angle. Remember, too, that if you choose the wrong type of paper the irregular pattern-matching could give unfortunate results.

Paper the wall alongside the window and then round the window itself, moving on to the wall below the other side of the sloping ceiling (see step-by-step photographs). Finally, you can paper the dormer cheeks.

Chimney breasts and fireplace surrounds

Special rules apply to chimney breasts. For a start, since they are a focal point in the room, any pattern must be centralised. The design of the paper will affect where you begin to hang the wallpaper. Where one length of paper contains a complete motif, you can simply measure and mark off the central point of the chimney breast and use a

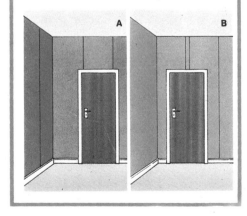

PAPERING AN INTERNAL CORNER

1 *Hang the last full length before the corner. Then measure the gap (see Ready Reference) to determine the width to be cut from the next length.*

3 *Measure the width of the matching offcut strip of paper and use a plumbline to mark a guideline on the wall this distance from the corner.*

2 *Cut from the next length a piece which will overlap 12mm (¹/₂in) round the corner. Then paste and fix it in position so it fills the corner gap.*

4 *Hang the offcut so its cut edge overlaps the matching edge of the first corner piece and its 'good' edge aligns with the vertical guideline.*

FLUSH WINDOWS

1 *Fix the last full length of paper before the window and pull the excess across. Cut round the sill and fix the paper beneath it.*

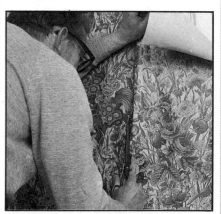

2 *You can then trim off the excess paper which runs alongside the window. Now press and brush the pasted paper into position.*

3 *Work along the wall underneath the window, fixing, creasing and trimming as you go. Afterwards you can fix the paper on the other side of the window.*

plumbline at this point to help you draw a vertical line down the centre. You can then begin hanging the wallpaper by aligning the first length with this line.

On the other hand, if it is the type of paper where two lengths, when aligned, form a motif, you will first have to estimate the number of widths which will fit across the chimney breast and then draw a line as a guide for hanging the first length of paper so the combined motif will, in fact, be centralised.

Your order of work should be from the centre (or near centre) outwards and you will then have to turn the paper round the corners at the sides so you form an overlap join with the paper which will be applied to the sides of the chimney breast. Follow the usual techniques for measuring and papering round external corners, remembering in particular not too take too much paper round the corner.

When it comes to fireplace surrounds, there are so many varying kinds of mantelshelfs and surrounds that only general guidance can be given. Usually the technique is to brush the paper down on to the top part of the wall and then cut it to fit along the back edge of the mantelshelf. You can then cut the lower half to fit the contours of the surround. If it's a complicated outline then you'll have to gradually work downwards, using a small pair of sharp scissors, pressing the paper into each shape, withdrawing it to snip along the crease line, then brushing it back into place.

If there is only a small distance between the edge of the mantelshelf and the corner, it's a lot easier if you hang the paper down to the shelf and then make a neat, horizontal cut line in the paper. You can then hang the lower half separately and join the two halves to disguise the cut line.

PAPERING ROUND A DORMER

1 Where the dormer cheek meets the junction of the wall and ceiling, draw a line at right angles to the wall on the ceiling by the dormer cheek.

2 Draw a vertical line at right angles to the first line on the dormer cheek. You can then fix the first length of paper in place on the dormer cheek.

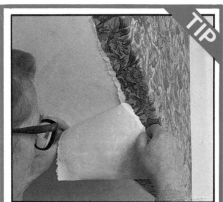

3 Work along towards the window, trimming as you go. Gently tear along the overlap to feather its edge so you won't get a bulky join later.

4 At the window, crease along the side of the frame by running the edge of the scissors along it. You can then carefully trim along the creased line.

5 Return to the small gap which needs to be filled at the narrow end of the dormer cheek; fix this piece in position, crease and trim.

6 Mark a straight line on the sloping ceiling to serve as a guideline for fixing the first length of paper on the underside of the dormer cheek.

7 Cut a piece of paper so it reaches from the point you have marked up to the window and brush it into position ensuring that it covers the feathered edges of the overlap.

8 At the junction of the wall and ceiling you will have to cut round awkward angles. You can then go ahead and brush the paper into its final position.

9 Finally, you can brush the strip of paper which fills the gap between the wall and the underside of the dormer cheek into position to finish off the dormer area neatly.

HOME DECORATING

Tiling

CERAMIC TILES for small areas

Ceramic tiles are easy-clean, hygienic and hard wearing. By starting with a small area in your home where these qualities are needed – like splashbacks or worktops – you'll not only grasp the basics but also gain confidence to tackle bigger things.

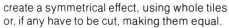

Modern ceramic tiles are thin slabs of clay, decorated on one side with coloured glazes. These are baked on to give the tile a hard, glassy surface resistant to water, heat and almost all household chemicals. The clay from which tiles are made, which is known as the biscuit, varies and you need to know the differences before you choose the tile to use. The thinnest ones with a pale coloured biscuit are good on all vertical surfaces (including doors where extra weight puts stress on the hinges).

If the biscuit is reddish/brown it has been high baked (vitrified). The thicker and darker coloured it is the more strength the tile has — floor tiles, for example, are usually big in size as well as thick in biscuit.

Work surfaces need tiles that are strong to withstand weights of heavy pots, while splashbacks and bathroom surfaces can take lighter, thinner ones.

Types of tiles
Within each range of tiles there are usually three types. *Spacer* tiles have small projections on each edge called lugs which butt up to the neighbouring tile and provide the correct space for grouting (with these it is very hard to vary the width of the grouting). *Border* tiles are squared off on all sides but are glazed on two adjacent edges — these give a neat finish to outer corners and top or side edges. *Universal or continental* tiles have no lugs and are square on all edges. All three can be used successfully in small areas, but do remember that if tiles do not have lugs you have to include grouting space in your calculations — the thinnest tiles need to be spaced by nothing more than torn-up pieces of cardboard, 6mm (¼in) tiles are best with a matchstick width in between.

Tiles are sold by the sq metre, sq yd, boxed in 25s or 50s, or can be bought individually. Boxed tiles usually advise on adhesive and grout needed for specific areas. When buying, if there's no written information available always check that the tile is suitable.

How to plan the layout
When tiling small areas you don't have much space to manoeuvre. The idea in all tiling is to create a symmetrical effect, using whole tiles or, if any have to be cut, making them equal.

Knowing about the different sizes of tiles helps in the planning. For example, if you know the width and height or depth of the surface you intend to tile, you can divide this by the known size of tiles until you find the one that gives the right number of whole tiles. Remember that the width of grouting has to be added to the measurement with non-lugged tiles – and except with the very thinnest tiles this can be slightly widened if it saves cutting a tile.

If you're prepared to incorporate cut tiles into the planning remember:
● on the width of the tiled area, place equal cut tiles at each end
● on the height, place cut tiles at the top edge
● on the depth (eg, window-recesses) put cut tiles at back edge
● frame a fitting by placing cut tiles at each side and the top

A mix of patterned or textured with plain tiles is best done first on metricated graph paper. This will help you see where you want the pattern to fall.

Fixings should be made in the grouting lines where possible. Some tile ranges have soap dishes, towel rails etc attached to tiles so they can be incorporated in a scheme, but if these don't suit your purposes, you can drill the tiles to screw in your own fitting.

A working plan
All tiles should be fixed level and square so it's important to establish the horizontal and vertical with a spirit level. Draw in the lines with pencil. If you plan to tile where there is no support (eg, on either side of a basin or sink) lightly pin a length of 50 x 25mm (2 x 1in) timber below the tiling line – the batten will prevent the tiles slipping.

On doors you may have to consider adding a timber surround to keep the tiles secure as they will be subjected to movement (also see section on *Adhesives* below).

Adhesives and grouting
The choice of both of these depends on where the tiles are to be fixed. In a watery situation (eg, a shower cubicle or a steamy kitchen) it is important to use a waterproof variety of both, even though you might have

Ready Reference

TILE SHAPES AND SIZES

Ceramic tiles for walls are usually square or oblong in shape. The commonest sizes are shown below. The smaller sizes are usually 4mm (⅝in) thick, while larger tiles may be 6mm (¼in) or more in thickness.

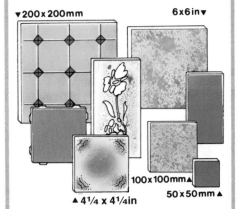

▼200 x 200mm

6 x 6 in ▼

100 x 100mm ▲

50 x 50mm ▲

▲ 4¼ x 4¼in

HOW MANY TILES?

Square or oblong areas
● measure lengths and width of the area
● divide each measurement by the size of tile you're using, rounding up to the next whole number if you get a fraction
● multiply the two figures to give the number of tiles needed

Awkwardly-shaped areas
● divide area into convenient squares or oblongs
● work out each one as above adding up the area totals to give the final figures

Patterns using two or more different tiles
● sketch out design on graph paper, one square for each tile (two for oblong tiles); use colours to mark where different tiles fall
● count up totals needed of each pattern, counting part tiles as whole ones

Add 10% to your final tile counts to allow for breakages

ADHESIVE/GROUT

For each square metre of tiling allow:
● 1.5kg (about 1 litre) of adhesive
● 150g of grout

TIP: AVOID NARROW STRIPS

Less than about 25mm/1in wide is very difficult to cut. When planning, if you see narrow strips are going to occur you can:
● replan the rows to use one less whole tile with two wider cut pieces at either end
● or increase the grouting space slightly between every tile in the row

HOW TO HANG TILES

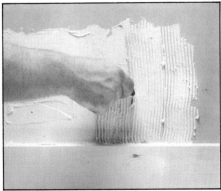

1 Spread ceramic tile adhesive to cover 1 sq metre, then 'comb' with notched spreader. To support tiles where no other support exists, pin a horizontal timber batten to the wall.

2 When positioning tiles it is important to twist them slightly to bed them. Don't slide them as this forces adhesive between joints.

3 Form even grouting spaces between tiles without lugs with pieces of matchstick. Or you can use torn-up cardboard from the tile packaging or similar if you want only a narrow grouting space.

4 Remove matchsticks or card after all tiles are hung, and grout 12-24 hours later. Press grout into the spaces using a small sponge or squeegee, making sure no voids are left in either vertical or horizontal spaces.

5 After 10 minutes, wipe off excess grouting with soft cloth. Use fine dowelling (sand the end to round it) to even up and smooth the lines. Fill any voids that appear with fresh grout to prevent water penetration.

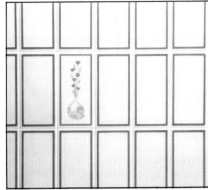

6 When grouting is dry, polish the tiles with a soft cloth so the area is smooth. All the surface needs now is an occasional wipe-down although non-waterproof grout may tend to discolour as time goes by.

to wait for 4-5 days before exposing the tile surface to use.

All ceramic tile adhesives are like thin putty and can be bought ready mixed in tubs or in powder form to be made up with water. They are what is known as thin-bed adhesives in that they are designed to be applied in a thin layer on a flat even surface. The spread is controlled by a notched comb (usually provided by the manufacturer but cheap to buy where you bought the tiles) to make furrows of a specified depth. When the tiles are pressed on with a slight twist, the adhesive evenly grips the back of the biscuit.

Special latex-based adhesives (usually, two-part products which have to be mixed before using) have much more flexibility and are good for tiles where there is any movement (eg, on doors).

Spread the adhesive on an area no more than 1 sq metre (1 sq yd) at a time, or it will lose its gripping power before you have time to place the tiles. If you remove a tile, before refixing comb the adhesive again.

Grout gives the final finish to the tiled area, filling the spaces between the tiles and preventing moisture getting behind them and affecting the adhesive. Grouting can be done 12-24 hours after the last tile has been pressed into place. Grout can be standard or waterproof (with added acrylic), and both are like a cellulose filler when made up.

If you only make up one lot of grouting, you can colour it with special grouting tints – but remember that it's hard to make other batches match the colour. Waterproof grouting cannot always take these tints.

Press grout between the tiles with a sponge or squeegee and wipe off excess with a damp sponge. Even up the grouting by drawing a pencil-like piece of wood (eg dowelling) along each row first vertically, then horizontally. Do this within 10 minutes of grouting so it is not completely dry.

Leave the tiles for 24 hours before polishing with a clean dry cloth. Wash clean only if a slight bloom remains.

Tiles should never be fixed with tight joints for any movement of the wall or fittings will cause the tiles to crack. Similarly where tiles meet baths, basins, sinks etc, flexibility is needed – and grout that dries rigid cannot provide it. These gaps must be filled with a silicone rubber sealant

Techniques with tiles

To cut tiles, lightly score the glaze with a tile cutter to break the surface. Place the tile glazed side up with the scored line over matchsticks and firmly but gently press the tile down on each side. If using a pencil press on one side, hold the other. Smooth the cut edge with a file. Very small adjustments are best done by filing the edge of the whole tile.

CUTTING TILES

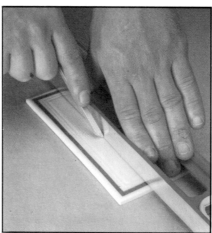

1 Before a tile will break, the glaze must be scored — on the edges as well as surface. Use a carbide-tipped cutter against a straight-edge.

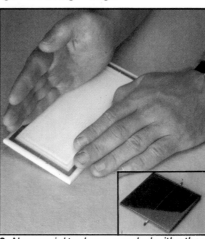

3 No special tools are needed with other tile-breaking methods. For medium thick tiles use a pencil, for thin tiles use matchsticks.

2 Another type of cutter has 'jaws' which clasp the tile during breaking. (It also has a small 'wheel' for scoring through the glaze on the tile).

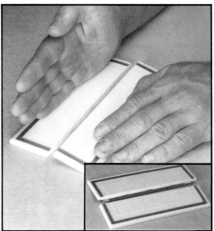

4 Place pencil centrally under tile and score line, hold one side and press firmly on other. With thin tiles, press lightly both sides.

To remove a narrow strip of tile, score the line heavily by drawing the tile cutter across the tile more firmly several times in the same place. Then use pincers to 'nibble' the waste away in small pieces and smooth the edge. Glaze on broken tiles is as sharp as glass, so be careful not to cut yourself.

Templates for awkwardly shaped tiles are not difficult to make. Cut the shape in card, place on a tile and score a line freehand with the tile cutter. Any straight score marks can be deepened afterwards, using a straight edge for support. Then nibble away the waste with pincers. If there's a large amount to be cut away, score the waste part to divide it into sections, then nibble away. A good tip is to do this on a soft or padded surface so the tile doesn't break in the wrong place.

Suitable surfaces

The ideal surface for tiling is one that's perfectly flat, dry and firm. Small irregularities will be covered up, but any major hollows, bumps or flaking, need to be made good.

Plastered walls and asbestos cement sheets: perfect for tiling, but wait a month after any new plastering to allow the wall to dry out completely. Unless surface has been previously painted, apply a coat of plaster primer to prevent the liquid in the tile adhesive from being absorbed too quickly.

Plasterboard: again, ideal for tiling as long as it's firmly fixed and adjacent boards cannot shift. (If they did the joins would probably crack). To prepare the surface, remove all dust, wipe down with white spirit

Ready Reference

TOOLS FOR TILING

Tile cutter: essential for scoring glaze of tiles before breaking them. Score only once (the second time you may waver from the line and cause an uneven break).
Pincers: these are used for nibbling away small portions of tile, after scoring a line with the cutter. Ordinary pincers are fine for most jobs, but special tile nibblers are available.
Special cutter: combines a cutting edge (usually a small cutting wheel) with jaws which snap the tile along the scored line.
Tile file: an abrasive mesh, used as a file to 'shave' off small amounts.

TIP: TO DRILL A TILE

● make a cross of masking tape and mark the point where you want the hole
● drill after adhesive and grouting have set using lowest speed or a hand drill with masonry bit — too much speed at the start will craze the tile
● once through the glaze, drill in the normal way

● cut tile into two along line corresponding with centre point of pipe; offer up each half to the pipe
● mark freehand semi-circles on tile to match edge of pipe; score line with tile cutter and nibble away waste with pincers

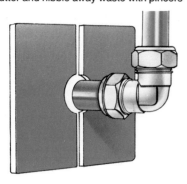

SHAPING TILES

5 *Edges of broken tiles need to be smoothed off — use a special tile file mounted on wood, a wood file or rub against rough concrete.*

6 *To cut an awkward shape, make a card template. Place it on the tile and score glaze on the surface and edges with the tile cutter.*

7 *On a soft surface, use pincers to take tiny nibbles out of the tile. If you're over enthusiastic you'll break off more than you intended.*

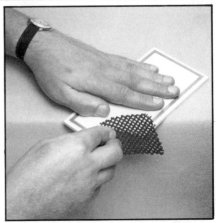

8 *Once the waste has been slowly but surely nibbled away, smooth up the edge. Files are also useful when a whole tile needs a slight trimming.*

to remove grease, then treat with primer.
Paint: old emulsion-paint needs to be cleaned thoroughly with sugar soap or detergent to remove all traces of dust and grease. Gloss paint needs to be cleaned thoroughly; remove any flaking paint then roughen up whole surface with a coarse abrasive to provide a good key for the adhesive.
Wallpaper: DO NOT tile directly onto wallpaper, as this can be pulled away from the wall by the adhesive. Strip it off completely.
Wood and Chipboard: perfect for tiling as long as it is flat and adjacent boards cannot shift. Treat with an ordinary wood primer.
Laminates: joins and small, minor blemishes in the surface can be covered up so long as the entire sheet is soundly fixed and absolutely flat. Its smooth face must be

roughened with course abrasive to provide a key for the tile adhesive.
Old ceramic tiles: the thin biscuit ceramic tiles are excellent for tiling over as they add little to the wall's thickness and won't protrude beyond existing fittings. Loose and cracked tiles will have to be removed. Scrape out the grouting surrounding the tile using an old, thin screwdriver or something similar, then, beginning in the centre and working outwards, remove the tile using a club hammer and cold chisel.

Small sections or mis-shapen pieces (as around a new fixture) can be built up level with neighbouring tiles with cellulose filler.

The area should then be sealed with plaster primer or emulsion paint to finish the surface.

CERAMIC TILING WALL TO WALL

Ceramic tiles are an ideal decorating material for they make a room look good for years and require virtually no maintenance. But covering several walls with tiles is a large-scale job which needs a methodical and careful approach if you are to achieve the best results.

The all-in-one look that wall-to-wall tiling can give has to be planned carefully to avoid expensive and time consuming mistakes. How to do this may depend on whether you want to include special patterns in the design, but following certain rules will give a desirable symmetry to the look.

One of the hardest tasks will probably be choosing the tiles for there's a vast array of shapes, sizes and colours available. Having picked out the ones you want though, don't buy until you've done the planning – for the plans of each wall should tell you whether the pattern will work in the room or would be lost in the cutting or amid the fittings.

Plans on paper also give you an instant method of working out how many tiles to buy (counting each cut one as a whole, and adding 2-5% for unintended breakage) including the number which will need to be border (two glazed edges) or mitred (on square or rectangular universal tiles) for the top row of half-tiled walls or external corners. Buy all the tiles at once, but do check each carton to make sure there's no variation in the colour (this can occur during the firing of different batches).

Planning on paper

The best possible way to start planning for a large expanse of tiling is not on the wall, but on paper. Graph paper is ideal, particularly if you intend including a mix of plain and patterned tiles, or a large motif that needs building up. Of course, advance planning is also essential if you're tiling round major features like windows, doors, mirrors, shower cubicles and so on.

You need separate pieces of graph paper for each wall you intend tiling. Allow the large (1cm) squares on the paper to represent your tiles — one for a square tile of any size, two for a rectangular tile; this will give you a scale to work to. Now mark up sheets of greaseproof paper with your actual wall sizes using the scale dictated by the tile size on the graph paper. Measure and outline on the see-through paper the exact position and in-scale dimensions of all fixtures and fittings (see the planning pictures on page 44).

At this stage, the objective is to decide

how to achieve the best symmetrical layout for your tiles — the 'ideal' is to have either whole or equal-size cut tiles on each side of a fixture.

First you have to mark in the central guide lines. For instance, on *walls with a window* draw a line from the sill centre to the floor, and from the centre of the top of the window to the ceiling. If there are *two windows* also draw in the central line from floor to ceiling between them. Mark the centre point above a *door* to the ceiling and also indicate the horizontal line at the top of the door. In the same way draw in a central line from the top of a *basin or vanity unit* to the ceiling.

For all these lines use a coloured pen for you have to be aware of them when deciding where whole tiles should be positioned. But they're only the starting point — other potential problems have to be looked at too.

Place the see-through paper over the tile sizes on the graph paper so you can see how the tiles will fall in relation to the guide lines. Now take into account the following important points:
● The first row above the lowest level — either the floor, the skirting board or a wall-to-wall fitting — should be whole tiles. If necessary, change this to prevent a thin strip being cut at the ceiling.
● Check where tiles come in relation to fittings. If very thin strips (less than 38mm/1½in) or narrow 'L' shapes would need to be cut, move the top sheet slightly up, down, left or right till the tiles are of a cuttable size — areas to watch are around windows, doors and where one wall meets another.

Placing patterns

When you are satisfied that you have a symmetrical and workable arrangement you can tape the top sheet in the right position on the graph paper, then start to plan where you're going to position your patterned tiles. Use pencil this time in case you change your mind and want to make adjustments. These are the points to watch:
● Don't place single motif patterns at internal corners where they would have to be cut — you won't find it easy to match up the remaining piece on the adjacent wall.

Ready Reference

TILING SEQUENCES

You can use the 'step' method (see page 55), or build 'pyramids'. Here are the sequences for different bonds.

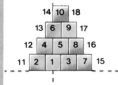

Running bond staggers the tiles. Place the first one centrally on your vertical line.

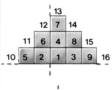

Jack-on-Jack has the joints lined up. Work either side of your vertical line.

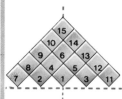

Diamond bond puts plain or outlined tiles at an angle. Place the first centrally on the vertical, fill in 'triangles' last.

● If the pattern builds up vertically and horizontally over four or more tiles, 'centre' the pattern on the wall so that cuts are equal at both ends. If pattern loss can't be avoided with designs of this type at least it can be kept to internal corners.

● Whole tiles should be used on both faces of external corners.

Now butt each of the wall plans up to the other to make sure that the patterns relate both vertically and horizontally.

Planning on the wall

When there are no complicated tiling patterns involved and walls are free of interruptions such as windows, it's often easier to do the planning directly on the wall itself. Here, the simple objective is to place the tiles symmetrically between the corners. And to do this, all you need is a tiling gauge which you can make.

A tiling gauge is like a long ruler, except that it's marked off in tile widths. Use a long, straight piece of timber ideally about 25mm square (1in square) and remember to include the grouting gap between tiles as you rule off the gauge. If you're using rectangular tiles, mark the widths on one side, the lengths on the other.

Holding the gauge against the walls —

first vertically, then horizontally — tells you instantly where the whole tiles will fit in and where cut tiles will be needed. But first you must find the centre of each wall. Measure the width — doing this at three places will also tell you if the corners are vertical (hang a plumb line or use a spirit level to make absolutely sure) — and halve it to find the centre point. Use the tiling gauge to mark this vertical centre line with a pencil, then hold the gauge against it. Move it up or down until you have at least a whole tile's width above the floor or skirting board — this can be adjusted slightly if it avoids a thin piece of tile at ceiling height — then mark off the tile widths on the vertical line itself.

Now hold the tiling gauge horizontally, and move it to left or right of the vertical line if thin pieces of tile would have to be cut near windows or fittings, or to make cut tiles at both ends of the wall equal. Following this adjustment, mark the wall and draw in a new vertical line if necessary. The wall can now be marked horizontally with tile widths. Keeping to the same horizontal, mark up adjacent walls in the same way.

At corners, whether internal or external, don't assume they're either square, vertical or even. An internal corner is the worst place to start your tiling for this very reason, but it

doesn't matter if you position cut tiles there. On external corners use the tiling gauge to work inwards in whole tile widths.

You can also use the tiling gauge to check that your graph plan is accurate, and make any necessary adjustments.

Putting up battens

Once you have determined that your plan is correct, fix a length of perfectly straight 50mm x 25mm (2in x 1in) battening across the full width of the wall — use a spirit level to ensure that the batten is horizontal. Use masonry nails to fix it in place but do not drive them fully home as they will have to be removed later. If using screws the wall should be plugged. The batten provides the base for your tiling and it's important that its position is correct.

If more than one wall is being tiled, continue to fix battens around the room at the same height, using the spirit level to check the horizontal. The last one you fix should tie up perfectly with the first. If there are gaps, at the door for example, check that the level either side is the same, by using a straightedge and spirit level to bridge the gap.

Once the horizontal battens are fixed, fix a vertical batten to give yourself the starting point for the first tile. Use a spirit level or plumb line to make sure it's positioned accurately.

Fixing tiles

Begin tiling from the horizontal base upwards, checking as you work that the tiles are going up accurately both vertically and horizontally. Work on an area of approximately 1 sq metre (1 sq yd) at a time, spreading the adhesive and fixing all the whole tiles using card or matchsticks as spacers as necessary. Make sure no excess adhesive is left on the surface of the tiles.

Next, deal with any tiles that need to be cut. You may find the gap into which they fit is too narrow to operate the adhesive spreader properly. In this case spread the adhesive onto the back of the tiles.

When all the tiling above the base batten has been completed wait for 8-12 hours, before removing the battens, and completing the tiling. Take care when removing the base batten that the tiles above are not disturbed — the adhesive is unlikely to be fully set.

Dealing with corners

Your original planning should have indicated how many border or mitred tiles you will need for tiling external corners or for the top line of tiles on a half-tiled wall. You will find external corners, those which project into the room, in virtually all tiling situations — around boxed-in pipework , or around a window or door reveal, or in an L-shaped room.

Where you are using universal tiles at an

PLANNING TILE LAYOUT ON PAPER

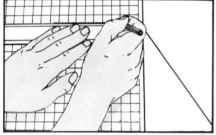

1 On graph paper with large (eg, 1cm) squares, let each square represent one whole square tile. Strengthen the grid lines with coloured pen if necessary.

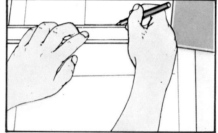

2 On tracing paper, draw the outline of each wall to be tiled, and mark in doors and windows. Use the scale 1cm = the actual tile size (eg, 150mm).

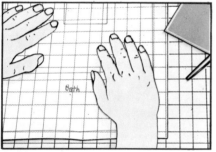

3 Place greaseproof over graph paper and move it around till you get the most manageable size cut tiles, especially near fixtures, ceiling and floor.

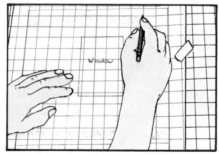

4 Tape the top sheet in place, then mark the pattern in with pencil. Do each wall the same so that the alignment of the horizontal is correct.

external corner, start at the corner with a whole tile — it should project by the depth of the mitre so that the mitre on the other face neatly butts up against it with a fine space for grouting in between.

With window reveals the correct method is to tile up the wall to sill level, cutting tiles if necessary. Fit whole tiles either side of the reveal, then again cut tiles to fill the space between those whole ones and the window frame. Attach whole border or mitred tiles to the sill so they butt up against the wall tiles. If using square-edged tiles the ones on the sill should cover the edges of those on the wall so the grouting line is not on the sill surface. If the sill is narrower than a whole tile, cut the excess from the back — not the front. If the sill is deeper than a whole tile, put cut tiles near the window with the cut edge against the frame. Continually check the accurate lining up of tiles with a spirit level.

Some vertical external corners are not as precisely straight and vertical as they should be and this can lead to problems of tile alignment. The use of a thick-bed adhesive will help to straighten out some irregularities where a corner goes inwards (a thin-bed helps where the wall leans outwards). Buying a 'flexible' adhesive will give you both qualities. As a general rule it is

PLANNING ON THE WALL

2 *Use a plumb line to check that the wall is vertical.*

1 *(inset) Mark the tiling gauge in tile widths (and lengths if they are rectangular).*

3 *Draw verticals down the wall, marking off the exact tile widths to give an accurate guide.*

4 *Check each horizontal with a spirit level, then mark tile positions from floor to ceiling.*

5 *Place horizontal batten at least a tile's width above floor or a fitting using masonry nails or screws.*

6 *Fix vertical batten and begin to tile where the battens meet. Spread adhesive to cover 1 sq metre (1 sq yd).*

Ready Reference

TACKLING TILING PROBLEMS
Whenever a fitting, a door or window interrupts the clean run of a wall, it becomes the focal point of the wall. So you have to plan for symmetry *round* the features. Here are some guidelines:

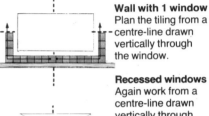

Wall with 1 window
Plan the tiling from a centre-line drawn vertically through the window.

Recessed windows
Again work from a centre-line drawn vertically through window. But make sure that whole tiles are placed at the front of the sill and the sides of the reveals. Place cut tiles closest to the window frame.

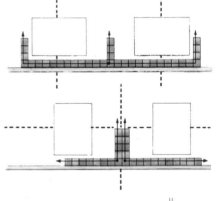

Wall with two windows
Unless the space between the two windows is exactly equal to a number of whole tiles, plan your tiling to start from a centre-line drawn between the two.

Wall with door
If the door is placed fairly centrally in the wall, plan your tiling from a centre-line drawn vertically through the door. If, however, the door is very close to a side wall, the large expanse of wall is a more prominent focal point. So plan the tiling to start one tile's width from the frame. If the frame is not exactly vertical, you'll be able to cut tiles to fit in the remaining space.

Jem Grischotti

MAKE YOUR OWN TILE BREAKER

1 *Use a timber offcut wider than the tile as the base. Use 3mm (⅛in) ply for the top and sides.*

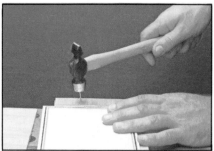

2 *Stack ply strips on both sides till the same height as the tile, then pin. Nail on the top piece.*

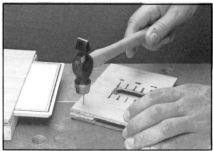

3 *The breaking part needs to be as wide and deep as the tile, with the opening on the top a half tile long.*

4 *Score the glaze on the top and edges with a carbide-tipped cutter. Put the tile into the main part.*

5 *Slip on the breaking part so the score line is between the two. Hold one side while you press the other.*

6 *The tile breaks cleanly. This aid costs nothing and will save you time when tiling a large expanse.*

TILING CORNERS

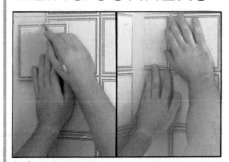

1 *At an internal corner, mark amount to be cut at top and bottom. Break the tile, then fit in position.*

2 *File the remainder until it fits the adjacent area with enough space left for a fine line of grout.*

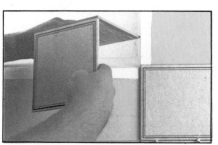

3 *On a window sill, use a whole tile at the front and make sure that it overlaps the one on the wall-face underneath.*

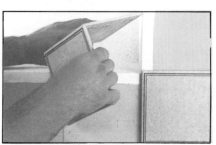

4 *Mitred edges of universal tiles and glazed edges of border tiles give a better finish to external corners.*

better to concentrate on lining up your border or mitred tiles perfectly vertically with only minute 'steps' between tiles, then bedding spacer or ordinary tiles behind to correspond with the line. Don't forget that if you do have to create a very slight stepped effect, you can reduce the uneven effect between the corner tiles and others by pressing in extra grouting later.

Internal corners seldom cause serious problems as cut tiles can be shaped to suit fluctuations from the truly vertical. Don't assume when cutting tiles for a corner that all will be the same size — the chances are that they will vary considerably and should be measured and cut individually. Another point: don't butt tiles up against each other so they touch — leave space for the grouting which will give the necessary flexibility should there be any wall movement.

Tiling around electrical fittings

When tiling around electrical fittings it is better to disconnect the electricity and remove the wall plate completely so that you can tile right up to the edge of the wall box. This is much neater and easier than trying to cut tiles to fit around the perimeter of the plate. Cut tiles as described in the illustration on pages 41 and 42 and fit them in the normal way with the plate being replaced on top, completely covering the cut edges of the tiles. This same principle applies to anything easily removable. The fewer objects you have to tile around the better, so before starting any tiling get to work with a screwdriver.

You have the greatest control over the end result if at the planning stage you work out where you want to place fittings such as towel rails and soap dishes, shelves and the like. Some tile ranges offer them attached so it's only a matter of fitting them in as you put the tiles up.

Tiling non-rigid surfaces

On surfaces which are not totally rigid or which are subject to movement, vibration or the odd shock, tiles should not be attached using adhesive which dries hard as most standard and waterproof types do. Instead use adhesives which retain some flexibility. These may be cement-based types with a latex rubber content, or acrylic adhesives. You may have to surround a non-rigid surface with wooden lipping to protect the tiles.

TILING AROUND FIXTURES

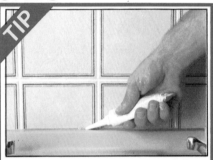

1 *At awkward corners use card to make a tile-size template. Place it on the tile and score the shape, then gently nibble out the waste with pincers — the smaller the bits the better.*

2 *Where basins, baths, kitchen sinks or laundry tubs meet tiles, seal the join with silicone caulking to keep out water. Caulking comes in various colours to match fixtures.*

3 *After the adhesive has had time to set, the tiles are grouted both to protect them and to enhance their shape and colour.*
Accessories can be bought already attached to tiles, can be screw mounted after drilling the tile, or if lightweight can be stuck on to tiles with adhesive pads.

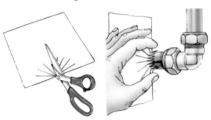

Flooring

STRIPPING TIMBER FLOORS

Sanding wooden floorboards is dusty, time-consuming work, but it's not difficult. You'll find the effort well worthwhile when the boards are transformed into an attractive floor surface.

Using floorcoverings can be expensive, particularly if you have to deal with passages, stairs or landings as well as main rooms. As an alternative you could decide to leave a wooden floor uncovered after treatment to make it an attractive surface in its own right. Since timber is one of the most versatile flooring materials there is, it will fit in with most styles of decor, whether modern or traditional. It's extremely hardwearing and easy to look after. And, just as important, it has a warmth you don't get with most modern floorings of comparable durability.

You can, if you wish, lay a new timber floor, if the old one is rotten or in a bad state of repair, finishing it with stains or varnish to bring out the natural beauty of the wood. But the chances are you won't need to go to this expense. You may well have a wooden floor already which you've covered up. The old floorboards may not look much when you first expose them but if you sand them smooth to take off the uneven top layers engrained with dirt you'll be surprised how beautiful they can become, especially after they've been coated with varnish to make the grain pattern clear.

Checking out the floor
Of course, ordinary floorboards are not intended to be displayed, so you cannot guarantee good results. A particularly unattractive, inferior grade of timber may have been used. Or the boards may have been badly laid or badly looked after. The only way to find out is to lift any floorcovering and see for yourself. You can make a preliminary survey simply by lifting a corner of the floorcovering; but to be absolutely sure the whole floor should be exposed.

When you lift the existing floorcovering, take care to remove any fixing nails and the remains of flooring adhesive. Many flooring adhesives are soluble in white spirit (turps) or petrol. But obviously, if you're using petrol you must ensure the room is adequately ventilated. Don't smoke while you're doing the work.

The look of the timber grain is important, but here much depends on personal taste. Some people like wooden floors to have

even, restrained grain patterns; others feel that, unless the pattern is striking and irregular, the floor doesn't look like real wood. It's up to you, but do allow for the fact that any grain pattern will become slightly more pronounced once the boards have been sanded and sealed.

You should also see if the floorboards have been stained, and if so, whether or not the staining covers the entire floor: it was once popular to stain the edges and cover the central unstained portion with a carpet or linoleum square. If the staining has been carried out over the whole of the floor area there shouldn't be any problem with sanding and sealing later. Thoroughly sand a trial area by hand to get an idea of the finished result. If you don't like the way the floor looks, you can try restaining it experimentally; alternatively try to lighten or remove the existing wood stain with a proprietary wood bleach. Border staining can be more of a problem because of the need to match the border with the unstained part of the floor. Again, experimenting with stains and bleaches is the only answer; make sure you sand the test area first. If, when later you come to tackle the job in earnest, you give the floor its main sanding

after staining, there is a risk that the old and new stains will respond in rather different ways.

Preparing the surface
When you've got a good idea of what the final result will look like, you can turn your attention to the physical state of the floor. Are there lots of large gaps, wider than 2 or 3mm (up to ⅛in) between boards? If there are, the finished floor may well turn out to be excessively draughty so you will have to fill the gaps before sanding. To maintain the floor's 'natural' look involves tailoring a fillet of timber for each gap and you may well decide, as a result, that a wooden floor simply isn't worth the effort. Watch out, too, for signs of excessive localised wear resulting in dips and ridges that no amount of sanding will remove. And, finally, check for signs of woodworm. This must be treated, but, remember, woodworm treatment will not restore the appearance of the affected wood.

If, at this stage, things don't look too promising, there are three remedies to consider which may provide you with the solution you require.

The first is a cure for gaps. All you do is lift every single board and re-lay them closer together: not difficult but very hard work. Next there is the remedy for boards disfigured by wear or woodworm, and you can also use it to overcome the problems associated with stained boards. Again, all you do is lift and re-lay the boards, but this time, you re-lay them with what used to be the underside uppermost. This is also very hard work, and there is a possibility that the underside of the boards may look no better; a good builder should have laid the boards with the worse side face down when the house was built.

Because of the amount of work involved with both of these solutions it's best to consider them as a last resort. You could instead adopt the third remedy: give up the idea of sanding the existing boards and cover them with new ones. Such 'non-structural' boards are available in a variety of hardwoods and softwoods, so the results can be very rewarding indeed in that you will end up with a very attractively coloured and grained floor surface. However, this type of floor is likely to prove very expensive and rather tricky to lay. The actual techniques involved will be covered in a later article.

If, on the other hand, you check the boards and discover that they are suitable for sanding, you should fill any gaps and make sure there are no protruding nails or screws. These should be driven well below the surface otherwise there could be dire consequences when you are sanding (see *Ready Reference*). Giving screws an extra half a turn should do the trick; otherwise unscrew them, drill out a deeper countersink and replace them. For nails which cause you a problem you will need a nail punch (if you don't have one you can use an old blunt nail instead) to drive the offending nails home so they can't cause any further nuisance.

Sanding the floor

Sanding floorboards is in essence, no different to sanding any piece of natural timber. You must work your way through coarse, medium and then fine grades of abrasive until you achieve the desired finish. It's simply that you are working on a larger scale than usual.

However, this question of scale does create a few complications. First, there will be a great deal of dust flying about, and a lot of noise, so you must protect yourself with the appropriate safety equipment (see *Ready Reference*). You must also take steps to stop the dust being trodden all round your home. Second, the job will be far too large for sanding by hand and, in any case, the average DIY power sander wouldn't be up to the task. What you need are two special floor sanders, and these you will have to hire. (See below for tips on hiring.)

The first sander looks a bit like a lawn mower, but is in fact a giant belt sander and its role is to tackle the bulk of the floor. It has a revolving rubber-covered drum set on a wheeled frame which can be tilted backwards to lift the drum from the floor. You wrap a sheet of abrasive round the drum to provide the sanding surface. There is a bag attached to the sander into which a fan blows the wood dust and particles produced by the sanding process. The second sander is a sort of heavy duty orbital sander, and it is used to tackle the parts the main sander cannot reach. It works on the same principle as the large sander (you attach an abrasive sheet to a rubber pad) but, being small and lighter, it's easier to manoeuvre.

You won't be able to rely entirely on these labour-saving devices, though. After machine sanding there will be small unsanded patches left, usually at the edges of the floor and these

will have to be sanded by hand or scraped with a shave hook or some other form of scraper.

The need to hire equipment raises a further complication: careful planning is needed to keep the cost to a minimum. As always, the best way to start is by shopping around the hire shops in your area to find the best price. In particular, look for firms that give discounts for extended periods of hire (for example, one where the weekly rate is cheaper than say, four or five days at the day rate) and find out how much flexibility there is in allowing you to switch rates should you decide to keep the sanders for a day or two longer than originally anticipated. This is important because, although it's only sensible to keep the period of hire to a minimum by doing all the preparation (punching nail heads below the surface and so on) before you pick up the equipment, and returning it as soon as you've finished, floor sanding is physically very demanding, and may well take longer than you think.

Check up, too, on the cost of the abrasives. If there is a marked difference in price between two shops, it may be due to the fact that, while one offers ordinary glasspaper, the other offers a more modern synthetic paper which will last longer and clog less readily, and so works out cheaper than it appears. You will also encounter differences in the way abrasives are provided. For example, some shops will give a refund for any abrasive you don't use. A point to remember here is that as it's difficult to estimate exactly how much abrasive you will need it's wise to take an amount which appears surplus to requirements. If you take this precaution you will avoid the annoying situation where you have to down tools and buy extra abrasive.

PREPARING THE FLOOR

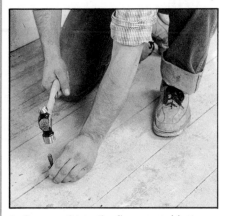

1 *Go over the entire floor, punching all nail heads well below the surface. If screws have been used, check they're adequately countersunk.*

2 *Cut thin fillets of wood to fill gaps between the boards; hammer them in, protecting the edges of the fillets with a block of softwood.*

3 *Plane the fillets flush with the surrounding surface, taking off a little at a time to prevent chipping and splintering.*

ORDER OF WORK

After you have checked that the floor is in a suitable condition for sanding, with gaps filled and no protruding nails or screws, you should adopt the procedure indicated below when using the large and small sanding machines. The arrows indicate in which direction the sander should be moved.

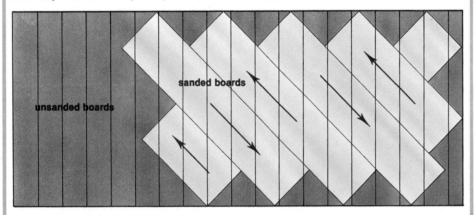

1 *Use the large sander in a diagonal direction across the boards in order to flatten them out and remove thoroughly the top dirt-engrained layer.*

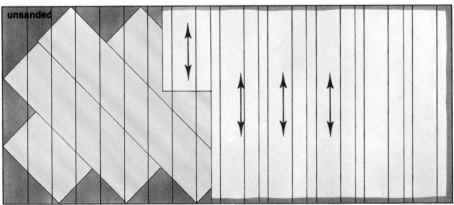

2 *Work in strips along the boards. Work down a strip, then with the machine on, move back along the strip. Switch off when you reach your starting point.*

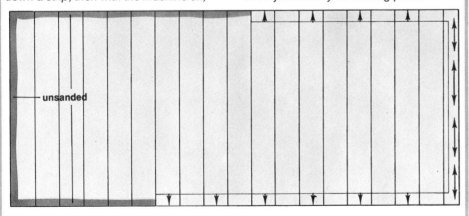

3 *When the floor has been sanded as in (2), with first coarse, then medium and fine abrasives, you can use the small sander on the perimeter of the floor.*

Ready Reference

PUNCH NAILS DOWN

Make sure there are no protruding nails or screws in the floor surface before you begin sanding, because:
● if screws or nails are less than 2-3mm (1/12-1/8in) below the surface of the boards there's a good chance they will tear the abrasive sheets
● a protruding nail will cause an explosion of flying bits of abrasive which can be dangerous; it may also damage the sander.

KEEP DOORS AND WINDOWS CLOSED

To prevent dust from permeating other areas of the house, keep doors closed. Close the windows, too, to allow the dust to settle so it can be vacuumed up.

SAFETY EQUIPMENT

Sanding is extremely dusty, very noisy work, so you should wear the appropriate equipment to protect yourself. A mask, to prevent you from breathing in dust, is a must; you should also consider ear muffs to protect your ears from the din, and goggles so dust and flying bits of grit don't get in your eyes.

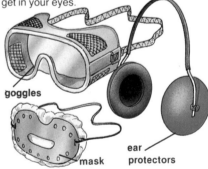

goggles

mask

ear protectors

ELECTRICAL SAFETY

To prevent nasty accidents, you should make sure the electrical cord is out of the path of the sander. One way to do this is to drape the cord over your shoulders as you are working.

FLATTEN WARPED BOARDS

Use the weight of the sander to flatten the edges of any warped boards in the first **stage of sanding** by running the sander diagonally across the boards.

SAND WITH THE GRAIN

When you are sanding in strips down the length of the room in the second stage of sanding, work in the same direction as the grain of the timber or you will cut deep, difficult-to-remove scratches in the surface.

SANDING AND SEALING THE BOARDS

1 Fit a large floor sander with a coarse grade of abrasive; the paper is locked into a slot in the revolving drum of the machine.

2 You can now start sanding the floor by running the sander diagonally across the floorboards to remove the rough and dirty surface layer.

3 Continue sanding the floor in this way until the bulk of the floor area has been treated; the sander will flatten out any warped boards.

4 Sand a strip down the length of the room. Work in the same direction as the boards and allow the sander to pull you along.

5 Sand this strip again, dragging the sander backwards. Repeat for the rest of the floor. Afterwards, sand using medium then fine grades of paper.

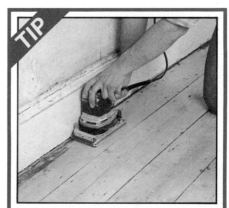

TIP

6 Use a small sander to sand round the perimeter using progressively finer grades of paper. Work in the direction of the grain.

7 You can use a shave hook to scrape stubborn areas at the edges. Other areas that the machines have missed will have to be sanded by hand.

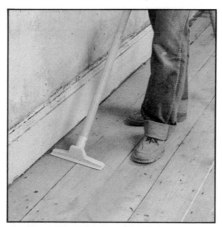

8 Allow the dust to settle, then vacuum the floor clean, paying particular attention to the gaps between the floor and skirting.

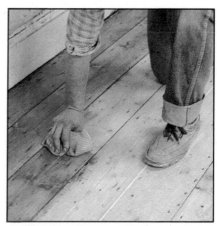

9 To reduce the amount of sealant needed, apply polyurethane varnish, diluted with white spirit on a clean cloth to prime the boards.

Finally, you should make sure that the shop from which you hire the equipment will give you adequate tuition on how to use and clean the sanders. If you damage them through misuse, or return them dirty, you will have to pay more.

Finishing the floor

Having dealt with the sanding, the final thing you have to consider is how to finish the floor: that is, add to its decorative quality and protect the boards from scratches and other types of wear.

If you feel that the boards are too dark to leave as they are after sanding you can apply bleach to lighten them. Use a proprietary wood bleach and follow the manufacturer's instructions for applying it. The fumes from the bleach can be at the least unpleasant and at worst dangerous, so make sure you keep the windows open and wear a protective face mask.

You may want to change the colour of the boards, as well as lighten them. You could use coloured polyurethane varnish for this, but as the surface of the floor becomes subject to wear, so the colour may become thin in some places, highlighting the wear more strongly than you would wish. So it's better to use wood stains which colour the timber itself and then seal with clear polyurethane varnish. Again apply the stain according to the manufacturer's instructions as to the number of coats needed. Work in the direction of the grain when you are applying the stain. (Stains, which come in a variety of colours, allow you to go in for different attractive decorative effects.)

Polyurethane varnish is by far the best choice for sealing the floor, simply because it is so hardwearing and easy to look after. You should choose a brand that is available in large cans rather than in the small tins you are probably familiar with. You'll need a lot to give the floor the two or three coats it requires, and buying such a large amount in small cans can work out very expensive. It's up to you whether you choose a polyurethane giving a high gloss, a satin look or a matt finish; it all depends on the style of the room as a whole. However, it's worth bearing in mind that a very high gloss will show marks more readily and may make the floor rather slippery.

Care and maintenance

To look its best, a wooden floor should be kept free of dust; regular vacuuming will attend to this. If you like a shiny look you can polish it with a proprietary floor polish. Dirty marks can be removed with a damp cloth or mop; more stubborn marks may require treatment with a proprietary cleaner. Where the finish or floorboard has been slightly damaged, such as by a cigarette burn, you will have to sand down the affected area until the signs of damage are removed and then apply polyurethane to reseal it. If there is more extensive damage you will have to remove the affected floorboards, replace them (or use them with the undamaged side face up), sand to provide a smooth surface and reseal.

Take care when you are moving bits of furniture about that they don't scratch the surface (see *Ready Reference*). There's not much point in spending the time and energy it takes to get an attractive varnished wooden floor surface only to spoil it in a few careless minutes.

10 *Follow the priming with at least two, preferably three, coats of polyurethane varnish applied with a brush, working with the grain.*

11 *Allow each coat to dry, then rub lightly down with medium glasspaper to provide a key for the next. Use a damp cloth to remove dust.*

floorboards

cloth

LAYING FOAM-BACKED CARPET

Having wall-to-wall carpet is most people's idea of floorcovering luxury. You can even lay it yourself if you choose the right type of carpet.

carpet from Allied Carpets

Carpet is warm and luxurious underfoot, a good insulator, which is particularly important in flats and upstairs rooms, and still something of a status symbol when fitted in every room – particularly in the bathroom. Modern methods of weaving carpets, and the development of new synthetic fibres, have made some forms of carpeting relatively inexpensive, but it is silly to buy carpet just because it is the conventional thing to have; or for its luxurious image and status.

Consider whether it is a practical proposition for your home. Carpets in bathrooms where there are young children splashing about, (or where the lavatory is situated in the same room) may not be a wise choice. Carpets in kitchens (even the special 'utility' area type) are not always practical at the cooking/washing up end of the room, (although the eating end can be carpeted to co-ordinate with a more easycare surface at the 'business' end of the room). In family rooms, childrens' bedrooms and playrooms, halls and dining rooms, a washable surface may be the answer, softened with large cotton rugs (these can be cleaned in a washing machine), a carpet square or rush matting. But for the sitting room, master bedroom, stairs and corridors, there is really no substitute for carpet.

Choosing carpets

So how do you decide exactly which type of carpet to buy? Of course, you will start by looking for a colour or pattern you like, but a trip to a local carpet specialist or department store can often result in complete confusion once you have seen the range. As a general guide, you should choose the best quality (and consequently the most expensive) you can afford for heavy 'traffic' areas such as hallways, stairs, landings and main living rooms. You can then select the lighter weights and cheaper grades for the rooms which get less wear, like bedrooms, bathrooms and so on.

The carpet industry has produced a labelling system which divides the carpets into categories. In each case the label gives details of how the carpet is made, what fibres have been used and how durable it is likely to be.

This is quite a useful guide, but you should also ask for advice from the salesman. Here are some of the terms it helps to know.

Carpet weaves

The traditional types of carpet are known as Axminster and Wilton, terms which refer to the way they are woven.

An **Axminster** carpet is usually patterned and has an extensive choice of colours within the design. The backing is jute or hessian, sometimes strengthened by polypropylene. Different fibres and blends of fibres are used, but an Axminster is frequently woven in an 80 per cent wool and 20 per cent nylon mixture, and also from acrylic fibres, which resemble wool in appearance and feel.

Axminsters come in many different widths, up to 5m (16½ft) wide. They also come with bound and finished edges, known as carpet 'squares', although they are not necessarily square in shape. This type of carpet can be turned round within a room to even out the wear.

A **Wilton** carpet is usually plain or two-tone, although there are some patterned Wiltons made with a restricted number of colours. The carpet is generally close-textures with a velvet, looped, twist-and-loop, or a mixed cut-and-loop pile (called sculptured or carved). Any yarn not used on the face of the carpet is woven into the backing, to add to the thickness, and the backing is usually jute

or hessian.

Different fibres and blends of fibres can be used in the construction, but Wiltons are usually made with 100 per cent wool pile, the 80/20 blend (as Axminster) or from an acrylic fibre.

Wilton carpet is woven in widths from 700mm (27in) to 2m (6ft 6in), which are then seamed together when the carpet is to be fully fitted; 3.75m (12ft) widths are also available in some ranges and can be bound to form a carpet 'square'.

Tufted carpets are a more modern type which has been developed during the last 25 years. Tufted carpets come in many different fibre mixtures including wool and wool blends. Widths vary from 1m (3ft) to 5m (16½ft). The tufts are 'needled' into a ready-woven backing and anchored by adhesive; when the main backing is hessian, this can be given a coat of latex to secure the tufts. Foam backing can then be stuck to the main backing; a high-quality foam-backed tufted carpet does not need an underlay.

Bonded carpets are made face-to-face, with the carpet pile held between two specially-treated woven backings. The carpet is then 'sliced' down the middle at the finishing stage, and becomes two carpets. The pile can be cut to different lengths to give a carpet with a texture ranging from a shaggy pile to a velvety velour. Fibres can be wool, wool blends or several different synthetics, and the carpet is

179

usually plain. Widths are as for Axminster carpets.

Needlefelt or needleloom carpet is not really woven. A fibrous material is needled into a strong backing to create a looped ribbed pile or one which looks like dense felt. The fibres used are normally synthetic and the carpet has a rather harsh texture. The backing can be resin-coated hessian or foam, and the surface can be printed or plain. Various widths are available.

Broadloom or body?
These are terms used to describe the width of carpet. **Broadloom** carpets are 1.8m (6ft) or more wide, and are the practical choice for fitted carpets in all but the smallest rooms. **Body** carpets are usually 700 to 900mm (27 to 35in) wide, and are intended for use on stairs and in corridors, although they can be seamed together to cover larger areas.

Carpet fibres
All the carpets previously mentioned can be made in several different types of fibre or different blends, which creates still more confusion.

Acrylic fibres are the synthetic fibres most similar to wool. They have long-lasting qualities, and good resistance to flattening, but are not quite so springy as wool. They tend to soil more easily than a natural fibre, but they can be treated to resist staining and to be anti-static. Acrylic fibres come under many brand names, such as Courtelle and Acrilan.

Nylon is a hardwearing fibre, which has a characteristic shiny look. It soils easily, and can look flat and sad if it is the only fibre used in the carpet construction, but when added to other fibres it increases the durability con-siderably. Nylon is frequently used in an 80/20 mix with wool.

Polyester is a soft fibre, used to create fluffy light-duty carpets. It is not very hard-wearing and does become flattened easily, but it can be blended with other fibres.

Polypropylene is a fairly tough fibre, which is often used to create 'cord' effect carpet. It does not absorb liquid, so it is often used for carpet tiles and carpets for kitchen and utility rooms.

Viscose rayon is not used very much these days, and has poor wearing and soiling qualities, but it can be used as part of a blend of fibres quite successfully.

Wool is the traditional carpet fibre, and no real substitute for it has yet been found. Wool is warm, hard-wearing, resilient and does not soil easily; from the safety point of view it also resists the spread of flame. It is used alone, or blended with other fibres. The most widely-used blend, 80 per cent wool and 20 per cent nylon, gives the best performance.

Other carpet types
Apart from the diferent methods of carpet making, and the various blends of fibres, you will find there are many other words in the carpet salesman's vocabulary, which loosely cover what might be called carpet styles, or types.

Cord carpets, for example, come in several styles. Originally the only type was a haircord, which was made from natural animal fibres, and was very hardwearing. This is now very expensive and is not frequently used, but there are some blends of animal hair with synthetic fibres available, and some much cheaper cords which are not particularly hard-

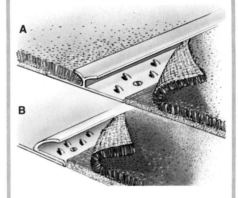
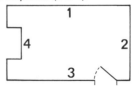
PREPARING THE FLOOR

1 *Lift old floorcoverings completely, and remove all traces of underlay. Nail down any loose boards securely with 38mm (1½in) nails.*

2 *Use a nail punch and hammer to ensure that all the nail heads are flush with, or driven below, the surface of the boards.*

wearing. Other types of cord carpet include the Berbers, which have a looped pile and look homespun. Originally these were made from un-dyed, coarsely-woven wool, by Berber tribesmen. Now they are made in many different fibres, including blends of wool and synthetic fibres. These are often called Berber-style.

Hardtwist is a curly, crush-resistant pile, which is sometimes called twist pile. This is frequently found in high-quality Wiltons, in wool or wool blends, but may also be found in all-synthetic carpets.

Shag pile carpets have a long pile, which can be plain or kinked and with a richly textured shaggy surface. The pile needs raking if it is very long, to maintain its appearance, and it is not a practical carpet to choose for areas which get a lot of wear, on stairs, or in halls for example.

Shadow pile is another fairly new development in carpet style. The pile is dyed so it has contrasting colour or tone, usually darker at the base, lightening towards the tip. The pile is usually shiny (synthetic fibres) and when the carpet is walked on the dark tones show as 'shadows'.

Sculptured pile is usually made by combining a looped and cut pile to form a self-coloured pattern, although sometimes different colours can be used. Fibres can be natural, synthetic or a mixture of both.

Printed carpets are another fairly recent development. The carpet is woven and then a design is printed on the surface via computer-controlled dye injection systems. They often resemble Axminsters in colour and design, but on closer examination you can see the pattern does not go right through to the backing. The fibres used in this range are usually synthetic, and the pile is frequently very close and sometimes looped or corded.

Planning and estimating

As with any other floorcovering, start your planning by taking accurate measurements of the room at ground level with a steel tape or yardstick. If possible, work out a scale plan on squared paper, marking in the recesses, corners, angles, projections and so on. Take this with you when you shop for carpet, so the salesman can work out exactly how much you need. It is usual to multiply the room measurements to get square yards or square metres, and you will find most carpeting is sold by the square yard or metre, although some types are still sold by the linear yard or metre.

With the more expensive types of carpet with hessian backing, it is wise to call in an expert to lay the carpet for you, unless you have had a great deal of experience laying other types of carpet and floorcovering. Otherwise you risk marring an expensive carpet if you make a cut in the wrong place; what's

LAYING THE LINING

1 Unroll the lining down the length of the room. Smooth out the strip and staple down both sides 50mm (2in) in from the edge.

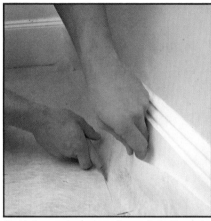

2 Using a sharp handyman's knife, cut off a strip of the lining 38mm (1½in) wide between the line of staples and the skirting board.

3 To fit the lining into an alcove, lay the strip up against the face of the chimney breast and make a cut with your knife in line with its corner.

4 Staple down the cut end of the length as before, after ensuring that it is perfectly flat. Then cut off the border strip next to the skirting board.

5 Continue covering the rest of the floor with the lining, overlapping each succeeding strip with the previous one by about 25mm (1in).

6 Stick double-sided self-adhesive tape down all round the edge of the room where you have cut off the strip of lining. Do not remove the release paper.

POSITIONING THE CARPET

1 *Unroll the carpet parallel with the longest wall, and position it so that there is an overlap at the skirting board all round the room.*

2 *Roughly trim off the excess carpet with a sharp handyman's knife to leave a 75mm (3in) overlap all round; cut through the foam backing behind.*

3 *At fireplaces gauge the depth of the alcoves using your cutting knife as a guide. Add 75mm (3in) to allow for the final trimming.*

4 *Cut into the alcove as you did with the lining. Make the first cut parallel with the side of the chimney breast and allow the tongue to fall into place.*

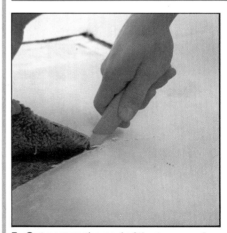

5 *Cut across the end of the tongue of carpet that fits into the alcove, taking care not to cut into the pile underneath the tongue.*

6 *At the corner of the chimney breast, make a diagonal cut on the underside of the carpet, and trim across the face of the chimney breast.*

Ready Reference

CUTTING IN AT DOORWAYS

At doorways carpet should extend to a point under the centre of the door. To get an accurate fit round architraves and door stops, start making release cuts in the overlap at one side of the door opening, until the tongue falls neatly into the door opening. Then trim it to fit neatly under the threshold strip.

COPING WITH BAY WINDOWS

It's often easier to cope with odd-shaped bay windows by trimming the two flanking walls first. Then
● pull the carpet down the room until its edge is across the 'mouth' of the bay

● measure the depth of the bay, and cut a strip of wood to match this measurement
● use it to trace off the profile on the carpet, marking the line with chalk

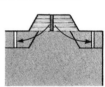

● trim along the marked line and slide the carpet back into place against the wall containing the bay.

FITTING ROUND PIPEWORK

Where pipes to radiators come up through the floor, you will have to cut the carpet to fit neatly round them. To do this
● make an incision in the edge of the carpet, parallel with one edge of the pipe
● measure the distance between wall and pipe, and cut out a small circle in the carpet at this distance from the edge

● fit the carpet round the pipe.

FITTING ANGLES

1 To fit the carpet tightly into an angle, press your thumb firmly down into the corner as shown.

2 Pull up the corner, keeping your thumb in place, and make an incision just beyond the end of your thumb.

3 Cut cleanly across the corner in line with the incision, and press the carpet back in position.

TAPING SEAMS

1 Carefully trim the edges of the two pieces to be joined, and check that they butt neatly together.

2 Cut a piece of carpet tape to the length of the join, peel off the release paper and bed one carpet edge on it.

3 Position the other piece of carpet over the tape, and press it down firmly right along the join.

FINAL TRIMMING

1 Press the carpet tightly into the base of the skirting board with the back of an old knife or a pair of scissors.

2 Turn back the carpet and cut off the excess, using the score mark made by the knife back as a guide.

3 Peel off the release paper from the border tape and press the carpet firmly into place.

more, it will wear out prematurely unless it is tensioned correctly during installation. This involves fitting special toothed gripper strips all round the perimeter of the room, and hooking the carpet on to the teeth once it has been pulled taut across the room.

The foam-backed types are, however, easier to lay yourself, because tensioning is not necessary.

If you are having the carpet professionally laid, ask for a written estimate and check carefully to see whether the price includes underlay or not, and if not, how much extra this will be. With an expensive carpet it may be wise to get several quotes from different firms. Some firms quote a price for carpet 'laid', but again check to see whether underlay is included in the price.

There are several different types of underlay – at different prices. The cheapest is the conventional brown felt, but there are also rubber and synthetic foams, including one on a coarse hessian backing. Foam-backed carpets definitely do not need underlay.

Laying carpet

It is usual to plan and lay carpet so the seams (if any) come in the least obvious place and where the 'traffic' is lightest. When the carpet has to be seamed, both pieces must be laid so the pile is going in the same direction, otherwise the colour would appear slightly different on each side of the seam. The floor

should be clean, level and free from dust and debris. Punch down any nail heads that are proud of the floor surface, and nail down any loose boards. If the boards are very uneven, cover them with sheets of hardboard pinned down at 230mm (9in) intervals to disguise the ridges. Otherwise simply lay stout brown paper or nylon lining to prevent dust from blowing up between floorboards.

Never lay a new carpet down on top of an existing one; the worn areas will quickly transfer themselves to the new carpet. It is not wise to use old underfelt either.

Do not lay a carpet with a latex backing, or a latex underlay, in rooms which have underfloor central heating, as you could find it gives off an unpleasant smell.

LAYING HESSIAN-BACKED CARPET

There's no denying that laying hessian-backed carpet requires a fair degree of skill. But with care and some practice you can learn how to use a knee kicker to stretch this type of carpet into place and so provide a longlasting floorcovering.

M ost really heavy quality carpets will not have a foam backing and therefore need to be laid with a separate underlay. A traditional method of securing such carpet is to 'turn and tack' it; the carpet is folded under at the perimeter of the room and non-rusting tacks are then driven through the fold to hold it to the floor. The underlay is cut to size so it meets the folded-under edge of the carpet. The problem with this method is that the tacks will be visible and will leave indentations in the carpet; also, you are likely to end up with scalloped edges and the carpet will be difficult to remove.

Consequently, most carpets which do not have a foam backing are laid using a system without tacks: the carpet is stretched over wooden or metal strips containing two staggered rows of angled pins which hook into the back of the carpet. This method provides an invisible fixing and it's quite simple to lift the carpet off the pins if you want to take it up later. But it's a much more complex method of fitting and fixing carpet than sticking down a foam-backed carpet (see pages 54–58).

Your chief problem is likely to be the stretching process: if you stretch the carpet too much it will tear; if you stretch it too little there will be lumps, which apart from being unsightly, will wear through quickly because of their exposed position.

A good professional fitter will be able to get the tension right according to the feel of the carpet. So at the outset it's worth considering the benefits of calling in an expert. Your chief guideline here will probably be cost and value for money. Fitting charges are, in fact, similar whether you are laying an inexpensive or a costly floorcovering. So, obviously, the costs of professional fitting relative to an expensive carpet make more sense than with a cheap one.

Bearing all this in mind you may decide you want to go ahead and fit your own carpet. There are many examples of successful DIY carpet fitting and yours may well be one of them. To ensure a good result it is worth practising fitting techniques on an old carpet you're going to discard before you begin on your new one. And it's certainly worth

tackling a simple rectangular room, with no awkward alcoves or bays, first of all, so the job will not be too complicated.

Tools and equipment

After you have measured up you can order the amount of carpet and underlay you'll need. Take a scale plan of the room along to your supplier so he can work out how much you need and check with him on the type of underlay which will suit the carpet you have chosen. A good quality underlay improves the feel of the carpet underfoot and, by serving as a buffer between the carpet and floor, helps to ensure even wear. It will also compensate for small defects if the floor is level but not perfectly smooth. For extra protection against dirt and dust rising up through the floorboards on a wooden floor you can lay paper or nylon lining underneath, so you will need to buy this as well.

You will also have to buy adequate carpet gripper. Gripper strips (commonly called smooth edge) can be nailed or glued to the floor. Strips intended for nailing come complete with pins for fixing to timber floors or masonry nails for fixing to solid floors. You will, obviously, have to buy adhesive of a suitable type (check with your supplier) if you are going to glue the strips in place.

In addition, you will require hessian tape

and adhesive for joining lengths of carpet and, if you are going to fix the underlay, staples (and a staple gun), tacks, adhesive or self-adhesive tape.

You will probably already have most of the tools required for this type of work: knife, shears, tin snips for cutting the gripper, hammer, bolster chisel and steel tape or wooden measure. You will also need a knee kicker to hook the carpet onto the gripper. This is relatively expensive, so it makes sense to hire one if, as is likely, you don't intend to go in for regular carpet fitting.

Preparing the floor surface

The floor surface must be level, smooth and dry. Wood floors can be sanded or covered with hardboard or an underlay; if the only problem is protruding nails you should punch the nails down or countersink the screws. Damp may also be a problem which needs tackling at a more basic level. If the floor is concrete, or has a composite surface, unevenness can be treated with a self-levelling screed.

The first stages

If you have decided to fix a paper lining, you will have to spot-glue, staple or tack it to the floor. You can then fix the gripper in place;

FIXING GRIPPER STRIPS

1 Cut the strips to length and nail them down so there's a gap of just less than the carpet thickness between them and the wall.

2 Cut short lengths and lay them with small gaps between them to follow a curve. Use a minimum of two nails to fix each piece in position.

LAYING THE UNDERLAY

1 Roll out the underlay and then position it so one end just comes up to the edge of the gripper strips fixed along one wall.

2 Cut the underlay so the end of the first length reaches the edge of the gripper strips along the opposite wall. Cut and lay other lengths.

4 Neatly trim what's left of the overlap so it fits exactly up to the edges of the gripper strips in the same way as for straight lengths.

3 At a curve or an angle, leave an overlap, and cut it at intervals so it fits around the obstacle. Then roughly trim off the excess.

Ready Reference

TIP: AVOID BURIED PIPES
Solid floors often have pipes running close to the floor surface, so if there is a radiator in the room it's better to stick down the gripper along the length of the wall to which the radiator is attached rather than risk nailing it.

GULLY WIDTH
The space between the edge of the gripper and the wall is known as the gully. Its width should be slightly less than the uncompressed thickness of the carpet.

FIXING THE FIRST EDGE
To hold the carpet firmly down during stretching you will have to use what's known as the 'starting edge technique'. This is used to hook the carpet along the first two walls to be fitted; the carpet is hooked along the other two walls by stretching. Select a starting corner (one where you will have a reasonably uninterrupted run of walls is best) and follow this procedure:
● ease the edge of the carpet up the wall about 10mm (⅜in)
● rub your fingertips along the carpet over the gripper with a steady downward pressure so the back row of pins start penetrating the warp (A)
● use a hammer to press the carpet down between the gripper and the wall (B)
● don't try to turn the compressed carpet into the gully at this stage or you will release the pressure on the pins.

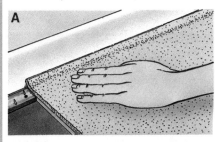

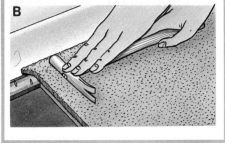

LAYING THE CARPET

1 Place the carpet roughly over the underlay, then adjust its position more exactly. Arrange it so the edges 'climb up' the walls all round.

3 Adjust the teeth of the knee kicker so they grip the carpet backing, hold the head down firmly, then 'kick' the pad with your knee.

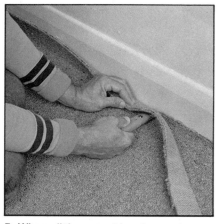

5 When all the carpet has been stretched and fixed in place, trim off the excess so there's about 10mm (³/₈in) lapping up against the walls.

2 Trim off most of the surplus so there's an overlap of about 50mm (2in) at the wall and floor join; this makes the carpet easier to handle.

4 When making the next 'kick' use a bolster to hold down the carpet where you made the previous one so it doesn't spring back off the pins.

6 Use a bolster or thin piece of wood to press the overlap neatly into the gully between the gripper strips and the walls ensuring a snug fit.

lengths of gripper can be placed end-to-end on straight walls. Recesses, bays and projections can be tackled by cutting the gripper into small pieces which you position to follow the contour of the wall. You can tack or stick the gripper down as you go along or when it is all in position. Tacking will also anchor the paper-felt lining. Where it is being stuck and a lining has been used, be careful to stick the gripper to the floor and not just to the lining, which should in fact be cut away within about 50mm (2in) of the wall all round the room.

With all the gripper satisfactorily in place, you can put down the underlay. It does not have to be fixed to the floor; lengths can simply be placed so they butt join without being secured. If you handle the carpet carefully, it should not disturb the underlay when you pull it over. If you feel happier securing the underlay, you can spot-stick it to the subfloor or anchor it to board floors with tacks or a stapling gun and tape successive lengths together where they abut.

If you have stuck the gripper down and it has been in place for the time recommended in the manufacturer's instructions, it's worth going round and trying to pull it off to make sure the adhesive has set really hard.

Laying the carpet

Unroll the carpet and place it roughly in position with the excess 'climbing up' the walls. Make sure the pattern (if any) is square and that the pile is leaning away from the light to prevent uneven shading in daylight. Position it so any seams will not be in areas of hard wear, such as doorways. You can roughly trim the overlap so the carpet is less cumbersome to handle when you are fitting it. Make sure you have left nothing under the carpet which shouldn't be there. You can then walk all over it and leave it to settle so that it flattens out.

As with foam-backed carpet, when you are trimming the carpet, and specially when you are cutting down into the overlap so it will fit round a corner or curve, make sure you do not cut too deeply or you will ruin the final effect. This and getting the tension right are likely to be your two major problems. Go round the room hooking and stretching in the required direction (see Ready Reference). Once you have hooked the carpet, stand back and take a look at it. It may not look straight and you might feel that it would be worth taking it off and starting again. Remember that one of the benefits of the tackless gripper method is that it's easy to hook and unhook a carpet so that you can get the adjustment right.

Where the carpet meets another type of floorcovering in a doorway, you can secure it with a threshold strip. You simply nail this down and then press the carpet onto the pins in the strip.

TRIMMING EDGES

1 *Where the corner forms a curve, cut down into the overlap so the carpet will fit round the curve; take care not to cut too deep.*

2 *At an external angled corner turn the carpet back and cut diagonally at the corner for a short distance and then straight towards you.*

3 *Trim off the bulk of the overlap, let the carpet flap back against the walls and then trim the overlap again for a perfect final fit.*

JOINING LENGTHS

1 *Lay the lengths of carpet so they butt against each other, then cut a length of hessian tape and place it so it fits beneath the two edges.*

2 *Use a small carpet offcut to spread adhesive along the tape. Take care that you don't get adhesive on the front of the carpet.*

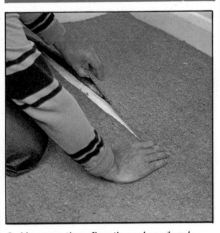

3 *You can then flap the edges back into position so they are held in place by the adhesive, and press the carpet down firmly along the seam.*

Ready Reference

STRETCHING CORRECTLY

To fit the carpet properly you should carry out the stretching and hooking in the following order:

● start at corner A and hook the carpet about 300mm (12in) along walls AB and AC. Stretch from A to B and hook on about 300mm (12in) of carpet along wall BD

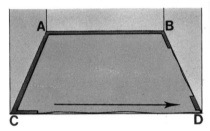

● hook the carpet along the full length of wall AB, then repeat in direction A to C. Stretch the carpet from C to D and hook it on. Stretch across the width of the carpet from wall AB as you hook onto wall CD

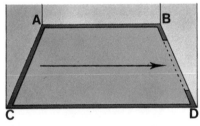

● stretch across the full length of the carpet from wall AC as you hook on the wall BD.

ADJUSTING THE KNEE KICKER

There are two sets of pins of different widths in the head of the knee kicker. The thinner pins are adjustable, so the amount they project from the head can be increased or decreased. You adjust them to suit the type of carpet, so:
● if you are laying a shag pile carpet, the thinner pins should project enough to grip the carpet backing; if they are too short they will snare the pile; if too long, they will become embedded in the underlay and will pull it out of place
● for smooth pile carpets you will need to use the thicker pins only.

LAYING CARPET ON STAIRS

Carpet provides an attractive covering for stairs, and will cut down considerably on noise levels in the home. Fitting a stair carpet is relatively straightforward providing you use the right techniques.

If you intend to fit a stair carpet you will first have to make sure that the carpet you have in mind is a suitable type. Since stairways are subjected to a lot of use, the carpet must be durable and hardwearing. The label on the carpet may help you make your choice; for example, carpets suitable for light wear only may be labelled as 'not recommended for stairs'. On the other hand, some ranges will be labelled as being specifically suited for use on stairs and others as being suitable for the whole house, including stairs. If the staircase is very heavily used and you require the carpet to last a long time, you will have to go for one of the toughest quality.

Foam-backed carpets are generally unsuitable for stairs; the cheaper light-weight ones tend not to be sufficiently durable and the heavier ones can be too inflexible to fit properly. You should also avoid carpets with a long pile which could impede movement and make the edges of the treads more difficult to locate. Again, some carpet patterns may obscure the outline of the treads or make people feel dizzy. Carpets with these kinds of patterns can be a safety risk, especially where elderly people will be using the stairs.

After you have chosen the carpet you must decide either to call in a professional to lay it or to go ahead and lay it yourself. The complexity of the job is a factor to take into account here; for example, if you want to cover a spiral staircase with a carpet fitted 'edge to edge', that is across the complete width of the stairs, it would normally be advisable to have a professional installation. A straight flight is likely to cause less problems, particularly if you intend to have a carpet runner which simply runs down the centre of the stairs and doesn't cover the complete width.

Measuring up

You will then have to work out how much carpet you'll need. The amount will be affected by the way you intend fitting the carpet: that is, edge-to-edge or as a carpet runner. If you have decided on an edge-to-edge fitting and the staircase is a regular width all the way up, you may find that this measurement

coincides with one of the regular widths in which carpet is supplied. If the staircase is narrower than a regular width, you can buy the regular width, trim the carpet to size and seal the cut edge. Where the staircase is a width which is going to waste a great deal of carpet in trimming you might decide to buy broadloom carpet and cut it into strips to match the stair width.

To calculate the length of stair carpet required you should add the height of all the risers to the depth of all the treads and then add on an additional 38mm (1½in) for each step to allow for the space taken by the underlay. Where there are curved nosings at the edges of the treads you will also have to allow for these – add 50mm (2in) for each nosing. Where you are using a carpet runner you can add on an extra 500mm (20in) to the length so you can reposition the carpet later to even out wear (see *Ready Reference*).

On a curved staircase measuring up is more complicated. You will have to calculate the bends separately, taking the largest dimensions of the winder treads which go round the corners.

As well as the quantity of carpet, you will also have to work out how much underlay to order. The underlay is cut in strips, with a

separate piece used for each step. Order an amount of underlay which will ensure that each strip is big enough to cover the treads and lap round the nosing so it can be secured to the riser beneath. Check with your supplier about a suitable type of underlay to use with the carpet you have chosen (remember that the better the quality the more wear and sound insulation it will give).

The preparation

As when you are fitting carpet on a floor, the stair surface must be in a suitable state; both treads and risers should be flat, smooth and dry. Check that they are in sound condition; this may involve nailing down loose treads or removing and replacing faulty treads or risers with new timber.

Unless you happen to have bought one of the few types of foam-backed carpet which are suitable for stairways you will have to fit an underlay before you go ahead and lay the carpet. And before you do this, if you are using the tackless gripper system, you will have to nail the gripper strips to the treads and risers. Fix the grippers to the back of each tread and the bottom of each riser so the pins face into the angle. The gap between the grippers on tread and riser should be

FIXING THE GRIPPER AND UNDERLAY

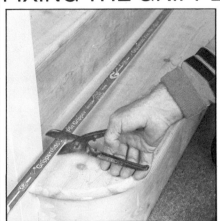

1 Use tinsnips to cut the gripper to size; its width should match that of the tread, measured where the tread meets the riser.

2 Fix the gripper strips to the treads by driving in the nails with a hammer; check that the gripper's teeth are not flattened as you do this.

3 Fix the gripper to the risers; there should be a gap of 15 to 18mm ($^5/_8$ to $^3/_4$in) between the gripper strips on the tread and riser.

4 On a landing, nail the gripper strips in place so the gully between the strip and wall is just less than the carpet thickness.

5 Place a strip of underlay in position on the landing and then trim it so it reaches the edges of the gripper strips.

6 Trim the underlay on the landing so it just reaches down to the edge of the gripper strip fixed to the first riser beneath the landing.

7 Use a staple gun to fix the underlay securely in place on the landing and then to fix it above the gripper strip on the riser beneath.

8 Work down the stairs, continuing to cut strips of underlay to size and fixing them in place between the gripper strips.

9 Where there is a bullnose tread at the bottom of the stairs you will have to cut the underlay so it fits the shape of the curved tread.

equal to about twice the thickness of the carpet, to allow the carpet to be tucked down between the grippers. If you are using special right-angled stair grippers, you don't have to worry about a gap. Where you are fixing a carpet runner you should cut the gripper strips 38mm (1½in) shorter than the width of the carpet so the method of fixing won't be obvious when the carpet is finally fixed in place.

You will have to cut the underlay into strips so there is a separate piece for each step. If you are fitting a carpet runner the width of the underlay should be about 38mm (1½in) less than the width of the carpet so it won't be visible under the carpet edges. Where you are using gripper strips, each piece of underlay should just reach the edges of the gripper strips on the tread above it and the riser below it. If you are using tacks to fix the carpet, each piece of underlay can be slightly longer, but you must allow enough room (ie, stair uncovered by underlay) to drive in the tacks which secure the carpet. The underlay can be tacked down, or, to make the job go more quickly, you can use a staple gun to staple it in place. If you are using a carpet runner, you should make sure the underlay is centrally placed (measure and mark off its position before you attempt to secure it). At the same time as you mark off the position of the underlay you can mark the position of the carpet runner so it too will eventually be centrally placed. Care taken at this stage will save you spoiling the look of the stairs later.

Where you are fitting edge-to-edge carpet, treat a landing as you would a floor; that is, cover it with underlay, except that the underlay should lap down over the edge of the landing onto the first riser beneath it. Where you will be fixing the carpet with gripper strips this overlap should reach to just above the gripper strip which you have fixed in place on the top riser.

Laying the carpet

Of the various methods you can use to secure the carpet in place, stair rods provide the simplest one and the tackless gripper system the most difficult (but it also gives the most 'professional' look). Don't forget that if you are using a foam-backed carpet, you can use stair rods instead of special right-angled grippers to hold it in place. You may already have stair rods holding an old stair carpet which you want to replace: these can be removed and used again. Or you may choose to buy new ones; they come in a range of types, including simple streamlined ones and more ornate versions, so you should be able to choose a variety which gives you the look you want for your staircase. Remember that it is simple to move a carpet if you have used stair rods to secure it and that they are the easiest of the various fixing methods to

take up and re-fix. So do bear this in mind.

With the next method, tacking, you should start at the top tread. First, centre the carpet if it is a runner and allow an extra 13mm (½in) for turning under where the carpet meets the top riser. This riser will be covered by the carpet which laps down from the landing. Turn the allowance under and tack the carpet down in one corner, then stretch it so it fits smoothly across the tread and tack it down at intervals of about 100mm (4in) across the riser. Then continue down the stairs, tacking it at the edges in the angles formed by the treads and risers. Make sure it's firmly stretched over the nosings as you go. To complete the job, drive in more tacks at 100mm (4in) intervals across the risers at the angles between treads and risers and, where you have made an allowance for moving the carpet at the bottom, tack up the sides of the folded-under carpet on the bottom step.

For an invisible fixing you will have to use the tackless gripper system. You can use a bolster to stretch and fit the carpet over the gripper strips (see step-by-step photographs) and in this case you should again begin work from the top downwards. But, if you prefer, you can instead use a knee-kicker to get the tension you want, in which case you will be working from the bottom step upwards. With the roll of carpet resting further up, push the carpet into the gully on the first (bottom) step so it is tightly held. Then roll the carpet further up the stairs and, using the knee-kicker on the second tread to pull the carpet tight, push the carpet into the gully between this tread and the second riser. Continue in this way, pulling the carpet tight (but not too tight) as you go, until you reach the top of the stairs.

Left-over carpet at the top and bottom can be tucked into the top and bottom risers and tacked firmly down. Sometimes it is tucked under another carpet at the top and bottom of the stairs; sometimes it continues to meet another carpet, and at other times it is finished with a binder bar. It all depends on the existing arrangements at the top and bottom of the staircase.

On stairs with winders where you are fitting edge-to-edge carpet, you will have to cut separate pieces for each step (see *Ready Reference*). To help you get the shape right it's worth making a paper template of each winder and using this as a guide when you are cutting the carpet.

Where you have cut the carpet to width from a wider measure you will have to seal it at the edges before you lay it. Otherwise the backing will fray, tufts will work loose from the edges and the appearance of the carpet will be spoiled. To seal the edges, run strips of latex adhesive along the underside and allow it to dry before you go ahead and fit the carpet.

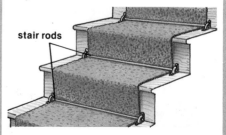
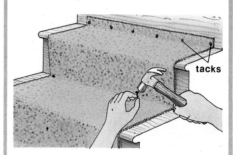
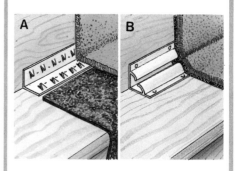

FITTING THE CARPET

1 Cut the carpet so it fits the landing and overlaps onto the riser beneath. Stretch and fix it in place using a knee-kicker.

2 With the carpet hooked in place on the gripper at one side of the landing, use a bolster to push the overlap down into the gully.

3 On the other side of the landing, where the carpet and the balustrade meet, cut into the overlap so you can fit the carpet round the corner.

4 Fix the rest of the carpet on the landing and then use a bolster to press the carpet down onto the gripper strip on the riser beneath.

5 With the carpet loosely secured, go over it again with the bolster, this time tapping it with a hammer to fix the carpet firmly in position.

6 Trim off the overlap with a sharp knife to expose the gripper strip fixed to the tread below the riser where the carpet is secured.

7 Again use a bolster to push the carpet down onto the gripper on the tread; go over it again, tapping the bolster with a hammer.

8 Unroll the length of carpet down the stairs and press the folds securely in place onto the gripper strips with your bolster.

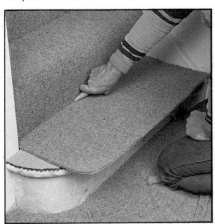

9 Finish a straight flight by trimming the carpet off at floor level; with a bullnose tread, cut it off below the last-but-one riser.

CARPETING A BULLNOSE TREAD

1 *If you have a bullnose tread at the foot of the flight, lay a piece of carpet across it and cut it 50mm (2in) bigger than the curve all round.*

3 *Then cut up to the edge of your thumb with shears to get the correct depth of the zig-zag cut. Cut in this way right round the curve.*

5 *Cut a piece of carpet to size so it fits along the exposed riser under the bullnose tread; then press it round the curve.*

2 *Make zig-zag cuts in the overlap where it fits round the curve. First of all press the carpet under the edge of the tread with your thumb.*

4 *Use a hammer to fix carpet tacks along and under the edge of the bottom tread to hold the carpet neatly and securely in place.*

6 *Nail the width of carpet in place at the sides of the riser and along the top; don't nail along the bottom, where tacks would be visible.*

Ready Reference

COPING WITH HALF-LANDINGS

Where the staircase changes direction at a half landing, treat it as two sets of stairs when you are laying carpet, whether you are fitting carpet edge-to-edge or using a runner.

WINDING STAIRS

Where you are laying carpet on winding stairs, you can use one of two methods to fit the carpet to the winders:

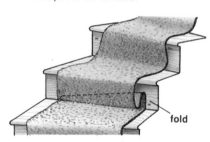

fold

● where you are fitting carpet edge-to-edge, use a separate piece of carpet for each winder. Fix additional gripper strips to the sides of the treads

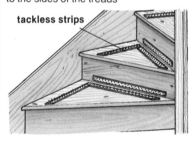

tackless strips

● where there is a carpet runner, leave the gripper strips off the risers of the winders and take up the slack with a series of folds which you can tack in place using 40mm (1½in) non-rusting tacks.

MOVING CARPET RUNNERS

You can move a carpet runner to equalise wear if you allow an extra 500mm (20in) when first laying it. Tack the carpet at the top and bottom with the extra 500mm tucked under the bottom step, to act as an underlay. Move the carpet (*before* signs of wear become obvious) as follows:
● start from the top and remove the tacks carefully so you don't damage the carpet
● gently ease the carpet off the grippers (or remove tacks or stair rods), move it and then fit it back on to them
● as you move the carpet up, insert strips of underlay on the bottom tread and riser.